Third Edition

Promoting
YOUR
School

This book is dedicated with equal measures of love, respect, and gratitude to my mother, Mary Tullis Rexroat Kunde, a teacher and one of the first women principals in both Oklahoma and California; to my father, Uriah Thomas Rexroat, Head Teacher of the first public school in Southwest Oklahoma Indian Territory and who later served in the Oklahoma legislature; to my uncle, Dr. David Sherman Tullis; and my aunt, Beulah Baker Tullis. Finally to Jerry Emmett, a great teacher and a remarkable human being. All are examples of great teachers, administrators, and human beings.

Third Edition

Promoting
YOUR
School

—— Going Beyond PR ——

Carolyn Warner   *Foreword by Jay Mathews*

CORWIN
A SAGE Company

For information:

Corwin
A SAGE Company
2455 Teller Road
Thousand Oaks, California 91320
(800) 233-9936
Fax: (800) 417-2466
www.corwinpress.com

SAGE India Pvt. Ltd.
B 1/I 1 Mohan Cooperative
    Industrial Area
Mathura Road, New Delhi 110 044
India

SAGE Ltd.
1 Oliver's Yard
55 City Road
London EC1Y 1SP
United Kingdom

SAGE Asia-Pacific Pte. Ltd.
33 Pekin Street #02-01
Far East Square
Singapore 048763

Printed in the United States of America.

Library of Congress Cataloging-in-Publication Data

Warner, Carolyn.
Promoting your school: going beyond PR/Carolyn Warner.—3rd ed.
    p. cm.
ISBN 978-1-4129-5812-7 (cloth)
ISBN 978-1-4129-5813-4 (pbk.)
1. Schools—Public relations—United States. I. Title.

LB2847.W36 2009
659.2'9371—dc22   2008049673

This book is printed on acid-free paper.

09 10 11 12 13 10 9 8 7 6 5 4 3 2 1

Acquisitions Editor:	Arnis Burvikovs
Associate Editor:	Desiree A. Bartlett
Production Editor:	Libby Larson
Copy Editor:	Teresa Herlinger
Typesetter:	C&M Digitals (P) Ltd.
Proofreader:	Wendy Jo Dymond
Cover Designer:	Monique Hahn
Graphic Designer:	Lisa Riley

Contents

List of Resources and Sample Documents

Foreword

Educators will often tell you that schools get too much negative coverage in the press. That may be true from their perspective. Just one or two stories about bad cafeteria food or missing textbooks may be too much for some people. But I have been reading education stories in *The Washington Post* and other newspapers, as well as watching them on television, for 40 years, and most of those stories have been positive.

We education reporters know that our readers are mostly parents, teachers, and students. They want to know what is happening in schools. They have invested so much time and hope in those places, they are much more pleased to read happy stories than nasty ones. Carolyn Warner, an extraordinarily experienced veteran of education news coverage in America, understands that. Notice how upbeat and optimistic her suggestions are for promoting one's school. She knows that we journalists (well, most of us at least) are well-brought-up and friendly people, motivated not by a desire to make schools look bad but by a need to make enough money to eat and pay the rent. We know we will not be able to do that if we don't write a lot of interesting stories and get them to our editors on time.

Reflect for a moment on the kinds of newspapers that do most of the education reporting in this country. They are the opposite of *The Washington Post*. They are small, not big. They are very local, not regional or national. They are often weeklies, not dailies. And what do the editors of those small papers want to see, first and foremost, in their school stories? Blood? Tragedy? Corruption? Nope. They want to see names—names of students, names of parents, names of teachers, as many names as possible. Why? Because people *love* to see their names in the paper and are more likely to buy it if the editors and reporters make a great effort to mention lots of local folks.

Former Arizona state school superintendent Warner also appreciates a unique advantage that educators have when dealing with reporters. People become teachers because they want to help kids. They are, in my view, among the most humane people I know. I have covered business tycoons, and bureaucrats, and politicians. When I made mistakes in stories about people like that, they never took my phone calls again. But whenever I make a mistake in a story about a teacher—and I have done that many times—the teacher will take my call or answer my e-mail the next day, without hesitation. She will explain to me what I did wrong, and tell me how I can do better the next time. She treats me just like the student she gave a D+ to on an exam. To her, all people are educable, and she treats them that way.

That is exactly the way we journalists should be dealt with, like slow-witted pupils who need more time and guidance to do our work correctly. Ms. Warner is too polite to say this in her book, but the best way to handle a conversation with any of us is to pretend we are about 12 years old. That way, you won't yell at us, you won't question our parentage, you won't hang up the phone. You will simply tell us how to do better and encourage us in that direction.

Sounds simple, right? It's not. This book is 264 pages long, and Ms. Warner has not wasted a single word. Forging a strong and healthy bond between a community and its schools can be hard work. It takes thought and preparation and teamwork. Ms. Warner has seen how this is done from every possible perspective. I may quarrel with some of her advice, but not much of it. And I suspect that wherever we differ—given that she has much more experience with these issues than I do—she is right and I am wrong.

So, enjoy the book. If I were you, I would use the table of contents to sample parts of the book that interest you most. But if you are an educator, or an active community member, for whom these issues are an important part of your life, I would read the whole thing.

And remember, the next time you see reporters like me, annoying and intrusive and demanding more than you can give, just smile and say you are so impressed with our good questions, and will be happy to help us with our story. We mean well, usually, even if it doesn't sound like it. You should not pat us on the head, but treat us like the occasionally impatient and clueless girls and boys we are, and all will work out fine.

—Jay Mathews
Washington Post *Education Columnist, 2008*

Preface

The first edition of *Promoting Your School* was published in 1994. Because of its success, Corwin asked me to update it with new material on the challenges facing education in the 21st century. The second edition, published in 2000, came out on the cusp of the explosion in technology that is still going on. Today, as we have prepared this third edition, even more rapid advances in technology continue to direct the ways we communicate. So we have done even more research on the most effective applications of technology. Educational leaders who participated in the first and second editions of the book were asked for additional input. From elementary and secondary state school "Principals of the Year" to "Superintendents of the Year" to school public relations experts from around the country—all were invited to contribute. As a result, this new edition contains updated examples of how these experts are taking full advantage of the latest technology in school and district communication efforts. Students and educators alike are increasingly sophisticated in their knowledge and use of computer technology and all its possibilities, so examples have been added throughout this edition showcasing some of the best practices in use today in public education. There is no better way to increase the confidence level of parents who want their children to be prepared to succeed both academically and economically in this changing world than to show them firsthand how educational change, creatively employed by educational leaders, is benefiting their children.

Promoting Your School is about communication. In this era of high-demand/high-performance expectations, schools struggle with their role in the community and with their ability to project an image that is both positive and honest. Academic requirements have increased at the same time that schools have taken on countless new responsibilities—responsibilities having nothing to do with the classic "three R's" that traditionally have been fulfilled by extended families, community agencies, and religious institutions. *Promoting Your School* was written with these realities in mind, and to simplify at least some aspects of the life of all school leaders by helping them draw upon a wide array of school and community resources to build a support base of human, material, and financial capital.

Parents who believe their children are getting a quality education in your school or school district will not "vote with their feet" by withdrawing their children from the public schools and enrolling them in a private school—and then lobbying for state funding to pay their tuition! If you honestly and openly involve parents and the greater community in your efforts to improve your school or your district, they will reward you not only with their time and support but also with the most precious asset they possess—*their children.*

Moreover, America's businesses have come to understand that a well-trained, well-educated, properly motivated workforce is the most powerful asset any company can have—especially if that company wants to be a player in the global economy of the 21st century. Employers are increasingly willing, even eager, to partner with schools to assist in developing such a workforce.

As it is with the private sector and with parents, it will also be with the community at large. Households that have no school-age children need tangible demonstrations of getting their money's worth before they will even consider paying more in taxes to support somebody else's children. It is up to you and your school teams to demonstrate the value of the education tax dollar.

So, more than ever before, it is "Job #1" for schools and school leaders to build and strengthen the four-way partnership between schools, parents, community, and the private sector. Today's high-demand/high-performance–era educational leaders must be able to successfully communicate the needs, problems, goals, successes, challenges, and educational priorities of their schools. Stakeholders who know the truth about public schools have demonstrated a remarkable willingness to be supportive not only with their time but with their resources as well.

But you have to tell them! You have to *communicate* with them! The *entire* community has to be told. It is up to *you* to see that the message gets out, and to remember that some of your best communicators are your students, staff, parents, and community members.

Throughout this book, the word *marketing* is used. You have to market (sell) your school and your district to the external constituencies of parents and community and employers, as well as to the internal constituencies of students, teachers, and staff. Every group must be given a reason for caring about what happens to your school.

No single book can answer every question or foresee every eventuality, but the strategies contained in this book *can* provide you with a map to help you and your team get to where you want and *need* to go. Most of these techniques and strategies are drawn from the actual successful experiences of schools all across the United States. Still others are taken from real-world business and political situations in which collaborative, communicative leadership has overcome bureaucratic tradition and inertia.

There are 13 chapters in this book. Each chapter deals with a separate component of communicating/marketing challenges and offers strategies for how to meet them. Unlike a novel or a biography, this book isn't necessarily designed to be read from beginning to end, or chapter by chapter. Communicating/marketing/selling your school or your school district is the only "plot," and there is a certain amount of duplication from chapter to chapter, since some basic marketing techniques obviously apply to more than one strategy or project.

Thus, each chapter is something of a stand-alone "cookbook" intended to provide hands-on strategies, tips, how-to's, lists, and resources for reaching and enlisting your essential audiences. The emphasis is on the practical and the doable rather than the theoretical.

Clearly, every tip and technique will not work for every school. Although some of this information may be old hat or didn't work for you, it may be new to someone else and may work well in another school environment or community. Also, remember that just because an idea has been around a long time doesn't mean it's not a good one.

This book is written to be used by all school and district administrators, new to the position or experienced, and at schools or districts, large or small; rural, suburban, or urban; elementary, intermediate, or secondary. It recognizes that principals and district administrators come to this task with varying levels of expertise in communications and marketing but that they are united by a common desire to help their schools be the best that they can be.

The book is also intended to be used, or at least to be helpful, to leaders of PTA/PTO organizations who want to be effective and supportive school advocates; to business leaders who realize that, without quality public schools, they have no economic future; to community members who understand that good schools make strong, healthy neighborhoods; and to elected and appointed public officials who understand the relationship between high-achieving public schools and an enhanced quality of life for their constituents.

The resources and samples at the end of each chapter were drawn from a wide variety of sources. A survey instrument was sent to "Principals of the Year" in all 50 states and to selected other school administrators—several hundred in all—soliciting items from their "arsenal of tricks." Other techniques and concepts were gleaned from school public relations professionals and other communication experts. The goal throughout was to avoid reinventing the wheel and to seek out what works best from the practitioners who are in the arena, marketing their schools day in and day out.

Selecting which material to include was a challenging task. The standards were to select those resources/samples that (a) seemed to best represent successful practices, (b) could be replicated outside their original setting, (c) covered as wide a spectrum of techniques and approaches as possible, and (d) could actually be implemented at the building level with building-level resources as well as at the district level, with a broader array of support. Every form, sample, example, or model is included in the book for one purpose only: *to be used.* Permission is granted to readers to copy, modify, or adapt any of this material for local school or district use.

Like the first and second editions, this new, third edition of *Promoting Your School: Going Beyond PR* has been very much a collaborative effort. Throughout the research process, I have received enormous and willing assistance from many of the best, most creative minds in education and from a number of outstanding national educational organizations and enterprises. I am grateful to the many educators who have shared so generously their ideas, advice, techniques, strategies, wisdom, and vision. Their contributions make up a large portion this book. With admiration and appreciation, those educators who contributed to both the original and second editions of *Promoting Your School* are acknowledged in Resource A at the end of the book.

Acknowledgments

My special gratitude goes to Eleanor Andersen and Jeri Robertson for their research, contributions, and updates to this edition of *Promoting Your School;* to David Bolger for his contributions to all three; and to Bethany Holder and Renee Davis for their tireless assistance in bringing this third edition to completion.

This book would not have been written without the inspiration, talents, and collaboration of all the people and organizations listed throughout the book. The credit goes to them. The errors of commission or omission remain mine alone.

PUBLISHER'S ACKNOWLEDGMENTS

Corwin gratefully acknowledges the contributions of the following individuals:

Bruce Deterding, Principal
Wichita Heights High School
Wichita, KS

Anne Roede Giddings, Assistant Superintendent
Ansonia Public Schools
Ansonia, CT

William A. Sommers, Program Manager
Southwest Educational Development Laboratory (SEDL)
Austin, TX

About the Author

Carolyn Warner has gained national stature as one of America's most articulate educational and public policy leaders. A product of pioneering Oklahoma stock, her father was an Oklahoma state senator, teacher, and newspaper publisher in whose honor the first public school in Oklahoma's Indian Territory was named. Her mother, also a teacher, served as a school principal in both Oklahoma and California.

With six children in the public schools, Carolyn Warner became an active parent volunteer and PTA member, and she began her public service career with election to the Phoenix Union High School District Board of Trustees. In 1974, public service became a full-time commitment when she was elected Arizona State Superintendent of Public Instruction, the first noneducator ever elected to this post. She was reelected to two additional 4-year terms. During her tenure, Warner became nationally known for her advocacy of educational accountability (both academic and fiscal); citizen participation in educational decision making; the integration of career and technical education and basic academic skills; and an unparalleled partnership with school administrators, teachers, and business leaders. Under her leadership, Arizona's Basic Skills and Employability Skills initiatives became national models, and were among the first educational materials to be printed in the Navajo language.

As a respected public policy leader, Warner maintains an active role in political and educational initiatives and organizations on both the state and national scene. Drawing on her vast experience in government, business, education, and communications, she heads her own firm, Corporate Education Consulting, Inc., which offers consulting, speaking, seminar, and training services focusing on education, workforce/workplace issues, leadership, and public–private partnerships.

Carolyn Warner is nationally known as a speaker of uncommon skills, giving over 30 keynote and seminar presentations per year. Her public speaking expertise is reflected in her bestseller, *The Last Word: A Treasury of Women's Quotes*. She is also the author of *Everybody's House—The Schoolhouse*, published by Corwin in 1997.

PART I

Establishing Communication

The Foundation of Success

"If you're the only one who knows something, it's a secret."

In days past, schools did not always need solid communication and public relations programs. The school was there, the teachers were there, parents sent their children, the law said so—and that was it!

Half a century ago, more than three-quarters of the families in both rural and urban communities across the United States had children in public schools. Today, fewer than one-quarter of families have children in public schools, leaving many community members with no direct line of communication with their local schools.

Thus, the traditional modes of communication from the school to the public—report cards, parent-teacher conferences, calls home when a child misbehaved, open house, flyers announcing special events, a newsletter, sporadic media coverage of special activities—were deemed adequate for keeping the community informed. But today, these methods, although still important pieces of a comprehensive communication plan, are simply not sufficient to build the broad-based support schools need to be successful.

The rightness of your "cause" (your position, your district's mission) aside, people just aren't going to take your word for it anymore. They want to see results, accountability, proof. Can you blame them for being skeptical in the face of the current, widespread public furor over the crisis in American education? However, it has been demonstrated that, over the long haul, communities will support a school system that exhibits a solid, measurable commitment to quality.

As a professional educator or public education supporter, you know that in most schools throughout the country, most educators are doing a good job with most students. Yet the public's knowledge of and confidence in public education does not always reflect these achievements. It is up to you to be the principal communicator, to make sure your community has the best possible image of your school, because it is their school, too. You must strive for constituency "buy-in."

Public schools are sizable financial enterprises. Many school districts, especially in rural areas, are their community's largest employers. School board members and administrators are responsible for managing large amounts of tax dollars. With that fiscal accountability comes the responsibility of informing federal, state, and local taxpayers (the stockholders in the enterprise of public education) in honest terms about how their money is spent, how their investment is managed, and what return they are getting from their dollars.

The siren song of "No new taxes!" is strong in this economic and political climate of deficit reduction and fiscal restraint. After all, it is easier to rationalize withholding financial, political, and even moral support from an institution than from the individual taxpayer who is struggling to pay the mortgage or to obtain affordable health care.

The school that takes its communication role seriously is the school that will receive the greatest public support when a program need arises or a crisis occurs. Public confidence cannot be bought. It must be earned through the daily actions of the entire school family and through a planned communication effort involving all education supporters, from the local school principal and PTA president to the district superintendent and the governing board.

THE COMMUNICATION PROCESS

What is communication? It is an exchange of information between people. Conveying information alone does not involve an exchange; it is simply the act of providing someone with data, a one-way flow. When we communicate with someone, what are we really attempting to do? Most of the time, we are trying to change or mold that person's attitude about something so that it becomes congruent with our own. Information is disposable; it can be presented, reviewed, or discarded—and with no attempt at changing attitudes, it may be simply a one-shot process. But you must make communication and attitude formation a continuous process.

Everyone involved in education is a communicator—a good one or a not-so-good one. As a principal or other educational leader, one of your major challenges is to build a schoolwide team of people who can effectively carry a positive message into the community about your school or district.

The communication process begins with determining what is currently being communicated about your school and deciding whether or not this is really what you wish to communicate. It then requires developing a strategy with an action plan that targets the opinion leaders within your community. These people will add their own perceptions to what is communicated and share their versions of the information with their constituencies. Local media will either reinforce the communication or add its own interpretation. Parents with students in your school will have their own assessments, as will your faculty and staff. This leads you back to Step 1, and the process begins over again. Once you understand the process of communication, you can begin to build understanding and support for your school.

THE FOUNDATION OF SUCCESS

DEALING WITH PERCEPTIONS

Educators tend to communicate with the public on the basis of facts, but the public does not always care about facts. Most people tend to function on the basis of individual perceptions. Each involved group operates according to a general consensus of what its members perceive. With the media adding its own spin, the public becomes confused and confidence levels toward schools drop.

As an example of perception, suppose two people witness a hit-and-run accident. When the police ask what color the car was, one witness says "gray" and the other says "green." Who is correct? The fact that the car was actually blue loses out to the perceptions of the witnesses.

Recognizing that perception is often more powerful than reality, how do you address this incongruity, a matter over which you may feel you have no control? First, you try to look at your school from the points of view of your varied constituencies. When you realize what their perceptions are and understand why, then you are ready to plan and work to bring perception and reality closer together.

As in any other major enterprise, good public relations and positive public perception are important keys to a successful school operation. These keys are almost as important to schools as what goes on in the classroom—because they greatly enable schools to be more effective in providing quality education.

OPINION LEADERS

There are diverse groups of people involved with the schools. As an educational leader, you at various times deal with the following people:

- Governing board members
- The superintendent's public information officer
- Central office staff
- Principals
- Teachers
- Support staff
- Students
- Parents
- Social service providers
- Community members
- Business leaders
- Legislators
- The media

Within most of these groups are individuals who function as opinion leaders. They are the people to whom others in the group turn for information and advice. How do you identify these citizens who have a following, who have credibility within the group, be it for their trustworthiness or for their expertise?

These opinion makers can be any number of informal leaders: the school secretary, the 25-year teacher, the president of the PTA, the local grocer or dry cleaner, the bank vice president. Always be aware that, in one way or another, these opinion leaders have an interest in the schools of their community.

One of the interesting characteristics of opinion leaders is that they are seldom the loudmouths in their group. The person who complains at every PTA meeting is not an opinion leader. An opinion leader, generally, is the one who stands to speak when it is important and has a valid statement to make. These citizens are usually activists and positivists, and it is vital that you cultivate their support.

GETTING THE WORD OUT

In spite of our best efforts to be effective communicators, we aren't always successful in reaching our desired goals. This is true for many professionals, but especially true for educators because they tend to be so focused and dedicated to simply getting the job done that it seems almost unprofessional to be seen and heard tooting their own horn. This terminal modesty is a dangerous by-product of dedication to the task at hand.

Former high school teacher, coach, and principal (and Governing Board President as of spring, 2008), Orin K. Fulton of Agua Fria High School in Avondale, Arizona, doesn't mince words: "Publicize throughout the community your student successes in everything—athletics, academics, performance groups, success rates. Don't hide your good qualities—flaunt them!" Here's a challenge for you:

- Inform the public about your school's programs and activities.
- Build confidence in what you, your faculty, and staff are doing for students.
- Restore the partnership between parents, teachers, and community in meeting students' needs.
- Rally support for the total educational program.
- Enrich the home, school, and community by improving educational opportunities for all.

Now, that's a tall order. How can you possibly accomplish all of those tasks? Chapter 2 will explain how to

- identify the image your school presents and identify the community's perception of your school.
- develop a strategic plan.
- develop an action plan to implement your strategic plan.
- become an educator who communicates and put your plans to work.

If community members are made aware of the quality work your school is doing in educating their children, they will support your efforts wholeheartedly. You, as well as the students and their parents, faculty, and staff—in fact, the entire community—will reap the benefits of such a partnership. Confidence in American education will be renewed—step by step, student by student, family by family, school by school, and community by community.

Let the communicating begin.

Commandments for Communicators

1. Thou shalt accept that it is *difficult* to communicate clearly.

2. Thou shalt know what thy message is.

3. Thou shalt define what thine objective is.

4. Thou shalt remember who thine audience is.

5. Thou shalt simplify.

6. Thou shalt repeat. Thou shalt repeat.

7. Thou shalt respect the power of the parable.

8. Thou shalt weave humor into the fabric of thine message.

9. Thou shalt analyze how thy message has been received.

10. Thou shalt stop when thou hast no more to say.

Source: John Jay Daly, Daly Communications, Chevy Chase, MD.

2

Making Your
Schools Stand Out

"Knowing where you stand isn't the same as standing out."

W hat makes your school different from others? Can you clearly define what is special and unique about your school? Can others on the staff? Can parents? Can your community? In an era of choice and local community involvement through participative management, not only must you be able to define your uniqueness, you must be able to demonstrate it as well.

There was a time when public schools were pretty much created from the same mold. No matter where you traveled throughout the country, you could reasonably expect to find the same basic program of instruction delivered in the same basic style. Even the school buildings tended to follow the same standard design.

For the most part, it was the private schools that offered specialized programs: some with a religious orientation; some with a college preparatory focus; and all designed to appeal to the special interests of parents or benefactors, if not of students.

As a tool to encourage voluntary school desegregation, public education expanded on the concept of magnet schools, a variation of the private school model. Magnet schools placed special emphasis on a particular academic program, such as science and technology, international studies, foreign languages, or the arts, to attract students to attend schools outside their own neighborhoods. Although magnet schools have achieved a certain degree of success, by definition, they generally lack the critical component of a supportive and involved community.

The successful school of the 21st century will work closely with the community, first to identify that community's most important educational needs and goals and then to design a program that meets those needs. The key is to create a dynamic program that also positions the school as an innovative and flexible institution within the community. Anything less will lead to schools being perceived only as part of the problem rather than as part of the solution.

IMPROVING YOUR IMAGE

Whether you realize it or not, your school already has an image. You don't have to have a communications plan in place for the public to have a perception of who you are and what you are about. Unfortunately, if you are not actively planning and managing what you communicate about your school, your perceived image could be that of "Just a school, I don't know if it's a good one or not," or even worse, "That's the school I don't want my child to go to."

Images are created (or re-created) by communicating your desire to serve your constituents, working with them openly and honestly to establish a relationship of trust, and consistently delivering the expected product or service. Douglas Pfeninger, principal for over 25 years at Dartmouth (Massachusetts) Middle School, acknowledges that his job of marketing is not so hard these days because "We have developed a reputation as a quality school. My 'selling' is our product over the years."

Susan Van Zant, principal of Meadowbrook Middle School in Poway, California, not only appears at all school events, she is out in front of the school at the end of each school day. Principal Nancy Saltzman of Broadmoor Elementary School in Colorado Springs, stands outside and greets the students every morning before school and does parking lot duty at the end of the day as well. Richard Janezich, principal of Brooklyn Center High School in Minnesota, takes this a step further. He believes that it is important for the principal to be visible in the community and attends as many civic meetings as he can fit in, from meetings of the city council and the chamber of commerce to those of civic groups such as the Rotary, Lions, Chamber of Commerce, and Veterans of Foreign Wars (VFW).

Establishing a relationship of trust can be as simple as validating and recognizing the students in the school. To parents, no one is more important than their child. If the principal validates their child, parents will be more trusting that their child's best interests will be met. Hanging students' pictures in the hallways is a way that Karen Bangert, principal of Wagonwheel Elementary in Gillette, Wyoming, shows that each child is important. Larry Clark, principal at Halifax County High School in South Boston, Virginia, arranges for weekly scheduled photo ops. When Ken Cazier of Star Valley Junior High School in Afton, Wyoming, presents "good deed" tickets, everyone knows he has found the "positive image" that Afton educators promote.

If your school's image needs improving, it will take planning and patience to achieve this. A plan is necessary to effectively target your needs, your audience, and your message. It takes time for people to assimilate the new messages you are sending about your school, especially if you must first overcome old, negative perceptions.

STRATEGIC PLANNING: THE KEY TO ORGANIZATIONAL SUCCESS

A strategic plan is the essential first step for the success of any organization, including a school. You have to have a clear vision of where your organization/school ought to be and of where the stakeholders want it to be. That is what the development of a strategic plan is designed to set down, in clearly understandable language. Once these fundamental strategic determinations have been made, you and your team are then ready to develop the elements of the school strategic plan into the various component plans that will move the school forward. (See example of Mount Vernon City Schools Strategic Plan at chapter's end.)

However—and this is a crucial point—a "set in concrete," lengthy, highly detailed strategic plan is as much an organizational dinosaur as top-down management. A good strategic plan should be a document that is in a state of constant development. Tom Peters, in his book *Thriving on Chaos* (1987), emphasizes that strategic planning is a process, not an end in itself. According to Peters, your strategic plan should have the following characteristics:

- Involves everyone—the whole team—in its development
- Is free of "you can't do that," "that will never work," and "we've never done it that way" assumptions
- Enables you to be flexible and constantly evolving
- Is developed on site by practitioners, not farmed out to planners
- Represents vigorous debate and creative thinking by all the stakeholders
- Contains a timeline for action and review

Once you and your team have begun living the strategic planning process, you are ready to develop the working components of your plan. The *hows* of this implementation process are the subjects of the chapters that follow.

Chapter 3 deals with assessing the climate and perceptions of your school among your internal school community (administrators and staff). This process is treated in its own chapter as a separate entity, but these assessments are obviously an integral part of the strategic planning process as well. You clearly cannot develop overall strategies, let alone tactics, if you don't have an accurate read on climate and perceptions. Like the strategic planning process as a whole, reflection and evaluation are ongoing events in the life of a communicating educational leader.

DEVELOPING A MARKETING PLAN

Your overall marketing plan should be considered the next logical phase in implementing your strategic plan. Steps toward developing a marketing plan are as follows.

Step 1. With the help of your school team, identify exactly what it is you wish to market to the community. Community perceptions are clearly a driving factor in reaching these marketing determinants. Your end product, obviously, is a well-educated student. But in today's social and economic climate, there are many "products" that the community expects schools to deliver. To produce these products, there may be a number of services, outcomes, or problems that require the support of the community. Among the products you may wish to market are the following:

- Involvement of parents
- Involvement of stakeholders who are not parents
- Volunteerism opportunities
- Early childhood programs
- Extended day programs
- Specialized curricula (science, technology, fine arts, career and technical education)
- Community-business partnerships
- Substance abuse programs
- Safety programs (gang prevention, "Stranger Danger," "Officer Friendly," weapons control)
- Health education (including sex education and HIV/AIDS information)
- Cultural awareness
- Environmental programs
- Academic achievement

- Adult/community education programs
- Statistical results
- Instructional strategies
- Teacher recognition
- Education foundations/scholarship programs

Step 2. Before you can create a plan to market your school and improve its image, you need to find out what people know or don't know about your school. This includes staff and students as well as community members. Design a survey to gather the necessary information so that you can better target your efforts when implementing your plan (see Chapter 12).

Step 3. Identify your primary or most important audiences. You may wish to group them into internal audiences (students, staff, volunteers, parent organizations) and external audiences (parents, stakeholders, business/civic organizations, clergy, media, elected/appointed public officials). Once you have identified these key groups, you must decide how you can best reach them with your message. Each group may require different information and a different communication strategy. This is targeting your audience and, if applied carefully, will save you time and effort in getting the right message to the right group.

Step 4. Determine how much of a budget you will have to support your marketing efforts. There is no point wasting time developing a creative and extensive marketing campaign if you cannot afford to pay for its implementation. Of course, if you have developed a good plan, you might market it to local employers and solicit business support for funding it. If your plan will yield an identifiable result for x dollars, don't be ashamed to seek out local resources to finance it. More and more businesses realize that good schools are good for business.

Step 5. Decide how you want to position your school in the community. *Positioning* means determining where you stand in relation to other schools and promoting your uniqueness. What is special that your school has to offer students? Parents? The community? Employers? The more generic a product or service is, the more challenging it is to differentiate it from similar products and the harder it is for the consumer to understand the difference between those providing the same service. With the growing trend of allowing choice within the public school system, you must be able not only to determine what characteristics make your school stand out but also to defend your claims.

Once you have determined your position, develop supporting messages in the form of a position statement or mission statement to use in communicating with your publics. This statement should be clear and concise and should focus on your unique attributes. (See sample mission statement from Mt. Edgecumbe High School at the end of this chapter.)

Step 6. Set a long-range goal for your campaign and write a goal statement as a guideline for your marketing team. Identify the objectives that will help you accomplish your goal and the action steps needed to achieve each objective. Each objective should support your position and the image that you wish your school to project in the community.

Step 7. Develop your marketing plan. Use the recommendations in the following chapters to develop your marketing plan into an action plan.

Step 8. Implement your marketing plan. The ideas and suggestions found in the following chapters will help you.

Step 9. Evaluate your efforts to determine whether or not your plan is a success. Create a timeline for evaluations as part of the plan. Decide in advance how you will measure your progress. You should review your status every few months or at least once a year. Remember, strategic planning and implementation is an evolving, ongoing process. To what degree have you met your objectives? Is your plan effective? How can it be modified to better meet your needs?

Step 10. Use your evaluation as a starting point to once again analyze what and how you need to market to the community and begin the planning cycle again. Remember, if you are going to stay on the cutting edge in providing educational services, you must continually revise and adapt to the needs of your market.

One evaluation tool you may want to consider using as part of developing your strategic and marketing plans is a Communication Audit. The National School Public Relations Association refers to this audit as "Your Blueprint to School Community Support." Its overview of such an audit is included as a resource at the end of this chapter.

IDEAS TO HELP YOU GET STARTED

There are an endless number of projects, programs, and events that will support your educational mission and help to enhance your image as well. They are limited only by your imagination and financial resources. Following are several model programs to help you begin to build your plan. All have been successfully implemented by schools around the nation.

School Profile. Prepare a card or brochure that gives a simple profile of your school. Describe the unique features of your school, including number of students and staff, test scores, special programs and activities, philosophy, and graduation requirements. This card can be distributed to new students, community members, and real estate agents and can be used by students when applying to colleges and universities. (See the Prescott Unified School District's Marketing Brochure at chapter's end.)

Signs. An area that is often overlooked is that of the signs around your school. Signs are effective message "snapshots." (Even those who complain about billboards read them!) As basic as a sign may seem, it is an important factor in the first impression a visitor has of your school. Wauconda Grade School in Wauconda, Illinois, has a big lighted sign on the front of its building. Do your signs welcome visitors, or do they simply tell them what they must do? Signs should help give visitors an introduction to the friendliness you hope they will encounter on campus. If you have a large non–English-speaking population, the signs could be bilingual.

Hang a large map of your school at the entrance door or near the school office. Along with room numbers, include each teacher's name, grade, and photo to personalize it and to help visitors find their way.

Marquees can be used creatively even when you don't have a special event to publicize. Use them to recognize students and staff, to thank volunteers, to ask for help on a project, or to display a special thought for the week. Some schools have used quotes so creatively that town residents have written letters saying how much they look forward to the new ones each week.

For special occasions and special announcements, North High School in Sheboygan, Wisconsin, rents mobile lighted billboards and places them in strategic locations on school boundaries.

Lobby Showcase. Turn your school lobby and hallways into showcases of student achievement. Have a "Wall of Fame" featuring photos of outstanding students and permanent plaques engraved with their names. Georgetown (Texas) High School has recruited a local supermarket to sponsor its Wall of Fame honoring outstanding student achievement.

Make your lobby into a colorful art gallery and announce upcoming displays in the school newsletter. Invite the community to stop in and view the artwork.

A portable bulletin board that can be moved easily to a meeting room, library, hall, gym, or cafeteria (wherever the public will be gathering) is excellent for promotion. Utilize technology to promote your school. Install an electronic "signline" that communicates to all who enter your building the outstanding people and events featured that week or month. Ask the computer classes to design banners that can celebrate people and events.

Student Recognition. Involving the entire school and community in recognizing and rewarding students is an excellent way to market your school. Academic achievement letters, improvement awards, "Student of the Month" certificates, bumper stickers—anything that emphasizes student achievement, participation, and your school's focus is fitting. Solicit help from local businesses in providing incentives and rewards for students, such as discount cards, coupons, or certificates. Be sure that parents are informed when their child is recognized.

Staff, Volunteer, and Board Member Recognition. Superintendent Dr. Kevin Settle of Mount Vernon City Schools in New York highlighted how his district utilizes programs to honor those in the schools.

a. Each month we recognize the employees of one of our cafeterias as the "Food Service Staff of the Month." As superintendent, I, along with the Food Service Director and Building Principal make a surprise visit to the cafeteria and make the announcement. We present them with a banner to hang in the cafeteria along with a plaque that has the school and month inscribed. A picture is taken for the local newspapers and the school newspaper. Pride in the appearance of the cafeteria, the quality of the meals, initiative of the workers, morale of the workers, and the number of meals served has increased substantially since we started this program.

b. Every spring we honor our volunteers. Special invitations are mailed to everyone who has volunteered in any capacity with our schools. The administrators are responsible for cooking the hot dogs and hamburgers and serving the volunteers. Each administrator has an apron with his/her name embroidered. We take turns mingling with the volunteers and eat with them. During an appropriate time when the crowd is the largest, I tell them how important they are to the success of our schools, and the administrators perform a thank-you song or a cheer. We give door prizes and everyone leaves with a personalized certificate of appreciation and small gift.

c. Illinois declared the first "School Board Members Day" on November 15, 2007. Although it was not well known, Mount Vernon City Schools provided several forms of recognition for our school board members. I read a resolution (see the following sample) at the November meeting, [and] presented each member with a certificate of appreciation and satchel embroidered with "Mount Vernon City Schools, Board Member." They proudly use them to take information to and from our board meetings. I also sent information to the local newspapers and asked them to write an editorial thanking all school board members for their work. Next year we are going to hold our November meeting in one of our schools, and invite all former school board members living in the area to a reception honoring them for their past service.

School Board Members Day Resolution

WHEREAS, School board members are elected to sit in trust for their diverse communities, and in that capacity are charged with meeting the community's expectations and aspirations for the public education of their children; and

WHEREAS, School board members are entrusted with the guardianship and wise expenditure of scarce tax dollars; they are responsible for maintaining and preserving the buildings, grounds, and other areas of the school district that the community has put in their trust; and

WHEREAS, School board members are responsible for providing leadership that ensures a clear, shared vision of public education for their schools, that sets high standards for the education of all students, and requires the effective and efficient operation of their districts; and

WHEREAS, School board members adopt public policy to give voice to that leadership; they are also responsible for the regular monitoring of the district's performance and compliance with state policy; and

WHEREAS, School board members selflessly donate countless hours to public service with no compensation; and

WHEREAS, Employers are supportive of their employees who serve as school board members, generously lending support and time; employers give their employees the opportunity to better serve the needs of the school districts and citizens they represent through sometimes tremendous sacrifice to the employer; and

WHEREAS, Decisions made by school board members directly impact the quality of life in their communities, placing them at the front line of American democracy; therefore, be it

RESOLVED, BY MOUNT VERNON CITY SCHOOLS, DISTRICT 80, that we proclaim November 15, 2007, as "School Board Members Day" as a way to honor those citizens who devote so much of their time and energy for the education of our children.

Dated this 14th day of November, 2007.

(sample from Illinois Association of School Boards)

Source: Dr. Kevin Settle, Superintendent, Mount Vernon City Schools, Mount Vernon, NY.

Off-Campus Displays. Ask local businesses and public offices to display student work. Offer to decorate their offices with student art at holiday times. Put student-made posters in local storefronts to announce upcoming school events.

Staff Inservice. Plan a special staff training about your community and your school's role within it. This is especially effective if your school is located in a large metropolitan area where new faculty and staff may not be familiar with the immediate area or the relationship between your school and the local community. Emphasize the influential role that individual staff members can play in communicating with specific organizations as well as with the community at large to get the word out about your school.

Honoring the Family. If at all possible, designate one or more nights during the week to allow for family time. With the advent of so many extracurricular activities, it is difficult for families to find time for themselves. Principal Deborah Binder-Lavender has established Monday nights as "Family Night" at Thornton High School in Thornton, Colorado. Meetings, practices, performances, and games are not allowed after 6 p.m.

Staff Involvement in Community. Staff members are most often the first line of information to the community. This is true especially of nonteaching staff who are community residents. Their participation in various organizations reflects directly on the school and demonstrates a commitment to the community at large. Encourage and recognize the members of your staff who involve themselves in the community. Everyone who works in your school is important to your marketing success, and everyone must be an informed part of your marketing team.

Key Communicators. These are the opinion leaders in your community. Once you have identified them and cultivated their support, keep them informed through personal contact, special newsletters, or quarterly meetings (preferably all three). Invite them to special events. Call them regularly to update them on issues and concerns impacting your school. Ask their opinions, and listen to what they have to say. These people can be invaluable in quelling rumors and disseminating positive information. John Richardson, principal of Sunnyslope Elementary School in Port Orchard, Washington, has found key communicators from all areas of the community to be extremely helpful in promoting a positive image of the school.

Speakers Bureau. Create a school speakers bureau and offer free presentations to local organizations. Include teachers, students, and volunteers who can speak enthusiastically about the school and its specific programs. Participating in state or national education programs will give additional credibility that will cause your speakers to be viewed as experts in the eyes of meeting planners. Following a trip to China sponsored by the National Association of Secondary School Principals (NASSP), Principal Douglas Pfeninger (Dartmouth, Massachusetts) received numerous speaking invitations from service clubs, church groups, and other community organizations. His presentations on education in the Far East also afforded an excellent opportunity to tout his own school's programs. Principal Alan Chmiel of Fall Mountain Regional High School in Alstead, New Hampshire, is one of a select group of high school principals who speaks for the Jostens Corporation on positive school climate.

VIP Program. Once a month, invite influential members of the community to spend a morning visiting the school. Consider inviting the mayor, your state legislators, city council members, the Chamber of Commerce president, and outstanding business leaders. Have students meet the VIPs and give them special badges. Provide a tour of the school and lunch with student representatives. Give the VIPs an opportunity to sit in on a class and, if possible, to talk with teachers.

Teacher for a Day. Invite community leaders and school patrons to become a "Teacher for a Day" and get a hands-on view of education. Match them with certified staff members who volunteer to host guest teachers. Prior to the actual day of the project, hold a get-acquainted, lesson-planning meeting for the guest teachers and their teacher hosts. Hold a reception at the end of the day to recognize the volunteer teachers and receive their feedback. The proven benefits of this project are increased community support, new respect for teachers and the challenges schools face, a better understanding of the social problems that impact your students, and the creation of new business partnerships as a follow-up to the program. Not bad for a day's work!

Student for a Day. Parents at Halifax County High School in South Boston, Virginia, and Pearl High School in Pearl, Mississippi, are invited for a "Back to School Day." Parents attend their child's classes and are responsible for all assignments and class activities. The program has become extremely popular and gives parents an unusual opportunity to find out what is going on.

Community Assessment Visit. If you are prepared to deal with real input, both negative and positive, invite a team of community members to conduct a critique in the style of an accreditation evaluation. This provides a focused visit for your guests and can also assist in changing community perspective about the daily challenges facing the school. Such a visitation brought a real turnaround in the community's view of Aurora (Ohio) High School. These visitations could be expanded into both facilities audits and performance audits (with respect to the non-instructional business of your school).

Community Awareness Day. Plan a daylong event featuring the historical background and cultural influences of your local neighborhood or community. Invite community elders to share their experiences and local artisans to display their crafts and skills. Involve students in projects such as creating a historical timeline of the community, building something with the materials originally used (such as an adobe house), or reenacting an important community event. At Sedalia Middle School in Sedalia, Missouri, the students from the Dreamweavers team made special invitations for a celebration of their work for parents and others who helped them complete a portfolio project on various aspects of the community. The celebration was so successful that it made the front page of the local newspaper.

Cultural/Arts Festival. Highlight the various ethnic cultures represented in your school population with a special festival. Invite parents to assist students in sharing the foods, clothing, arts, and traditions of their heritage. Show how each culture contributes to making your school and community unique and special. Mainland High School in Linwood, New Jersey, sponsors a Teen Arts Festival to showcase student talent, during which time the school is open to the public. Ravenel Elementary School in Seneca, South Carolina, sponsors a popular annual "Artists on the Green Day," a celebration of local artists who exhibit their work and conduct creative workshops for students and community members.

Maintaining Traditions. Principal Gary Phillips of Fayette County High School (FCHS) in Fayetteville, Georgia, is very proud that his school has been able to sustain several traditions through the years, especially at graduation ceremonies. As they come to see their grandchildren graduate, many grandparents remember walking between rows of yellow and white flowers at their own graduation ceremonies. Awards given to students each year demonstrate a tradition of generosity from alumni who are grateful for the fine start they received at FCHS. Nancy Richmond, principal of Amsterdam Elementary School in Belle Mead, New Jersey, creates a school scrapbook during the year and makes the current and past books readily available to students and visitors.

Civic Projects. Encourage student involvement in civic projects such as recycling, adopting a stretch of highway for litter control, tree planting, or other community beautification efforts. A very special Cultural and Racial Equality (CARE) Committee has been organized by students and staff at Sauk Rapids High School in Minnesota. This committee was organized to promote diversity and traditions and to upgrade the curriculum and school policies to provide for a caring/nurturing school environment. Principal Gary Damore of Paradise Valley High School in Phoenix, Arizona, says that getting involved in community projects such as Skateboarding Park and Crosswalks for Schools has helped the school project a positive image within a large urban setting.

School in the Mall. Hold classes in a local shopping mall for a day (perhaps during Education Week). Most people won't visit a school if they don't have children in attendance. By taking the schools to the public, you can reach those who otherwise would not have an opportunity to see education in action.

"Ask the Principal" Sessions. Once a month, set up a table outside a supermarket or other agreeable, high-traffic business and be available to chat with community residents. Bring

handout information about your school. A variation on this is to walk your local school neighborhood or attendance area periodically, introducing yourself and asking residents if they have any questions or concerns about the school. This variant on "management by walking around" can pay significant dividends in increased community awareness, especially among households with no school-age children.

Community Talent Bank. Through your community contacts, identify those people with special skills or talents on whom you can call when the need arises. These could be people who are willing to help sew costumes for a play; who may have expertise in writing or producing newsletters; who are able to draw or paint; or who understand public relations, finance, or mass communications. Every community has a resource pool; it is up to your creativity and energy to tap it! Retired persons are often more than willing to help—they just need to be asked.

Place Mats. Have students design colorful place mats that include your school name and slogan or other information. Laminate them and find a local restaurant willing to use them, or present them to local hospitals, senior centers, and nursing homes.

Grocery Sacks. In cooperation with grocery stores, new sacks can be distributed to elementary, middle, or high schools for students to write or draw on. When displayed in the store, seasonal tributes in the form of poems, information, or drawings featuring a particular school can be rewarding for the student, school, and community.

School Bus Advertising. In some states, advertisements are allowed on the sides of school buses. The ads can highlight school or district successes, and offer a great opportunity to partnership with community organizations or business who will sometimes underwrite the cost of the school message with inclusion of their logo in the ad. These "moving billboards" travel not only throughout each district but also across the state for athletic and other competitions making them great visual tools.

Senior Passes. Offer free school activity and athletic passes to senior citizens in the neighborhood or at a nearby retirement residence.

Real Estate Breakfast. Invite local real estate agents to a breakfast or an open house at your school. Have students assist in presenting a brief program about the school. Provide packets that include information about instructional programs; extended-day options and extracurricular activities; awards received by the students, staff, and school; achievement test scores; school demographics; and school goals and philosophy. Realtors play an important role in marketing your school. You will know you have their support when real estate ads read "Located in _____ school attendance area."

Real Estate Signs. An extension of enlisting the support of real estate agents is to have signs made up for them to hang beneath their For Sale signs that read "_____ School Attendance Area: Dedicated to Education Excellence" (or whatever your slogan or position statement is). This helps potential buyers who are shopping for a school as well as a home and assists in marketing your school, too.

Welcome Wagon. Invite Welcome Wagon representatives to an orientation at your school. Provide them with school information to hand out to new residents.

Orientation to School. To make incoming freshmen feel more like a special part of the whole school community, students are welcomed with an Open House at Fayette County High School in Fayetteville, Georgia, where they may follow their new class schedule. Members of the Beta Club are stationed at key points in the hallways to assist the new students. The staff at Sussex County Vocational-Technical School in Georgetown, Delaware, go one step further. There is a home visitation program for all ninth graders and their parents. Parents can also have an orientation especially for them. Teachers run a class for parents during the mock school day Open House at Buffalo High School in Minnesota.

School Alumni Association. Recruit a high-profile community member who is a graduate of your school to help form an alumni association. The group should be organized to support school programs and activities through the continued involvement of former students. Build a mailing list through class reunion organizers, permanent record files, and advertisements.

Once you have located enough interested graduates, help them form a planning group, establish an organizational structure, survey alumni to find out their needs and interests, and invite others to participate. If the group can provide social activities, recognition, and meaningful involvement in the school, the alumni association will be of tremendous help to your school. Such groups often raise money for college scholarships.

School Mascot. Something as simple as the introduction of a school mascot (even at the elementary level) can have a tremendous impact on improving school spirit among students and staff. Hold a contest to select and name the mascot. Find someone who can design and assemble a costume. Announce the mascot's arrival days or weeks ahead to create an atmosphere of anticipation. Before introducing the mascot for the first time, have a series of activities to generate interest among the students. Staff members, parents, or even students could be recruited to wear the costume. You may or may not want to keep the mascot's identity secret, communicating only through gestures or interpreters such as the principal or a teacher.

The mascot could make regular appearances at school and community events and visit classrooms to reward good behavior, academic improvement, and perfect attendance. The mascot could visit classes prior to test week to encourage students to do their best.

A local or student artist might prepare a set of cartoon logos to use on printed materials. The mascot's picture could be put on posters, reward tickets, passes, and so on. A "Principal's Stamp of Approval" might be made up with your mascot's picture. The mascot should be linked to all special programs and events to be a constant theme and motivator for school and students.

School Slogan. Hold a contest for the slogan that best represents your school. It should be short and catchy and usable on all school materials. Good slogans are easy to remember and reflect the positioning of your school.

Homework/Calendar Hotlines. Providing telephone hotlines to parents and students is not only convenient for them, it is also a real time-saver for your staff. There are a variety of these interactive systems, both commercial and nonprofit, currently in use around the nation. You might find it helpful to study a system that is already online and evaluate whether your school and school district would benefit from this technology.

Articles/Ads. Send an editorial to the local newspaper. Write articles about your business partnerships for publication in their internal publications. Write an article about one of your programs and submit it to educational journals and newspapers. Encourage teachers to submit articles for professional journals as well. Don't be hesitant to toot your own horn in writing. (A listing of key national education media contacts for education associations and publications is included at the end of this chapter.)

Pearl (Mississippi) High School worked in conjunction with the local Chamber of Commerce to run a full-page ad in the state's largest daily newspaper. The ad was informative in nature and extremely effective in bringing to everyone's attention just how important the school is to the community.

Web Sites, Web Pages, and E-Mail. Most schools and districts have Web sites. Individual teachers, grades, or departments usually have Web pages on the school site. Many of these Web sites and pages are created and maintained by students. School information, announcements, grades, calendars, homework assignments, and so on can be entered and changed with ease. E-mail is a fast and easy way to contact individuals or several people at once. The Internet also offers instant messaging services that allow two or more people to have a dialogue. (See Chapters 4 and 13 for more detailed information regarding the importance of electronic communication.)

Radio Show. Radio is an effective way of getting your message out, particularly in small communities with fewer schools or school districts in their broadcast area. If you have your own show, you can be even more effective. This is feasible in smaller communities where stations are more likely to provide a regular weekly time slot for schools. Businesses that are regular radio advertisers could be encouraged to sponsor such a program. It is an excellent way to share information about local, state, and national education issues, as well as highlight your own school's outstanding programs and students. In larger communities, you can pursue invitations to participate on local talk show programs or suggest that one of your programs be the focus of a public service feature story.

Of course, the subject is moot if your school has the problem of Logan Rogersville (Missouri) High School, located in a rural/small suburban area with no local newspaper, radio station, or television station. In such a situation, Principal Emmett Sawyer has found he must rely on issue-specific publications and meetings as his best way of communicating with parents and patrons.

Cable Television. Another medium often overlooked is the local cable television network. Most carry some type of educational programming or may be willing to work with you to produce your own show or to provide a constantly running school events/bulletin board/calendar. Your district may even have its own cable station that you can tap into. Thornridge High School in Dolton, Illinois, has made its cable program an outstanding feature of the school. Aired on three different days for a total of five times a week is "Word on the Street," a bimonthly round-table discussion program that gives students a forum to discuss timely issues that impact the lives of young people. This 30-minute program was launched by the Advanced Radio and Television class. L'Ouverture Computer Technology Magnet School in Wichita, Kansas, has a daily student-produced TV show to communicate with students within the school.

REFERENCES AND SUGGESTED READINGS

Brown, J. L., & Moffett, C. A. (1999). *The hero's journey: How educators can transform schools and improve learning.* Alexandria, VA: Association for Supervision and Curriculum Development.

Kohn, A. (1997). *Education, Inc.: Turning learning into a business.* Arlington Heights, IL: SkyLight Publishing.

National School Public Relations Association. (1987). *Marketing your schools* (Pocket folder). Arlington, VA: Author.

Peters, T. (1987). *Thriving on chaos: Handbook for a management revolution.* New York: Knopf.

Ross, A., & Olsen, K. (1993). *The way we were . . . the way we can be: A vision for the middle school.* Kent, WA: Books for Educators.

Sherwin, R. M., & Ellis, B. (1989). *Promoting a positive image together.* Paper for Personnel Management Advisory Committee, Oregon Department of Education, Salem.

Sonnenberg, F. K. (1990). *Marketing to win: How you can build your client base in the new highly competitive service economy.* New York: HarperBusiness.

MOUNT VERNON CITY SCHOOLS STRATEGIC PLAN

The strategic plan for Mount Vernon City Schools is an extremely important document. The 5-year plan is the roadmap that guides the district. The vision and mission are clearly stated in the strategic plan, along with the basic beliefs from which the strategic directions, objectives, and action plans follow. From the strategic plan, the board of education develops its annual goals, which guide the superintendent's annual goals, which guide the principal's annual goals, which guide the teacher's annual goals. With all constituent groups fully informed and working toward the same vision and goals, the organization performs at a higher level. Following is a diagram showing the alignment of the components that guide the district and schools.

Mission: To challenge all students to seek a brighter future.

Mount Vernon City School District #80

Mount Vernon City Schools

Teaching for Tomorrow Today

District 80

Goal Alignment of Plans

Vision: Always seeking, always learning.

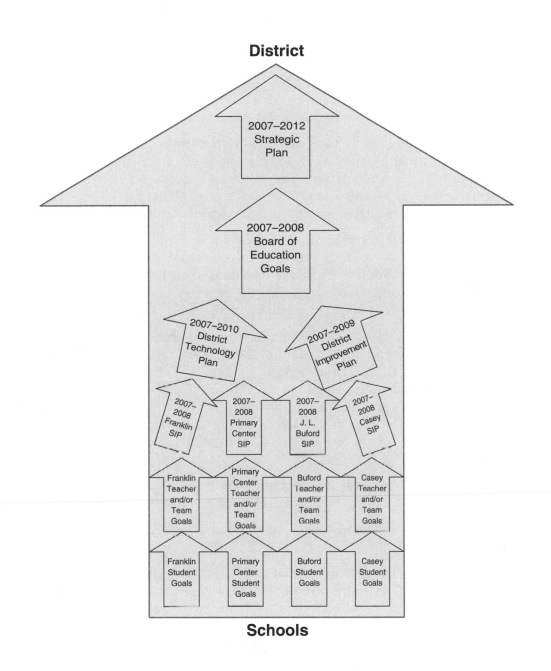

The purpose of strategic planning in Mount Vernon City Schools, District 80, was to bring into clear focus the long-range directions the school district would pursue to the year 2012. The vision guiding the Board in the implementation of its mission statement was best expressed as a hope that the collaboration of the members of the Board of Education, employees of the District, parents, and members of the community would produce a quality elementary education for each child enrolled in Mount Vernon City Schools, District 80. With this stated purpose and vision, the Board wished to pursue a strategic planning process that involved a quality representation of the Mount Vernon Community. The goal was to seek input from staff, parents, and other representatives of the community regarding the existing Strategic Plan and to engage them to assist the Board in the development and design of the new Strategic Plan that would serve to guide the District to the year 2012.

The following procedural process was recommended:

a. The Board clearly states its beliefs concerning the function of education.

b. The Board focuses on the planning with a clear statement of its concept of the mission of the school district and a clear statement of the vision it has for the district.

c. The Board identifies a Strategic Planning Group consisting of the District Learning Leadership Team and other selected members to effect a quality representation of the community. A representative of the Board of Education will serve as the chair. At least one-half of the membership of the Strategic Planning Group shall consist of community representatives not affiliated with educational programs.

d. The Board charges the Strategic Planning Group with the responsibility of reviewing the present Strategic Plan, which had a conclusion date of June 30, 2007. The Strategic Planning Group will analyze the status of each stated Strategic Direction and make reports to the Board regarding the progress of the plan. An initial report will be presented to the Board in February 2007.

e. The Board charges the Strategic Planning Group with the responsibility to assist them in the design and development of a Strategic Plan to guide the District for the period of July 1, 2007, to June 30, 2012. During the fall of 2006, the Strategic Planning Group will enter into planning activities for the purpose of development of the new plan. As specified in Section 130.00 of the Board Policy, the Plan shall consist of clearly stated action plans that will facilitate accomplishments of the stated directions. Each Action Plan shall be assigned a Chair to guide the established activities.

f. The Board charges the Strategic Planning Group with the responsibility of bringing a completed Plan to the Board of Education for adoption in March, 2007.

g. The Strategic Planning Group will be dismissed upon completion of the adoption of the 2007–2012 Plan.

h. The Board charges the District Learning Leadership Team with the responsibility of assisting them in the monitoring of the 2007–2012 Strategic Plan of the District. The District Learning Leadership Team will, on a regular basis, review each stated direction and associated action plan, and report to the Board any concerns or comments related to their progress toward goal attainment.

i. The Action Plan Chairs will make annual progress reports regarding their stated initiative to the Board of Education in June.

j. The Board will schedule annual Strategic Plan meetings for the purpose of reporting to the public the status of the plan's initiatives.

The following table shows an outline of the Strategic Initiatives and Objectives of Mount Vernon City Schools' 2007–2012 Strategic Plan. Although this outline does not contain the details such as the action plans with the timelines and people responsible for implementation, one can still see what an important communication instrument it is. At every monthly administrator meeting, the components are reviewed that should be addressed.

Mount Vernon City School District #80

2007–2012 Strategic Plan

Strategic Initiative #1: The educational program of the District will ensure appropriate learning opportunities to meet the diversified needs of all students, allowing them to interact in a global society.

Objective 1: Students will be provided an academic curriculum that allows them to meet or exceed the Illinois Learning Standards and Benchmarks.

Objective 2: Students will be provided educational experiences that promote understanding, tolerance, and respect of other people and their cultures.

Objective 3: Students will be provided opportunities to interact on an equal basis with other students.

Objective 4: Students will be provided learning time necessary to master the curriculum.

Objective 5: Students will be provided appropriate counseling, social, and health services to enable them to achieve at their maximum potential.

Objective 6: Students will be provided learning opportunities in the fine arts.

Objective 7: Students will be provided learning opportunities in the area of foreign languages and cultural awareness.

Objective 8: Students will be provided with programs to meet their special needs, including the following: special education, talented/gifted, and early childhood.

Strategic Initiative #2: The District will actively recruit, train, and retain highly qualified staff.

Objective 1: The District will actively recruit and employ qualified candidates from diverse backgrounds for all positions.

Objective 2: The District will provide professional development for all staff that is based on sustained, ongoing scientific research methods.

Objective 3: The District will provide incentives for employees to remain with Mount Vernon City Schools.

Strategic Initiative #3: Educational facilities must support the achievement of all students.

Objective 1: All District 80 facilities will support quality learning.

Objective 2: All District 80 facilities will support family and community needs.

Objective 3: All District 80 facilities will support current and future technologies.

Objective 4: Measures will be implemented to increase the safety and security for the District 80 schools, staff, students, and public.

Objective 5: The District will pursue the disposition and acquisition of property that is in the best interest of the future of District 80.

(Continued)

(Continued)

Strategic Initiative #4: The District will partner with parents and the community to strengthen communication and their involvement in the educational process.
Objective 1: The District will develop relationships and communication with parents to encourage their involvement in District 80.
Objective 2: The Board of Education, administration, and attendance centers will provide information about educational programs and student achievement to the Mount Vernon community.
Strategic Initiative #5: The District will seek and obtain funding and sponsorship for existing and enhanced educational objectives.
Objective 1: The Board of Education Budget Committee and Superintendent will devise a budget strategy and a budget that realistically reflects the relationship between the District's revenues and expenditures.
Objective 2: The Board of Education and Administration will seek additional forms of revenue to supplement District funds.

Source: Dr. Kevin Settle and Dr. Tyler Brown, Mount Vernon City Schools, District 80, Mount Vernon, IL.

MT. EDGECUMBE HIGH SCHOOL

Sitka, Alaska

Vision

An Innovative Learning Community Committed to Excellence

**We are INNOVATIVE, constantly striving to find and create better
ways of pursuing our goals and dreams;**

**We are all engaged in LEARNING, staff and students alike,
finding joy in its constant pursuit;**

We are a COMMUNITY that finds strength in our diversity;

We are COMMITTED to learner success and the MEHS mission;

We care deeply about EXCELLENCE in its many forms.

Mission

To Provide a Residential High School for Alaskan Students

Mt. Edgecumbe High School provides a comprehensive secondary educational
alternative, in a residential setting, for over 400 students, from more than
100 Alaska communities, preparing students to be lifelong productive citizens.

Source: Mt. Edgecumbe High School, Sitka, AK. Superintendent: Bill Denkinger; Academic Principal: Bernie Gurule.

The Communication Audit—Your Blueprint to School Community Support

The National School Public Relations Association (NSPRA) is among the nationwide organizations and companies that offer a comprehensive Communication Audit to school districts across the country.

NSPRA's Communication Audit process takes a snapshot of your current communication efforts, the climate for communication, the issues and image perceptions you are facing, and the communication needs and patterns of your target audiences.

Each NSPRA audit is different as each is tailored to your needs. The first question you will hear from NSPRA when you call to find out more about the auditing process is, "What do you want the NSPRA audit to accomplish for your district, service agency, association, etc.?"

NSPRA auditors review all current communication materials and techniques at the district and building level. The auditors talk with key representatives from target audiences and seek their honest opinions on the communication process, role, and effectiveness. The auditors also probe for key responses predetermined at the outset of the audit. (Remember the question, What do you want this audit to accomplish for you?)

The blueprint for success, the final report, then draws upon NSPRA's unique position of being on top of the best and latest communication techniques and plans, and tailors the recommendations to your specific needs.

Start Building Support With an NSPRA Communication Audit: The First Important Step to Build Support for Your Schools!*

- An audit demonstrates your commitment to improving communication.
- An audit demonstrates your willingness to listen and respond to community views—a major relationship builder in every audit we conduct.
- An audit will find out what major segments of employees, citizens, and customers think about your district's or agency's image.
- An audit will make definitive, workable recommendations for improving two-way communication and building community and staff support in your district or agency.
- An audit can lead to a practical public relations and marketing communication plan for your district or agency.

What Is a Communication Audit?

- Basically, it's a snapshot of a school district's communication needs, policies, capabilities, activities, and programs.
- It's an assessment of the effectiveness and credibility of present district, agency, and school publications and other communication and marketing activities.
- It involves a review of the district's or agency's public relations/communication policies.
- It takes a look at your demographical data, long-range plans, and past surveys of parent/staff/community attitudes.
- It examines your budget, current plans, and staffing patterns of the public relations/communication efforts.
- It reviews coverage by the local newspaper, radio, and television media.
- It uses focus groups of 8–10 people representing citizens, parents, business people, administrators, teachers, support staff, and other key audiences whose support is needed to improve communication in your district or agency. Focus groups help NSPRA communication experts assess the institution's image, communication pattern, and gaps.

- It delivers a 50- to 60-page Communication Audit report, which (1) reviews existing policies and printed material; (2) summarizes comments of focus group participants; (3) gives practical, down-to-earth recommendations to help improve communication efforts; and (4) makes certain you are receiving the biggest bang for your communication investment.

There Are Five Major Steps in an NSPRA Communication Audit:

1. Making the decision to do it.

   Nothing is more important in building trust and support between your organization and the public you serve than the quality of your communication efforts. Are you addressing the community's concerns? Are you communicating with citizens effectively? Does your staff understand and support what you're trying to do? If you cannot answer with a resounding "YES," you will benefit from an NSPRA Communication Audit.

2. Analyzing the current program.

   NSPRA's communication consultants will review your existing policies, publications, strategies, media relationships—every aspect of your internal and external communication efforts.

3. Listening to your audiences.

   The core of the audit is hour-long focus groups that are representative of your internal and external audiences. Focus groups can generate a lot more useful information than most surveys because a trained facilitator can probe the feelings behind the opinions. Each audit is different, so the number and composition of focus groups vary depending on the main mission of your audit.

4. Developing constructive recommendations for improving your communication program.

   Based on an analysis of your current program and the input from the focus groups, the NSPRA communication experts will make detailed recommendations for improving your communication and marketing efforts. Our experts are highly educated and experienced in the field and have had hands-on experience in school districts and agencies similar to yours.

5. Implementation assistance.

   Once the final report is received, NSPRA will coach you through the implementation steps. Examples include offering (1) sample materials and policies; (2) contact with NSPRA colleagues who have successfully dealt with similar situations to yours; and (3) lists of additional products and services that can assist you in turning your recommendations into positive results.

Why Choose NSPRA for Your Communication Audit?

Experience

NSPRA has conducted more than 50 audits in the past 5 years for districts, schools, associations, and agencies similar to yours. Our experience also creates an efficient and timely process that saves you time and money.

A Treasury of Resources

NSPRA knows better than anyone else what's going on in school districts and agencies around the country and how that should be communicated for maximum effectiveness. NSPRA's "catbird seat" gives you the most up-to-date solution to your communication problems.

(Continued)

(Continued)

Economics

Time after time in bid competitions, NSPRA has been thousands of dollars lower than anyone else, and usually offers more services.

Corporate AND School Public Relations

We know and practice both corporate and school public relations. All audits are reviewed by NSPRA seasoned counselors with both corporate and school PR experience. So you receive the double benefit of tapping into the best advice of our corporate and school PR professionals.

When's the Right Time?

- When you want to improve communication and support for your schools.
- When a new superintendent or board majority takes office.
- When you are about to embark on a new initiative, such as year-round schooling, or when there are major changes in the community.
- When a new public relations professional comes on board.
- When a communication audit hasn't been done for 5 or more years.
- When you have determined that your public's perception is quite different from your present reality.

What Will I Get From a Communication Audit?

- Effectiveness of your current communication efforts.
- Establishment of priority audiences and the best channels to reach them.
- Image of your schools or agency by staff, community, and customers.
- Two-way communication techniques that will work for your district.
- Information and frequency desired by your priority audiences.
- Specific information sought by you from the audit.

Your NSPRA Communication Audit will culminate in a 50- to 60-page report that comments on the district's existing communication efforts, summarizes focus group responses, and recommends innovative and proven techniques for improving two-way communication in your district. The recommendations will be down-to-earth; effective; and, in many cases, will cost you little to implement.

NSPRA Audits Are Tailored to Your Needs

Each audit NSPRA completes reflects the first question we ask you: "What do you want an NSPRA Communication Audit to do for your district, agency, association, etc.?" From that first step, NSPRA plans an audit that will work best for you.

For example, in addition to the usual and basic communication questions we ask focus groups—What information do you want? What's the best way of getting it to you? How often do you want it?—we often ask key planning and awareness questions on such topics as year-round schools, building new schools, closing others, school reform, etc. Some audits are just for external audiences, while others only look at staff and related internal audiences. Many combine both into one audit.

Each NSPRA audit report is unique and reflects the direction you give to NSPRA at the very beginning.

Source: The National School Public Relations Association, Rockville, MD; www.nspra.org.

PRESCOTT UNIFIED SCHOOL DISTRICT MARKETING BROCHURE

Making the Smart Choice

AS A PARENT, your first concern is finding a school that meets your child's needs. If you're feeling a little overwhelmed by the process, you've come to the right place. This booklet will take you on a brief tour of Prescott Unified School District (PUSD), where you'll discover a world of choices built on a foundation of excellence that's more than a century old.

Whether you're looking for traditional or alternative, college prep or vocational, gifted or special education, you'll find the programs that meet your child's unique needs for learning and self-discovery. And no matter which one of our award-winning schools you choose, your child will fit right into a dynamic, safe, student-centered learning community, where the teachers are certified, the test scores are high and your child is valued, challenged and encouraged to succeed – from preschool through high school and beyond.

Governing Board Approved Curriculum based on Arizona State Standards

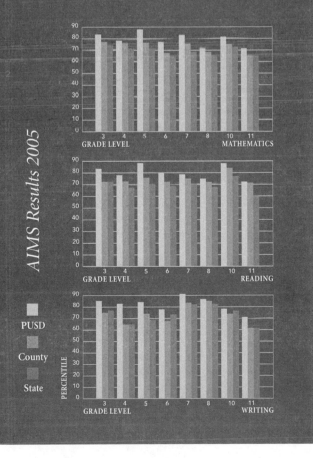

Our Mission

TO STRENGTHEN OUR COMMUNITY BY PROVIDING A DYNAMIC, SAFE EDUCATIONAL EXPERIENCE THAT ENCOURAGES EVERY CHILD TO SUCCEED IN AN INTEGRATED PROGRAM OF ACADEMICS, ARTS AND ATHLETICS.

Our Vision

TO BE THE PRESCOTT AREA'S MOST INNOVATIVE, EFFECTIVE AND RESPECTED EDUCATIONAL ORGANIZATION, FULFILLING THE PUBLIC'S TRUST.

AIMS Results 2005

MATHEMATICS
GRADE LEVEL

READING
GRADE LEVEL

PUSD
County
State

WRITING
GRADE LEVEL
PERCENTILE

(Continued)

(Continued)

doing your homework

EVERY FAMILY has different needs and priorities when choosing a school. That's why it's important to sort through the characteristics that are most important to you and your child. In addition to getting the basic tools needed to become a strong citizen, valued employee, entrepreneur or leader of tomorrow, you'll want to consider issues such as location, philosophy, parental involvement, test scores, music, arts, athletics, special needs, extracurricular activities and even transportation and food services.

The best way to learn more about all of the above is by visiting our schools. Be sure to observe some classes, meet some principals and teachers and see whatever else interests you. For most people, all it takes is one visit and they know.

To arrange your visit, simply call or e-mail our District Office, or contact the school directly (see the inside back cover for details). Before you visit us in person, feel free to drop in at **www.prescottschools.com**. We look forward to meeting you soon!

PUSD'S PRESCHOOL AND CHILDCARE PROGRAMS OFFER FAMILIES A SECURE, NURTURING ENVIRONMENT WHERE CHILDREN DEVELOP EMOTIONAL, LANGUAGE AND SOCIAL SKILLS ACCORDING TO INDIVIDUAL READINESS. CERTIFIED TEACHERS, BRIGHT CLASSROOMS AND SAFE PLAYGROUNDS MAKE FOR A POSITIVE SETTING WHERE FUN AND LEARNING ARE THE ORDER OF THE DAY.

Music   Art   Sharing

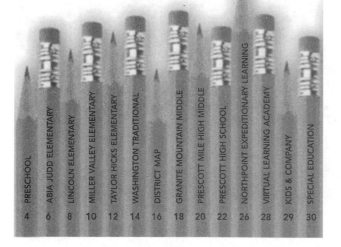

Preschools

DISCOVERY GARDENS
Early Childhood Center welcomes 3 to 5 year-olds for fun and learning. Offering a developmentally appropriate preschool, along with comprehensive special needs services, Discovery Gardens helps each child develop intellectual, physical, social, emotional and language skills according to individual readiness.

Discovery Gardens' facility is unmatched in the area with its colorful classrooms and "center" rooms, as well as a safe playground with tall shade trees. The curriculum is aligned with Arizona State Standards and uses a hands-on, center-based learning experience led by certified Master's level teachers.

Discovery
Gardens
early childhood center

Preschools are accredited by the National Association for the Education of Young Children

Approved   NAEYC Accredited   Department of Health Licensed

(Continued)

(Continued)

Abia Judd
Elementary School

A U.S. Department of Education Blue Ribbon School of Excellence and an Arizona A+ School, Abia Judd offers a well-rounded academic curriculum enriched by literature-based reading programs and hands-on math and science. The latest in computer technology sets the stage for mastering keyboarding and research skills that reinforce classroom studies. Distinguished for its parental involvement, Abia Judd has twice received the Arizona PTA of the Year Award.

*Photo left: Jane Robertson,
Arizona State Teacher of the Year, 2004*

Side-by-Side Reading   PTA   Cultural Arts Fair   Musi

91% OF PUSD 3RD GRADERS MET

OR EXCEEDED THE STANDARDS ON THE AIMS

READING EXAM, WHICH IS 20% ABOVE

THE STATE AVERAGE.

Spelling Bees   Physical Education   Student Newspapers

Miller Valley
Elementary School

Located in the heart of Prescott, Miller Valley is a bustling campus with a warm, friendly atmosphere. The school's strength lies in its faculty, a close-knit team of talented, highly trained homeroom and specialist teachers committed to helping every child become a lifelong learner. Chosen as an Arizona Literary and Fine Arts Site, Miller Valley offers comprehensive academic programs as well as enrichment programs and self-contained classrooms for exceptional students.

89% OF PUSD 5TH GRADERS MET OR EXCEEDED THE STATE STANDARDS ON THE AIMS MATH EXAM, WHICH IS 32% HIGHER THAN THE STATE AVERAGE.

Accelerated Reader   Libraries   Tutoring   Internet

(Continued)

(Continued)

Granite Mountain Middle School

New friends and new experiences go hand-in-hand at Granite Mountain. This welcoming environment provides the backdrop for gaining the skills – organizational, social, decision-making, leadership and service – that 6th through 8th graders need for continued academic success. Across the curriculum, students use the most modern technology and equipment to support their exploration of new subject matter alongside a child-focused faculty. From daily TV productions in the school's video lab to orchestra, fine arts and sports, students gain rewarding experiences and build the maturity and confidence needed for high school.

• 91% OF PUSD 7TH GRADERS MET OR EXCEEDED THE STANDARDS ON THE AIMS WRITING EXAMS.

• PUSD 8TH GRADERS SCORED AN AVERAGE OF 21% HIGHER THAN STATE SCORES ON AIMS READING, WRITING AND MATH EXAMS.

Yearbook   Geography Bees   Kids Voting   Honor Society

Source: Prescott Unified School District, Prescott, AZ. Kevin J. Kapp. Used with permission.

NATIONAL EDUCATION MEDIA CONTACTS

Education Associations

American Association of School Administrators
  (AASA)
1801 North Moore St.
Arlington, VA 22209
703-528-0700
Fax: 703-841-1543
www.aasa.org

American Educational Research Association
  (AERA)
1230 17th Street NW
Washington, DC 20036–3078
202-223-9485
Fax: 202-775-1824
www.aera.net

American Federation of School Administrators
  (AFSA)
1729 21st Street NW
Washington, DC 20009–1101
202-986-4209
Fax: 202-986-4211
www.admin.org

American Federation of Teachers (AFT)
555 New Jersey Ave. NW
Washington, DC 20001
202-879-4400
www.aft.org

Association for Career and Technical Education
  (ACTE)
(formerly American Vocational Association
  [AVA])
1410 King St.
Alexandria, CA 22311
800-826-9972
www.acteonline.org

Association for Supervision and Curriculum
  Development (ASCD)
1703 N. Beauregard St.
Alexandria, VA 22311
800-933-2723
Fax: 703-575-5400
www.ascd.org

Delta Kappa Gamma Society International
PO Box 1589

Austin, TX 78767
512-478-5748
Fax: 512-478-3961
www.deltakappagamma.org

National Association of Elementary School
  Principals (NAESP)
1615 Duke St.
Alexandria, VA 22314–3483
703-684–3345
Fax: 703-548-6021
www.naesp.org

National Association of Secondary School
  Principals (NASSP)
1904 Association Drive
Reston, VA 22091–1598
703-860–0200
Fax: 703-476-5432
www.nassp.org

National Education Association (NEA)
1201 16th Street NW
Washington, DC 20036–3290
202-833-4000
www.nea.org

National School Boards Association (NSBA)
1680 Duke St.
Alexandria, VA 22314–3407
703-838-6722
Fax: 703-683-7590
www.nsba.org

National School Public Relations Association
  (NSPRA)
1501 Lee Highway, Suite 201
Arlington, VA 22209
703-528-5840
Fax: 301-519-0494
www.nspra.org

Phi Delta Kappa, Inc.
PO Box 789
Bloomington, IN 47402
812-339-1156
Fax: 812-339-0018
www.pdkintl.org

Publications

The Education Digest
(accepts previously published
  material only)
PO Box 8623
Ann Arbor, MI 48107
313-769-1211

Education Week
4301 Connecticut Avenue NW, Suite 250
Washington, DC 20008
202-364-4114

Teacher Magazine
4301 Connecticut Avenue NW, Suite 250
Washington, DC 20008
202-686-0800

USA Today
(accepts commentaries only)
1000 Wilson Boulevard
Arlington, VA 22229
703-276-3400
www.usatoday.com

3

Internal
Communication

"Before you can sell the customers, you have to sell the sales force."

You've heard the saying, "Bricks and mortar don't make a school; people do." The way your school or school district is perceived by the community is due primarily to the image presented by the people in it—your faculty, staff, and students. Unless you plan to put all the students in the gym or cafeteria and teach them yourself and personally communicate with every parent and patron, you need to have a plan for making each person in your school an active member of the school team.

Each member of the school staff, from the custodian to the principal, is a key communicator with the community. Even substitute teachers are involved in carrying the image of your school back to the community.

Where do people most often go when they want the "inside story" on an issue or an organization? They seek out someone they know and trust who is directly involved with the source of information in which they are interested. All the favorable newspaper or radio or television coverage in the world will not overturn the negative or inaccurate report given firsthand by one of your employees to a neighbor.

Building good communication with your staff is vitally important. It is your best insurance against negative and divisive talk that originates in-house. Positive attitudes about your school are generated by the ripple effect created by good programs, good people, and good management. Staff members feel these effects first and pass these feelings on to students, who share them with parents, who transmit them to the community at large.

In order for all your school team members to be effective communicators and people who willingly promote an affirmative message about their school, they need to have a clear sense of the school's mission and goals and be fully informed about the school's program and the issues that affect it. This includes all staff, not just teachers. Instructional support staff, bus drivers, crossing guards, food service workers, secretaries, and custodians are all frontline communicators and are just as much a part of the school team as you and the teachers.

Today's leading superintendents recognize the connection between an effective communication program and student success. They understand the need to demonstrate accountability by delivering key messages about their schools and model good communication practices daily.

Here are some wise words and tips, with a focus on internal communication, from some communication-savvy administrators.

What does communication look like in a "world class" system?

"It has to be tailored to your school district/system. Communication is everyone's responsibility—from food service director to the board president. It has to be strategic, planned, flexible and it also has to be responsive."

"It's not just print or electronic; it must be mobile and multifaceted to reach out to diverse communities."

"Nothing will set back a district faster than poor communication."

"Everything the district does needs to be mission related, mission driven."

"Recognize you have to invest in good communication if you want it to truly be a world-class system, appropriately budget for it. Your school community must value communication and professional development."

"Good internal communication is essential. Whether it is the kindergarten teacher, the cafeteria worker or the bus driver—build on open and honest communication with internal stakeholders as well as having those conversations within your organization. Think of all those folks [district employees] as 'navigators' or 'key communicators'—everyone has a circle of influence outside of their job."

"We as educators need to be listening to our stakeholders as well—embrace what they are saying about our school and our district, and determine where we need to move with our mission."

"We need to make sure that the communication staff are helping us get an accurate database of key communicators. Listen to their suggestions and input about where we need to go with our mission. Sometimes, the folks who have the most influence are not necessarily the most high-profile in your community—but they have credibility and others respect their opinions."

"The cabinet [or executive council] needs to recognize that communication must be a major function of everything the district does."

If everyone is responsible for communication, how do you hold your staff responsible?

"Through the motivation and building capacity for people to see the power of good communication; creating a culture of encouraging people. You have to be encouraged to start small. Have the communication staff do a 'mini audit' at building level. By starting small with some great successes, your efforts pay off in the long run."

"If the administrative team understands the importance of great communication, then the culture of the district will reflect that."

"Practice good customer service. For example, talk to the secretaries about how they answer the phone with positive messages, or receive visitors with smiles."

"Ask, 'How do we serve our customers?' Look at the messages we're sending."

Source: National School Public Relations teleconference, Dec. 2007; panelists: Dr. Ken Bird Superintendent of Westside Community Schools, Omaha, NE; Dr. Sandra Husk, Superintendent of Salem-Keizer Public Schools, Salem, OR; and Dr. Rodney Lafon, Superintendent of St. Charles Parish Public Schools, Luling, LA.

TECHNIQUES FOR IMPROVING STAFF COMMUNICATION

Staff Meetings. Here are some suggestions that will assist you in transmitting information at staff meetings, as well as make the experience more pleasant for busy staff.

- Post agendas for your regular staff meetings. When the staff know the topics in advance, they come better prepared, and two-way communication is upgraded.
- Encourage participation and input from everyone.
- Stick to specific topics of interest to all. If you have subjects to discuss that involve only one or two teachers, meet with them privately.
- If it is necessary to review materials, send the information out with the meeting agenda so that pertinent questions can be asked during the meeting, which eliminates the need for additional time on the subject later.
- Don't waste staff time by calling a meeting to pass out information that could have been distributed through mailboxes or e-mail. Whenever possible, chair the meeting yourself—but have others actually present the material or the agenda. This gives you a certain objectivity in observing how the staff relate to an issue. It also involves more participants in the meeting.
- Limit the length of the meeting! By respecting everyone's time, you create an environment that allows you to deal productively with important issues. (Some educational leaders limit staff meetings to an hour—and always serve beverages.)

It is critical to lay the foundation of trust and two-way communication with all staff so issues can be dealt with before they are blown out of proportion. Although it takes time, the time spent creating relationships and dealing with issues while they are small saves much more time in the long run.

The system that has led educational leaders to several successful nonconfrontational contract negotiations in the past decade follows:

a. Chitchats
   - Every building has a representative from each grade who meets monthly with the building principal to discuss any issues, concerns, or ideas that need to be addressed. These are referred to as building chitchats. An agenda is created 3 days before the meeting, with items from the staff and principal so each group

may obtain the information needed to discuss the items. In nearly every case, issues are resolved at this level.

- If an item continues to be an unresolved issue, it is taken to the district-level chit-chat, which is also held on a monthly basis. This meeting is held in the superintendent's office with union leadership and others who may help resolve the issue. The building representatives may contact their union representative, who will contact the superintendent and have unresolved building issues added to the agenda. The superintendent may add issues to the agenda, which is determined three days in advance of the meeting so each group may obtain information and those involved may be invited to attend.

b. District Council
- Once a month, a more formal meeting is held at the Central Office, facilitated by the superintendent. Participants include one representative from each grade, principals, and a school board member. The union or administration may place items on the agenda that need to be discussed and communicated to the rest of the staff. This has served as an excellent way to obtain information about items and assures that nothing is overlooked by any constituent group.

c. Working Conditions Committee
- Once a month, a formal meeting is held at the Central Office with the support staff representatives. The superintendent facilitates this meeting. Support staff, union leaders, administrators, and a school board member all attend. The union or administration may place items on the agenda that need to be discussed and communicated to the rest of the support staff.

d. Learning Leadership Teams
- The Building Learning Leadership Team (BLLT) meets once a month. School is dismissed early and the staff meets to work on Critical Building Issues (CBIs). The CBIs must be linked to the School Improvement Plan and focus on student achievement.
- The District Learning Leadership Team (DLLT) also meets once a month. Members on the DLLT include parents, community leaders, teachers, support staff, a board member, and administrators. The DLLT starts with a luncheon and meets for an entire afternoon. One of the agenda topics is a review from each building about how they are progressing with their CBIs. This important topic assures that each building and the community leaders know what the other buildings are focusing on. The DLLT uses group processing techniques to determine Critical District Issues (CDIs), which they research and report back to the school board in the late spring each year.

At North High School in Sheboygan, Wisconsin, most staff meetings are by *affinity groups*—that is, secretaries, custodial staff, teacher's aides, department chairs, and so forth—so that the information shared can be as need-specific as possible. In this way, full-staff meetings can focus on topics of general interest and concern, thus saving time for everybody.

Staff Relations Team. A good way of communicating in schools with large staffs is to develop a staff relations team made up of teachers from each grade or subject level, several classified employees, and building administrators. The team meets often (once a week, or every other week) to discuss issues concerning the school and the district. Team members represent their colleagues by bringing questions and concerns to the table for discussion. The team members then pass on discussion results to their colleagues via grade-level and subject-area meetings.

Another way of communicating in schools with large staffs is to follow the lead of Gary Phillips of Fayette County High School in Fayetteville, Georgia. He divides his staff into four cluster groups. Each of the four assistant principals then presides over a cluster. This smaller-group approach allows for greater interaction and more effective communication.

Open Door Policy. Administrators who are available at all times to staff, parents, and students set the tone for a positive, caring attitude throughout the school. An open door sends a powerful message that you are there to help—or just to listen. But attitude is important as well. "The key," says Bob Kenison of Wauconda Grade School in Wauconda, Illinois, "is to be approachable." Deborah Binder-Lavender's twist on an open door policy is to be available to both students and faculty in the student commons. Every Monday at Thornton High School in Thornton, Colorado, Dr. Lavender sits at a table from 1 to 3 p.m. and allows people to stop by without an appointment and visit.

Be a Good Listener. Take time to get to know individual staff members. Ask about their families and their hobbies. Be visible around the campus and pay attention to the feedback you receive from staff. Eat lunch at different times and spend a few minutes visiting with staff members. Chat with them about how the year is going, what their classes are like this year, how they like the new math curriculum, and so on. Their answers will give you an idea of the image they are presenting to parents and community members, and provide you with a valuable tool to target areas needing improved communication.

Address Professional Needs of Staff. Do a "mini survey" at a staff meeting to determine what needs the school should address to increase staff effectiveness. When planning staff development programs, be attuned to staff suggestions and formulate programs that reflect these recommendations. Encourage teachers and staff to participate in schooling, training, workshops, inservice programs, and other activities that facilitate and improve their effectiveness. Grace King High School in Metairie, Louisiana, brings in outside speakers to talk on topics of current interest during teachers' lunchtime. Off-campus school retreats afford an excellent opportunity in a relaxed setting to share new teaching methods, to discuss the latest trends in education, and to develop a closer relationship among peers.

Staff Recognition. Recognition for special efforts can take many different forms. It is important that your staff feel they are valuable members of the team and that their efforts and input count. The most powerful recognition is daily acknowledgment of each individual's contributions to the success of the school team. This can be as simple as a welcoming greeting in the morning or verbal approval of a job well done. This personal touch is important whether you are from a small rural area or a large urban setting. Principals Ken Griffith (Guernsey, Wyoming) and Ben Grebinski (Regina, Saskatchewan, Canada) both attest to the effectiveness of this one-on-one with staff. As Grebinski states, "The personal contact takes time, but it is more productive." And Griffith says, "We are a small rural high school, so the individual phone or personal contact is still the most effective."

Successful teams do not generally single out individuals for special recognition. By rewarding one individual for being the best at something, you isolate him or her from the team and send the message that the rest of the team is not as important. Focus on recognizing staff through appreciation of efforts that promote teamwork.

Think about your personal leadership style. Do you offer praise freely, or is it given grudgingly and on an infrequent basis? As an educational leader, whichever style you model will be followed by your staff. The following are ideas for staff recognition:

- Write personal notes of appreciation.
- Take time to thank someone in person.
- Create a floating monthly award with an amusing theme.
- Hold drawings for free dinners or movie tickets donated by local businesses.
- Provide a special treat in the lounge such as doughnuts or ice cream sundaes.
- At full faculty meetings, recognize special occasions such as birthdays, weddings, births, and so on.
- Hold a barbecue at the completion of a successful project or event.
- Give posters with a theme promoting teamwork that can be displayed in work areas and classrooms.
- Sponsor an afterschool holiday get-together (and not necessarily on the last afternoon prior to Christmas break).
- Provide special buttons or pins.
- Create a staff committee to organize recognitions. After all, it's a team effort.
- Host an end-of-the-year party; you can enlist others to help you. But if this is the only full faculty or staff social gathering of the year, you've waited too long to get everyone together.

Address Personal Needs of Staff. An awareness and willingness to find out and meet the personal needs of staff members are greatly appreciated. Exhibiting this kind of caring attitude encourages the staff to become involved in supporting each other as well. Here are some suggestions for meeting personal needs:

- Sponsor a wellness clinic through the local hospital.
- Start a Weight Watchers at Work chapter.
- Organize an afterschool aerobics class.
- Create a cooperative child care group for staff taking evening classes.
- Hold a stress management workshop.
- Create a social activities club for single staff members.
- Develop a peer support network.
- Start a "sunshine fund" to provide flowers or small gifts for birthdays, weddings, births, funerals, and achievements.
- Arrange for coverage of a teacher's classes in case of emergency.

Staff Publications. Use your staff newsletter or e-mail to communicate information that does not need to be covered in a staff meeting. Many principals feel the need for a written bulletin (for faculty and students)—issued daily so that news doesn't become old news. The school bulletin from Dodgeville High School in Dodgeville, Wisconsin, is always printed on bright orange paper to draw attention to it and to distinguish it from other printed material.

Use E-Communication. Send announcements and important need-to-know information through all-staff electronic mailing lists. Create an all-staff E-Newsletter with current news and announcements at the district or school and distribute weekly. Post alerts and crisis information hotlines on the school or district's home page. Post crisis response letters (communication to parents and the school community informing them how an issue is being handled/addressed, with the safety of children/students at the school(s) being the top concern); post information on the school's Web site, or distribute it through the staff electronic mailing list and to your key communicators before you send it to the media, to keep staff in the know and rumors under control.

Intranet for Staff. Create an intranet for all personnel with updates and employee surveys. Post staff responsibilities during a crisis, the staff E-Newsletter, and daily or weekly announcements. Consider posting monthly podcast messages for employees.

Telephone Messaging Systems. Broadcast important crisis information updates or district reminders from the superintendent or principal through the district's phone messaging system. Caution: Verify facts and send only need-to-know information before transmitting crisis communication messages.

Encourage teachers to contribute monthly grade-level or department reports for a newsletter to update the rest of the staff on curriculum items and to pass on successful teaching tips.

Faculty/staff handbooks should include information about school and district policies, insurance and disability, absences and leaves, school philosophy, curriculum, staff conduct, retirement, grievances and complaints, evaluations, records, professional growth, and salaries. Consider a school supplement to the district's handbook that will cover any relevant local school issues or policies. The teachers at Paradise Valley High School in Phoenix, Arizona, have prepared such a supplement. To help teachers find strategies to enhance their teaching in block scheduling, teachers devised a handbook about teaching in the block that is full of helpful hints, answers questions, and addresses the concerns that are most likely to arise.

Staff Business Cards. Solicit local business funds to provide all employees at your school—faculty and staff—with their own business cards. This builds a sense of pride, self-worth, and ownership in your school. It says, "I am a professional, and I'm proud to let people know where I work."

Staff Crisis Updates. All staff members should be familiar with your crisis plan (see Chapter 11) and have a clear understanding of their roles. For them to function effectively in a crisis, however, they must have current information about the situation. Don't wait for regularly scheduled staff meetings to share crisis updates. If staff members are to effectively communicate the true status of a situation to concerned parents and community members, they must be apprised of current information as soon and as often as feasible. They need to get their information from you directly and not through the grapevine. When people are aware of situations but don't have accurate information, they begin to speculate. Speculation turns into rumor, which turns into misinformation that can be damaging to the school and difficult to undo. With proper information, your staff can assist in diffusing the impact of crisis situations on campus.

New Staff Orientation Program. Involve your veteran staff members in creating an orientation program for new staff. You could develop a special kit of "survival" materials to help them become acclimated. Establish a mentor or buddy system to pair newcomers with veterans teaching at their grade level or in their department. Hold monthly meetings for newcomers and their veteran partners so they might share their experiences.

Welcome Substitutes and Volunteers. People who spend time in your school as substitutes, student teachers, or volunteers become a part of your school team as well. Get to know them and encourage their participation in school activities. Include them in staff meetings when appropriate. Remember that they, too, are important sources of information to the community about your school.

Assemble welcome packets that include important information about your school: demographics, a map of the campus, a list of staff members, and so forth. Include a name tag that identifies each newcomer as a substitute, volunteer, or student teacher.

Make a sign in the lounge welcoming substitutes. Take a photo of each sub and place it on the sign, along with the sub's name and the class in which he or she is subbing. This makes substitutes feel welcome and serves as an icebreaker with other staff members. Do the same for volunteers and student teachers.

Be a Cheerleader. As an educational leader, you set the tone for your school, so don't be afraid to lead the parade. Look for things to celebrate, large and small, and when you can't find any, invent some. Positive attitudes are contagious, so spread yours around!

TECHNIQUES FOR IMPROVING STUDENT COMMUNICATION

The very best ambassadors for education are students. If students are not excited about learning and proud of their school, then school has failed them by not providing the kind of environment that nurtures success. This environment does not require the newest building or latest technological equipment. It does mean that educators must create, within whatever limited resources are available, a warm and caring climate that fosters self-esteem and a desire to learn.

Society places an enormous burden on schools. Today, educators must be all things to all children—and then some. Amazingly, educators continue to be up to the task, by willingly accepting the challenges and overcoming great odds on a daily basis. But as mentioned in Chapter 1, educators are often reluctant to toot their own horns. Students will do it for you if you include them in your communication network.

Be Enthusiastic. When you are excited about something, your students will be, too. Let the kid inside you show and children will respond tenfold. For many children, the enthusiasm shown for them and for their school is the only positive reinforcement they receive— and enthusiasm is definitely contagious.

Be Visible. Every child on campus should be able to identify you as the principal, no matter how big your school. Join in student activities. Jump rope. Shoot a few baskets. Participate in an art class. Eat lunch in the cafeteria. Attend athletic events, music concerts, and drama productions. Let students know that you are more than just the person who enforces the rules and metes out the punishment. Demonstrate your interest in students' activities with your presence.

Personalize Contact With Students. Work at learning the names of the students who aren't in your office all the time for discipline or who aren't on the student council or the honor roll. Conducting personal interviews with students allows administrators and guidance personnel at Archbishop M. C. O'Neill High School in Regina, Saskatchewan, to receive more accurate information about student issues, concerns, evaluations, and procedures. Another way to contact students and parents is to have an automated phone call-out system like they have at Meadowbrook Middle School in Poway, California. Even though you may not speak with students or parents personally, at least you know your message reached someone at the home.

Use Positive Body Language. Students are very sensitive to your body language and have an innate sense of your response to them. Learn to smile, wink, and nod in nonverbal acknowledgment of a child's presence. Remember that your most difficult student may be from an abusive home, and you may be the most caring presence in his or her life.

Student Recognition. Create as many ways as possible to reward and recognize students. You and your staff can design awards and certificates that meet specific needs. You are limited only by your imagination in what can be recognized. Let students create peer recognition awards as well. Recognition helps students build pride in themselves, their work, and their school. By praising students for their contributions to the school team and by recognizing individual and group efforts, you will build a positive school family that supports learning achievements. Included at chapter's end are some sample "Student of the Month" and "Recognition of Outstanding Scholarship/Excellent Attendance" certificates. To make these certificates special, have them printed on heavy, high-quality paper.

Create a Student Relations Team. Create a team of student representatives who meet with you each month to discuss issues and concerns, similar to the staff relations team. Involve them in establishing school rules and planning special events. Encourage them to take ownership of their ideas and decisions.

Student Communication. Establish a student newspaper. Publish a book of student poetry or creative writing. Encourage students to communicate through both the written and spoken word. Students can also take an active role with the daily announcements. These can be done using video or audio. Let the media classes have an active part in the production. Such student involvement is characteristic of Halifax County High School in South Boston, Virginia.

New Student Orientation. Just as you involve veteran staff in welcoming new staff members, involve students in creating an orientation program for new students. Put together a student survival kit and set up a buddy system to make new students feel a part of the school.

SUGGESTED READINGS

Guttmann, R. C. (1993). Community relations: Guidepoints to improving and keeping them strong. In J. L. & J. J. Herman (Eds.), *People and education: Vol. 1. The human side of school* (pp. 105–120). Newbury Park, CA: Corwin.

Hymes, D. (1993). An almanac of low tech communication ideas. *Journal of Educational Public Relations, 14*(4), 13–30.

Mendler, A. N. (1998). *Power struggles: Successful techniques for educators.* Bloomington. IN: Center for Professional Development and Services.

Mitroff, I. (1998). *Smart thinking for crazy times: The art of solving the right problems.* San Francisco: Barrett-Koehler.

National School Public Relations Association. (1986). *School public relations: The complete book.* Rockville, MD: Author.

Theobald, P. (1997). *Teaching the commons.* Boulder, CO: Westview Press.

Webster, W. E. (1996). *Voices in the hall: High school principals at work.* Bloomington, IN: Phi Delta Kappa International.

Student
of the Month

THIS CERTIFIES THAT

_____

_____

SCHOOL

_____   _____

CITY   STATE

has been recognized for outstanding achievement and is hereby awarded this certificate of distinction.

Given this _____ day of _____ 19 ___

_____   _____

Source: Dodgeville High School, Dodgeville, WI.

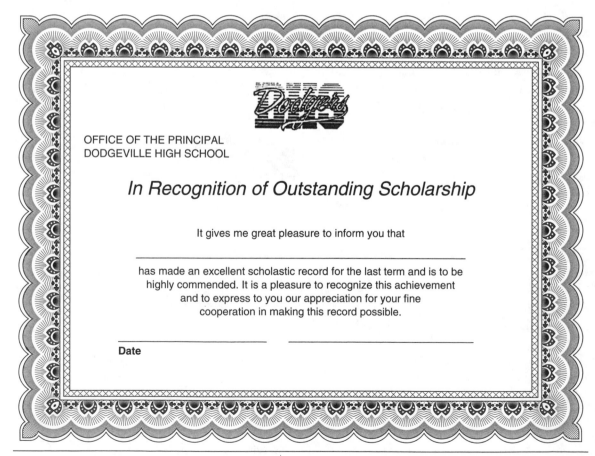

OFFICE OF THE PRINCIPAL
DODGEVILLE HIGH SCHOOL

In Recognition of Outstanding Scholarship

It gives me great pleasure to inform you that

_____

has made an excellent scholastic record for the last term and is to be highly commended. It is a pleasure to recognize this achievement and to express to you our appreciation for your fine cooperation in making this record possible.

_____   _____

Date

Source: Dodgeville High School, Dodgeville, WI.

Source: Dodgeville High School, Dodgeville, WI.

4

Publications/ Electronic Communication

"If you want it to be remembered, put it in writing."

One of the most important charges given to public schools is to teach children to communicate through the proper use of language. Throughout the elementary grades, the primary focus is on teaching and reinforcing the skills of reading, writing, grammar, spelling, vocabulary, and pronunciation. In high school, more advanced uses of language are emphasized through creative writing, journalism, speech, and drama.

As an educational institution, how much effort and emphasis does your school place on utilizing these same communication skills to educate, inform, and enlist the support of your principal constituencies? Because it is a given that your school should be doing this, this chapter focuses on the *hows* and not the *whys* of written communication from you and your school.

First and foremost, every written communication from your school must be well-written, grammatically correct, and free of errors. You can never allow these seemingly small details to slide because you are pressed for time or are dealing with other issues. Once a publication reaches the hands of the intended readership, an image of your school and your leadership is created that may be difficult to undo without a great deal of time and effort. Therefore, it makes sense to ensure the quality of any publication up front.

If a publication from your school contains typos or spelling and grammatical errors; if it has inaccurate, incomplete, or misleading information; if it is visually hard to read because the type is too small or too faint or the layout is cluttered; if it is written above or below the average reading level of your targeted audience, readers may well draw comparisons between the quality of the publication and the quality of education you provide. Such publications send this hidden message: "You, the reader, aren't very important to me, the writer." That is a message no school leader can afford to send—to anyone!

School publications are an important, and somewhat unappreciated, form of communication. Although traditionally they have been used as vehicles for providing information to parents, with the advent of site-based management and similar decentralization concepts, publications should be adapted by educators to provide information to other community groups as well.

There are a variety of publications that schools can use effectively. You may need a brochure for one project, a flyer for another, or an announcement on your Web site for a third. These days, everyone is inundated with incredible amounts of information on an enormous number of topics. Because people cannot possibly read everything available to them, most have become much more selective about what they do choose to read. Some simply do not read much of anything; others, especially older and retired people, avidly read everything that comes their way. As a result, school publications must be adapted to these varied and changing information needs. You want your patrons to choose to read what you send them, so you must make it easy and appealing for them to do so.

To create or improve your school's communications/publications plan, ask yourself four questions:

1. Who? Determine the publication's audience. Who do you want to read it? Is it for staff, parents, students, the community at large, or a special interest group such as parents of a particular student population? The targeted audience will determine how the publication is written and designed, as well as how it is distributed.

2. What? Determine the purpose of the publication. What do you want it to do? Is it meant to provide basic information about your school programs and activities; to report on local, state, or national educational issues; to enhance your school's image with the community; to ask for help; or to recognize achievement? Does the overall design reflect the purpose?

3. When? You will need to determine not only the audience and the purpose of the publication, but also the frequency. Is it a one-shot item or an ongoing effort?

   Whether you send it out weekly, bimonthly, monthly, or twice a year, if you are consistent, many in your targeted audience will begin to look for it. If the design is always the same in size and color, your intended readership will recognize it whether it is mixed in with their other mail, folded inside their child's backpack, or lying on the floor. Design the publication with those thoughts in mind.

4. How? Decide how best to communicate the information the publication is intended to disseminate; then determine a writing style to match. Is it appropriate for the audience and subject? Is it clear, focused, accurate, and interesting? Is the type size and style appropriate and easy to read? For example, publications for young children and seniors should use a large, clear typeface. Children like lots of graphics and illustrations. Is the reading level appropriate for the audience? (Use the Fog Index check discussed near the end of this chapter.)

NEWSLETTERS

Perhaps the most common type of published school communication is a newsletter. Desktop publishing by personal computer has greatly simplified the process of creating an attractive newsletter. There are several different commercially produced software packages on the market that are specifically designed for creating newsletters and similar publications. You can also buy graphics software that eliminates the need for pasting in "clip art" or having someone illustrate the page.

Sample school newsletters are included at the end of this chapter, from Fall Mountain Regional High School in Charlestown, New Hampshire, and Washington Jr. High in Toledo, Ohio.

The following guidelines consist of 10 commandments for a good newsletter.

1. Make it interesting. If no one wants to read your school's newsletter, you have wasted significant time and resources. Review your concept with others, including intended members of the target audience. Get, and use, constructive advice. Remember, a newsletter is intended to accomplish something for a specific set of readers; it isn't a diary.

2. Follow the 30–3–30 principle. That means your newsletter is written to provide pertinent information whether the reader has 30 seconds, 3 minutes, or 30 minutes to spend. This is why it is important to use headlines with action verbs, subheads within blocks of copy, strong lead sentences, and first paragraphs that address the content of the story. For an outstanding example of the application of this principle, study the presentation of the news in *USA Today*.

3. Have an easily identifiable masthead that is used consistently. The masthead should incorporate the following:
   - The name of the publication
   - The school name
   - An identifying logo (This could be the school mascot or a distinctive use of type.)
   - Publication date
   - Statement of purpose (Examples are "A Newsletter for Parents and Patrons" or "A Publication for Staff Members.")
   - The school address, phone number, and e-mail address (This can alternatively be placed at the bottom of the page.)

4. Leave lots of white space. You don't have to fill every inch of space available. If you try to do so, the pages will look cluttered and will be unappealing to the eye. Short paragraphs and a column format with plenty of space increase readability.

5. Use color for emphasis. In the interest of cost, most school newsletters use only one color of ink. However, you can "punch up" your newsletter by preprinting quantities of your masthead using two or more colors. These can then be run through the copy machine and printed on an as-needed basis. You can also stretch the use of color by using "spot color" or "screens" (shades of color or black/gray) to create varied shades or by overlapping two colors of ink to create a third.

   One caution on using screens created with desktop publishing and laser printers: The quality and appearance diminish with each generation run on a copy machine and quickly begin to look muddy or smudged. Run a proof copy first and evaluate the effect. You may be better off eliminating screens and using borders to highlight copy instead.

   If you opt for using colored paper for your newsletter, use soft neutral colors such as ivory, beige, or pastels. Brighter colors may attract attention, but they make the newsletter difficult to read. Save the neon colors for flyers.

6. Avoid endless columns of text. Use subheads, bullet copy, borders, graphs, and graphic art to add interest to the page and break up blocks of "gray" copy. Warning: Use art only if it relates to the story so it will be complementary rather than distracting. When using art, be sure that it is in the public domain or that you have purchased the right to use it, for instance, in a software package of clip art. Using comic strips from the local newspaper or other published art is in violation of copyright laws. No one is likely to go to the trouble to sue you, but it is unprofessional and could damage your credibility with key members of the constituencies you want to build a relationship with—especially the media!

7. Use consistent type elements. One of the pitfalls of computerized newsletters is the temptation to use every typeface available. Stick to one style of type for the body copy (text) and another for headlines. Body copy should generally be a serif type (letters with tails or flourishes that lead the eye to the next word) and headlines in sans serif (plain type without tails and flourishes) in a larger size than the body copy. Use bold or italic type for emphasis within a sentence. Never type body copy in all capital letters—it is the written equivalent of shouting at the reader. Most copy, including headlines, should be printed in standard upper- and lowercase for readability. By the same token, do not print entire paragraphs in bold or italic.

8. Use photos judiciously. Before you use photos in your newsletter, be sure that you can ensure good reproductive quality. You may be able to use a computer scanner to place the photograph in your publication. However, if the copy machine you are using is not capable of reproducing clear and identifiable copies, you are better off leaving photos out. If your newsletter is printed on a press, you can have the photos stripped in by the printer and you won't have a problem. Like art, photos are effective only if they add to the story. Caution: Photos taken by students or teachers are great to use in district or school publications as long as they do not require copyright permission—most do not if taken and used for school publications on school property, but be careful that all FERPA (Federal Education Rights and Privacy Act) laws are followed and that each student pictured has parental permission. All other copyright laws prevail. (Most school districts use an opt-out clause in the Student Handbook that parents will sign. Use good judgment and follow district policy with regard to photos posted on Web sites, especially those created by students.)

9. Use the best printer you can find. A laser printer is excellent, but if you don't have easy access to one, you might consider taking your newsletter to a local quick-print shop to have an original copy printed. For a minimal charge, they will print your newsletter on a high-quality laser printer or imagesetter. All you have to do is provide the computer disk with your newsletter copied on it exactly as you want it printed. You will then have a quality original from which to run your copies.

10. Make sure copies are clean and neat. Before you waste 800 sheets of paper running newsletters that turn out to be unreadable or crooked, take the time to run several proof copies and check them carefully for problems. While the copies are running, periodically pull one to make sure it still looks good. You are better off catching a problem halfway through and correcting it, rather than catching it after the fact. Paper is expensive—and so is your time!

Parent and Community Newsletters

Publishing a regular newsletter gives you a chance to inform patrons about the positive education stories that apply to their school and stories that the local media don't know about, don't have room for, or don't choose to cover. It can be a monthly, biweekly, or weekly publication, depending on available time, energy, and resources. As was mentioned earlier, the front pages of several sample newsletters are included at the end of this chapter.

Traditionally, school newsletters have been distributed to parents only. But as more schools move toward building-level decision making and a greater level of community involvement, educational leaders need to create a news link to people and organizations and businesses that do not have children in school—groups that have been "outside the loop" until now.

One effective way to produce a quality newsletter (and to make sure all the key points previously discussed are addressed) is to create a newsletter team responsible for preparing and publishing it on time. This team could include teachers from different grade and subject levels, a parent or two, and the school secretary. Seek out retirees in your community with a journalism or printing background who are willing to volunteer their help, or build a partnership with a local business that produces its own in-house newsletter and ask for assistance. Charge the newsletter team with responsibility for collecting information, writing articles, and preparing and designing the publication.

Principal Robert Ericson of North High School (Sheboygan, Wisconsin) uses students from the journalism department to write his monthly newsletter. He meets with the editors monthly and reviews with them the material to be included. The students contribute ideas, write articles, interview teachers, dig up facts about an event, and develop the artwork and appropriate graphics.

You may wish to produce two monthly newsletters—one aimed specifically at parents and one targeted toward your school's nonparent community/business constituency. A newsletter for parents and the community, or whatever combination of audiences you wish to address, can follow a regular format of presenting information by subject areas such as student achievements, calendars of events, curriculum updates, and tips for parents, or it can concentrate on a specific theme in order to provide comprehensive information about a topic or issue of interest.

If you are just beginning this process, use an early issue to survey your readers and gather input about the type of information that is most valuable to them. Just because you think your newsletter is terrific doesn't mean your readers find it relevant. If you are already in the newsletter business, it is wise to review the characteristics of a good newsletter periodically.

Typically, timely newsletters do the following:

- Discuss various curriculum programs and how they impact student learning. For example, the newsletter might explain in lay terms the benefits of the new science lab or the reasons for using cooperative learning techniques
- Highlight the achievements of students, staff, and volunteers
- Review school rules and regulations, and attendance and discipline policies
- Inform parents how much homework to expect at each grade level and provide tips on how they can help their children
- Provide age-appropriate reading lists and book reviews
- Address issues of concern such as drug and alcohol abuse, gangs, guns, safety, and teen pregnancy, and list community resources parents can access for help

- Feature an outstanding school program and provide in-depth information
- Share test results and explain how to interpret them
- Profile a staff member, student, volunteer, or business partner
- Explain how new legislation will impact your school, as well as your district
- Provide updates on the activities and decisions of organizations such as school site councils
- Provide updates on the activities of the PTA/PTO and student council
- Include district news and information of interest to parents and community members
- Address student health issues
- Solicit volunteers for specific projects or ongoing programs
- Offer special-focus issues on subjects such as building self-esteem, the importance of parent involvement, school–business partnerships, and cultural diversity
- Inform about projects affecting the school site (for example, construction, remodeling, repairs, weather damage, parking lot problems, landscaping, and beautification projects). Major site projects often impact the local neighborhood, and residents appreciate being informed in advance whenever possible

Staff Newsletters

Although your staff should receive copies of the school newsletter along with parents and patrons, there is a lot of other information they need to know in order to be effective in their jobs. A staff newsletter can help provide them with that information. The format should be simple and easy to read. Don't waste time with photos and graphics, because this should be a "quick read" publication, preferably one page front and back. Survey your staff and ask them about their information needs. Involve them in making it their publication.

Items for the staff newsletter might include the following:

- Information about colleagues: retirements, new staff members, illnesses, births, deaths, promotions, awards, and achievements
- Periodic review of policies, procedures, and state and federal mandates.
- Testing information
- Governing board actions or proposals (if your district does not have a publication for this purpose)
- New legislation affecting schools
- Grade-level reports
- Curriculum updates and adoptions
- Teaching tips and ideas
- Professional growth opportunities
- Ideas for communicating with parents
- School concerns and problems
- Upcoming events and meeting schedules
- News from around the district
- Student discipline information

Two examples of different staff communications are included at the end of this chapter: "Week in Review Form" from Paradise Valley High School in Phoenix, Arizona, and "Weekly Calendar" from Owen J. Roberts School District in Pottstown, Pennsylvania.

Student Newsletters

Don't overlook the importance of student newsletters in communicating the good news about your school. Although student newsletters are written by and for students, you can bet that parents read them, too. Under the guidance of staff or community volunteers, students can apply the techniques discussed earlier in this chapter to create interesting and informative newsletters.

Items for student newsletters might include the following:

- Student council information and decisions
- Interviews with staff members or community members
- Reports on classroom projects and school activities
- Information about school and district events
- Book and movie reviews
- Creative writing and poetry
- Homework tips
- Lunch recipes
- Information about community service projects
- Student profiles focusing on cultural diversity

Distributing Your Newsletter

How you choose to distribute your newsletter will depend a great deal on the frequency of your publication and your financial resources. Some possible distribution methods are

- *E-Mail.* Most schools collect parent e-mail addresses at registration. Recent parent surveys show that this is the new preferred method of delivery in most communities, especially among younger parents, and even in low-income areas where parents have access to computers at their local library or place of work. Inserting an opt-out clause is always recommended.
- *U.S. Mail.* Schools qualify for a nonprofit bulk rate permit, the cheapest postage rate available. You pay a yearly permit fee and a per-piece cost for each mailing. To take advantage of the bulk mail rate, you must mail a minimum of 200 pieces of the same item and they must be grouped by zip codes. Your district office may already have a bulk mail permit that you can use. You can also mail first class, which does not require grouping by zip code, but this is an expensive option best reserved for critical communications with individual parents.

  Obviously, you have access to an address list of parents, but you should also consider mailing to other residents in your school community. Through a specialty service, you can purchase mailing labels for all residences in a designated area, but these are expensive even for a one time purchase. You can also use a direct mail service, but again, this is expensive and you pay on a per use basis. Building your own mailing list is time-consuming but can be accomplished using city directories, volunteer help, and the assistance of organizations such as chambers of commerce that already have the lists you may need of businesses in your area.
- *Newspapers and Free-Throw Publications.* ("Free-throws" are free publications that are distributed to school neighborhood residents. Schools can usually include inserts through arrangements with the publishers.) Check with your local "free" newspaper

publisher or "Pennysaver" about inserting your newsletter for distribution in your attendance area.

- *Community-Based Drop-Off.* Ask permission to leave stacks of newsletters in the offices of doctors, dentists, real estate agents, veterinarians, and other professionals in your school community. Take copies of your newsletter to retirement homes and apartment complexes and ask that they be distributed. Some banks, restaurants, and grocery and convenience stores may also be willing to let you leave some newsletters on display. Be sure to get permission before leaving them, however, or they may end up being thrown in the trash by an irritated proprietor or store manager, which won't build a positive image for you or your school.

- *Door-to-Door Delivery.* Check with school-based scout troops or other student organizations to see if they might distribute newsletters door-to-door as a community service project or as a fundraiser. They may be willing to take it on as a regular project for much less than the cost of mailing.

- *Student Delivery.* The old standby is to send parent newsletters home with students. This works better in the primary grades than it does at the middle or high school levels. To conserve costs and cut down on waste, you might try sending the newsletter home with only the youngest child in a family. Be sure that some statement such as "A Newsletter for Parents" is near the masthead, so there is no mistaking for whom the publication is intended.

TECHNOLOGY TOOLS

Now that we are living in the 21st century, technology has added new dimensions to how organizations communicate, both internally and externally. Tried and true techniques and written materials still need to exist but many times are more easily disseminated to our audiences via this new format. This age of instant information using computers and cell phones is one that changes rapidly, and if we don't stay current, we can miss out on the best way to reach many of our students, parents, and community members. Without using technology, we also put people at risk during times of crisis or when immediate communication is needed.

Superintendent Dr. Paul Kinder of Blue Springs School District in Missouri highlights how his staff augments traditional communication vehicles with technology.

Communication occurs in myriad ways within our organization. While some are quite traditional such as newsletters to parents from teachers, others are much more advanced. The internal audience receives most information in an electronic format through e-mail, Web-based information, and communication boards within our management systems. Weekly information is sent to staff via a link to an online document. This includes information about our staff and their awards, and concerns, what is going on in our schools, and even a place for staff to share ideas and items. In addition, our superintendent [both] sends . . . legislative updates and communicates events and issues to the staff in an e-mail message weekly. Stories of success and information are published quarterly for our internal audience, and this is sent via a Web link to staff with computer access, and printed copies are sent to those without.

Our external communication is also multifaceted. It includes both formal and scheduled communication and informal communication that occurs as needed.

Parents are able to gain information about their student using our "Parent Connect" information portal. This allows parents to log on and see their child's grades, attendance, and daily schedule. In addition, parents can pay for school lunches online and can check out what their student is purchasing for lunch using our electronic payment and food management system. Parents are also afforded instant information in the form of an automated calling system. They receive a call within minutes of [the] decision to close school due to inclement weather, and this system also disseminates information about possible health issues in schools and notifies parents when a student is absent. Not only can each school use this system individually, but the district office has access and a phone call can be delivered within minutes to more than 13,000 parents and families.

The District publishes a quarterly magazine that highlights current events in our district and the awards that students, staff, schools, and community members have received. This also gives the district an opportunity to share information about programs of which our patrons may not be aware. These stories are also then uploaded to our Web site so it is made available to the world.

The Web site is a major form of our communication to our external audience. Ten years ago, the information remained static and most sites seemed to be an electronic contact sheet with a few photos. Today, our site is dynamic and provides the user a glimpse into our schools. Information is updated daily and calendars of events are provided for each school and the district as a whole to ensure all members have access to necessary information. Board policy is available online as well as the minutes from each meeting and agendas. This gives all patrons, parents, students, and staff equal access to information that impacts our learning community.

Technology has even impacted the way we transport students. Recently our buses have been tagged with Global Positioning Sensors that allow us to keep up-to-the-second accounts of our buses' locations and it also provides information about their rate of speed and time on route. This is especially important as a communication tool when we have concerns from patrons about our transportation services. It also allows our district to communicate with employees using accurate information about job performance in an arena where the supervisor cannot be present at all times.

E-Newsletters, Web Sites, and Online Media

As the number of schools utilizing e-newsletters and Web sites continues to grow each year, school communication professionals face new opportunities and unique challenges with each new digital communication option. There are many resources and tools available beyond the scope of this book that instruct readers in the use of the very latest technology tools to assist in school and district communication efforts.

Parents and other community members have come to expect at least a "Web presence" for information about their local schools and school districts.

According to Edward H. Moore, APR, in the National School Public Relations Association's (NSPRA) resource guide to *Mastering E-Newsletters* (2005), when it comes to technology, communication efforts are best served when things are kept simple. As Moore points out, in the same manner as the office and personal e-mail that most of us are used to receiving, e-publications are another method of getting electronic messages to many people quickly and efficiently.

The speed at which e-newsletters can communicate messages to as many recipients as you have e-mail addresses for, and be quickly forwarded to other interested recipients, has far surpassed traditional print newsletters. E-newsletters can include links to more detailed information where other Web sites of interest help readers better understand the story, and they also can be invaluable in helping collect feedback and data from readers.

How well e-publishing technology works in delivering school e-publications is crucial to e-publishing success. Choosing the right computer software and list management tools is as important as the content and design.

Web sites can also be effective or ineffective tools for school and district communication. In many schools, the duty of keeping the Web sites content current falls on the shoulders of already busy teachers or school secretaries. A good, easy-to-navigate Web sites with a simple, appealing, and user-friendly design is a great start.

Advanced technology designers (many of whom are students in Career and Technical Education programs) are now using the newest features of Internet "broadcasting" and "videography" to help tell their stories as well.

MONTHLY CALENDAR/MENU

An inexpensive and effective way to keep parents informed of upcoming events is to send out a one-page combination calendar/menu that can be posted on the refrigerator for quick reference. (Many schools are opting to post this information on the individual school's Web sites for parents to view online, preferring to "go green"/ environmentally friendly.) There are some great computer software packages available specifically for creating calendars. At the top of the calendar page, add the phone number of the attendance clerk, the office, and the homework hotline if you have one. Use the back side of the page to list student achievements such as student of the month, honor roll, improvement awards, and contest winners. This will get important information to parents and will save space in your regular newsletter for more detailed articles.

Many schools still print separate wall calendars or combination handbook/calendars. These look great. However, the downside is that they are expensive to print, and usually by the time school starts, some events have already been rescheduled.

PARENT/STUDENT HANDBOOKS

A parent/student handbook is an important publication that every school needs. It provides vital information about your school, district policies, and the guidelines for cooperation between parents and educators. Handbooks are most valuable to educators if they are to be used as a reference and guide for student conduct and similar purposes. Your handbook should contain general guidelines that allow you flexibility in dealing with a variety of situations while remaining within the boundaries of district policy. If rules and regulations are written in too much detail, you may find yourself boxed into a corner when dealing with a particular issue.

Involve your school site council or other parents and staff members in helping to develop the contents of your handbook. By including those who will be using it, you will end up with a publication that better serves the needs of your school. Even if your school district provides such a handbook to parents, a supplement addressing issues specific to your school would be very useful.

Subjects that should be included in the handbook are the following:

- Attendance
- Code of conduct
- Dress code
- Discipline
- Academics
- Student activities
- Student and parent rights
- Health care and regulations
- Transportation
- Safety programs
- Parent involvement
- Philosophy and goals

The brochure for Plymouth (Minnesota) Middle School is an excellent example of an easy to update, do-it-yourself handbook.

BROCHURES AND FLYERS

Brochures and flyers are useful for promoting specific programs or events. They contain topic-specific information, usually on one page, and sometimes on a front-back format. Due to space limitations inherent in this type of publication, your copy must be concise and to the point. If you try to include too much information, you may not have the space to make it look attractive. Decide on the most important information, and concentrate on presenting it in an interesting and understandable format. Some possible topics for brochures and flyers include the following:

- Preschool programs
- Kindergarten programs
- Special education programs
- Volunteer programs
- Afterschool programs
- School–business partnerships
- Homework
- Magnet programs
- Athletics
- Honors programs
- Fine arts programs
- Sex education-HIV/AIDS curriculum

Brochures

Good brochures use graphic art or photographs to add interest and break up the copy. You can also use borders, dashes, bullets, and white space to create an interesting look. If you plan to use photographs, it is best to use white paper and black ink; otherwise, the photos may not look natural. Add color by adding a second color of ink to headlines or art. If you use colored paper, stick to neutrals and pastels for readability.

The most common sizes used in brochures are 8½ x 11 inch (letter-size paper) or 8½ × 14 inch (legal-size paper). These sizes are also the easiest and least expensive to produce and can be used with most copy machines. Different looks can be created with different folds. Brochures can be folded in half, in thirds, in quarters, and with variations on these. You can get lots of ideas by collecting brochures that you find attractive and studying their layout and the different ways in which they are folded. Visit a local print shop and ask to see some samples.

If you don't have a folding machine, you may want to consider having a printer or a quick-copy outlet prepare your brochure. You may be able to talk the shop's staff into letting you provide the printed sheets and charging you only for the folding. Otherwise, be prepared to bring in the troops to fold your brochures by hand.

Flyers

Flyers generally are used to announce an event. They are usually one sided and contain a minimum of information, but that information is displayed in an eye-catching format. Use attention-getting, bright-colored paper for flyers, as there will not be a lot of copy to read. Extra-large type and graphics can enhance the message and entice people to read it. By using a computer to do your layout, you might fit two or three copies of your announcement on one sheet, then cut the sheet into halves or thirds after printing.

LANGUAGE

If there are a large number of non–English-speaking parents in your school community, consider producing anything you want parents to read, such as parent newsletters, brochures, flyers, handbook inserts, and calendars, in English on one side of the page and in another language on the other. Make sure your translations are done by someone who has a written and not just an oral knowledge of that foreign language.

SUGGESTIONS FOR BETTER WRITING

These writing suggestions were developed by Bob Grossman (1979), an educational public relations consultant:

- Nouns
  - Simplify complex nouns.
  - Look for nouns that can be changed to strong verbs.
  - Use specific nouns rather than general.
- Verbs
  - Strengthen verbs.
  - Reduce the number of linking verbs.
  - Use active, visual verbs.
- Other parts of speech
  - Eliminate needless adverbs.
  - Eliminate weak adjectives.

- Avoid too many pronouns.
- Avoid needless adverbs modifying adjectives.
- Eliminate excessive numbers of prepositional phrases.

- Vocabulary
  - Cut jargon.
  - Reduce the number of multisyllabic words.
  - Use vocabulary appropriate to the audience.

- Sentences
  - Strive for shorter sentences.
  - Vary sentence length.
  - Be careful of compound subjects and verbs.
  - Use subject–verb–object word order.

- Content
  - Concentrate on specifics rather than abstracts. Resist the temptation to be legally specific.
  - Get to the message quickly.
  - Organize thoughts into logical order.

- Style
  - Eliminate the word *there* when you can use active speech. (For example, instead of "There are a number of students who have signed up for the school picnic clean-up team" say the following: "A number of students have signed up for the school picnic clean-up team.")
  - Write in short paragraphs when possible.
  - Put words that demand emphasis at the beginning or end of the sentence.
  - Limit each sentence to one or two thoughts.
  - Don't overuse transitional words and phrases.

The Fog Index

The Fog Index is a device used to estimate the reading level appropriate for your publication. Keep in mind that most successful publications write to a general reading level of ninth grade or less. Try conducting a Fog Index on a sample story from a popular general publication (such as *Reader's Digest*, *USA Today*, or your local newspaper) and comparing it against your own writing.

- Step 1. Select a 100-word sample of writing.
- Step 2. Find the average number of words per sentence in the sample. If the 100th word is in the middle of a sentence, count the rest of the words in that sentence and use that number to compute the average.
- Step 3. Count the number of words in the 100-word sample that have three or more syllables. Do not count proper names or three-syllable verb forms ending in –ing, –ed, or –es.
- Step 4. Add the average number of words per sentence to the number of three-syllable words and multiply by 0.4.

The result is an estimate of the reading level (grade) required to understand your writing. The Fog Index is affected mainly by two factors: the level of vocabulary and the length of the sentences. The purpose of using the Fog Index is to make sure your newsletter copy can be understood by the intended audience.

Proofreading Tips

One of the bonuses of computer publishing technology is the ability to spell-check and grammar-check your writing. But that does not eliminate the need to proofread your articles, especially names and numbers that the computer cannot identify. It is worth a little extra time to ensure accurate copy.

- Have someone other than the writer proofread the copy. Better still, have more than one person proof it.
- Proof the copy backward, beginning with the last word. This helps to catch mistakes you may miss because of reading too fast (even though you're trying to read slowly and carefully).
- Mistakes tend to cluster. Watch for more than one typo in a sentence or paragraph.
- Watch for changes in typeface or type style that should not be present.
- Check the sequence of page numbers.
- Check accuracy of all callouts ("continued to page . . ." or "continued from page . . .").
- Check for complete parentheses, brackets, and quotation marks. Check that these punctuation marks face the proper direction.
- Check the spelling of all names.
- Check all addresses and phone numbers. Watch for transposed numbers.
- Check that photos and cutlines (or captions) match.
- Check carefully for all necessary punctuation marks. Omitted periods are easy to overlook.

REFERENCES AND SUGGESTED READINGS

Grossman, B. (1979). *Writing for school administrators.* Unpublished master's thesis, Glassboro State University, Glassboro, NJ.

Illinois Association of School Boards. (1987, Summer). *Five basic school publications. Communications tips.* (Newsletter available from IASB, Springfield, IL)

National School Public Relations Association. (1986). *School public relations: The complete book.* Arlington, VA: Author.

National School Public Relations Association. (1988, May). *Publishing made easy: But is easy better? It starts in the classroom.* (Newsletter available from NSPRA, Rockville, MD)

National School Public Relations Association. (2005). *Mastering e-newsletters.* Rockville, MD: Author.

Wildcat Happenings

Volume: 7 March Issue

2008

News & Events

March

4- FM Pride Night
6:30-8:00pm
at FMRHS

7&8- School Musical
"Sweet Charity"
7:30pm

11- Horticulture Trip
Boston Flower Show

12- All Sports Banquet
6:30pm

12- Site-Based
Committee Meeting
7:00pm

13- Parent/Teacher
Conferences 3-7pm

14- Early Release 11:25pm

21- PE Trip to
Springfield, VT

25- NH Higher
Education Network
6:30pm @ FMRHS

27-29- Montreal Trip

28-30- NYC Music Trip

8,15&29- SAT Prep
Keene Public Library
9:30-12:30pm

Parenting - A Tough Job

As I reflect on events of the last few months at FM I would like to begin this month's message with: Parents have a tough job. When a person makes the choice to become a parent the role does not come with an instruction manual. Therefore, it is understood that at times a parent may be disappointed in decisions made both by themselves and/or their child.

Communicating values has never been more important than it is today. When all is said and done, parents have far more influence over instilling values in their child than any other factor. Keep in mind: 1) kids get their sense of what's right and wrong from people they love and respect. No one has more influence over teaching values than a parent. 2) When it comes to teaching values, actions always speak louder than words. Respect for life, respect for other people, honesty, integrity, and responsibility… kids get these by watching the adults in their life. 3) Learning to love and respect themselves is incredibly important for any child. It is also the first essential step to helping a child learn to love and respect those around him/her.

We all know the child grows and eventually becomes a teenager. At this age parenting is challenged, the job gets harder, and it seems as though this generation rejects everything taught to them while growing up. As far as a teenager is concerned, adults know nothing.

Our values and beliefs are constantly challenged with most of our words seen as interference - emotions may run high. It is at this time parents, and the adults in the child's life, are more important than ever. During these last few months members of our school district have discussed the adoption of the core values: Respect, Integrity, Citizenship, and Responsibility. It is my belief that through our work together we may teach our youth how to be successful.

As educators we are constantly looking for ways to improve what we offer to our students. Currently, the high school administrators and faculty are looking at creating, and implementing, an Alternative Program – a school within a school to help students struggling to succeed be successful. We are also looking to: increase our block five credit recovery program, implement a two-tiered diploma, and renovate our 30 year old building to assist the students with being better prepared for the job force if this is the path chosen. These projects cannot be completed without your support. If you are interested in getting involved with our mission to improve lives, please contact me.

Mr. Thomas Ronning
Principal
tronning@sau60.org

JROTC

Written by Cadet 2nd Lt. Joe Hart

It's been another great month in JROTC! We've been very busy this month with in-class training, marching in the Newport Winter Carnival Parade, preparing for the Military Ball and more! With the new semester, we have hit the ground running with many new and returning cadets. We are working as hard as we can, always doing our best as an Honor Unit with Distinction.

We've already had several opportunities to go outdoors for PT in snowshoes this semester. We went through the woods and learned about our surroundings, and we held a snowshoe/sledding competition where two cadets in snowshoes pulled another who was in a sled across the football field in a race to be the fastest and to not lose any gear.

New cadets have had the opportunity to learn the basics of drill and ceremony, with the instructors teaching and the upperclassmen advising them. Over the past month, they have learned how to march in the Newport Carnival Parade, and how to perform Funeral Details. Cadets who have done Funeral Details before helped teach the other cadets who are not familiar with Funeral Detail Drill and Ceremony.

The Newport Winter Carnival Parade was a huge success! It was the best we have ever done at Newport in the twelve years we have marched there. Excellent job to all of the cadets who marched in the parade!

The Military Ball Committee kicked off with its first meeting this semester. It's very important that we get a good head start on planning for the Ball. It's a night for the cadets to be recognized by the community and it's our most important event of the year. This year, the Military Ball will be on Saturday, May 3rd. It is a blast for everyone. All cadets are strongly encouraged to participate! If you would like to be a part of the Military Ball Committee, you can see CO Kevin Martel, or if you are interested in the Silent Auction Committee, contact Cadet 2nd Lt. Patrick Colwell. Please take a part in the Military Ball, JROTC's greatest event of the year!

On February 14, Valentine's Day, all cadets from both semesters had their photos taken in uniform for JROTC record, and we hope to use those photos in the JROTC Yearbook.

Along with this, Cadets in the S-5 department, Cadet 2nd Lt. Hart and Cadet PFC Brewer, continue to work with the Alstead Veterans to finalize the Veterans' Roll of Honor for the Alstead Veterans' Memorial.

Overall, this month has been one of the greatest in JROTC! We're doing a great job, cadets! Keep it up!

Here's to another great month in the FMRHS JROTC!

HOO-AHH!

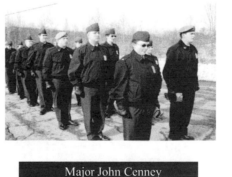

Major John Cenney
jcenney@sau60.org

March 2008

Source: Fall Mountain Regional High School; Thomas Ronning; 159 East Street, PO Box 600, Charlestown, NH 03603; 603-826-7756; Fax: 603-826-4430. Used with permission.

February/March 2008

The Cougar's Corner

Washington Junior High School – 5700 Whitmer Drive – Toledo, OH 43613

The Principal's Corner By Mr. Ibarra

Greetings everyone! We have returned from winter break and began second semester here at Washington. In reading this newsletter you will see many efforts to assist your child with academic success. Remember, even if you have not been very active in the past, It is never too late to become more involved in your child's education. Studies from the Parent Institute show that parent involvement produces:

- Higher grades and test Scores
- Better attendance and more homework completed
- More positive attitudes toward school
- Higher graduation rates
- Increased enrollment in education after high school.

Here are some things you can do to be involved with out having to volunteer:

- Encourage your child to read. Try reading aloud or listen to audio books. You may be surprised.
- Set aside a regular time and place for homework (and enforce it).
- Let your middle schooler know that effort, not intelligence, is the key to success in school.
- Visit the library together.
- Ask specific questions at the dinner table about school. Questions like: What was the most important thing you learned today? What do you think your history teacher will ask on the next test? Will provide more conversation than the standard "What did you do at school today?".

IMPORTANT PHONE NUMBERS

Principal's Office	473-8449
Assoc. Principal's Office	473-8451
Attendance Line	473-8483
Homework Hotline	473-8383

www.washloc.k12.oh.us/washington.html

WLS Weather Cancellation Hotline: 419-473-8499

Tardies

- Students who are tardy to school at 8:20 a.m. and after must report to the attendance office.
- Tardy to school is from 8:15-11:30 a.m.
- ½ day absence is from 11:30-12:00
- Any tardy to school after 12:00 is considered a full day's absence.
- Tardy students must report to the attendance office for an admittance slip.
- Unexcused tardies are, for example: missed my bus and I overslept.
- Excused tardy fall under the same reasons as excused absences.
- 5 unexcused tardies will result in an after school detention.

Mark your Calendar...

February 14
Valentines Dance
7-8:30 PM

February 15
Whitmer registration materials distributed
(through history classes)

February 18
Presidents Day
No School

February 21
Whitmer Q & A Night at Whitmer 7 PM

February 21
Conferences
(by appointment only)

February 22
Conferences
NO SCHOOL
(by appointment only)

February 28
Delayed Start – School starts at 10:15 AM

February 28
3rd Quarter interim grades sent home with students

March 13
Parent Club Meeting 7 PM in Library

March 21-28
Spring Break

April 4
End of 3rd Quarter Grade cards mailed home the week of April 14th.

April 28-May 1
OAT Testing week

(Continued)

(Continued)

From the
Associate Principal's Desk
Chris Kreft

Since returning from winter break, school days seem to be going by fast and our winter activities are moving forward. I just wanted to inform parents, students, and athletes that we have had some reports of theft from both the boys and girls' locker room and locker room lockers in the past month. We investigate theft reports and when items are recovered we return them to the rightful owners. While thefts at school are rare, there are some helpful hints that you might want to talk with your child about. First, if your child has something valuable, please try to leave it at home; do not bring it to school. Second, make sure that your child is reminded that every time he or she is away from their locker or locker room locker, make sure it is locked. Third, make sure that your child is reminded not to leave things of value outside of their locker when he or she is not present. And last, try to label, or some how identify, your child's belongings or equipment so that it can be easily identified if found or lost. Our goal is to prevent any thefts from occurring and to try to get belongings back to the rightful owners if they are taken. If your child has any information that may help in the return of things or equipment back to the rightful owner, please have your child contact either the Middle School Office or the school Resource Officer. In addition, coaches and teachers are keeping watch as much as possible. If you have any questions, you may contact me at school.

Students of the Month

September – Tallia LAbiche, Che'nae Coates, Michael Antoine, Zach Lindner

October – Terriva Williams, Kaleigh Brewer, Ericka Calendine, Seth Baer

November – Jordan Rushton, Megan Floering, Darrell Hutchen, Destiny Cunningham

December – Mallory Krell, Samantha Barber

January – Jeremy Koepfer, Andrew Plonski, Nicholas LaPoint, Justin Pfaff

Keep up the good work!

Nurse's Notes
Marie Kraus

There have been several new immunizations developed for adolescents in the past few years. There was a new Tetanus/Pertussis vaccine (Tdap) and the new cervical cancer vaccine for girls (human papillomavirus-HPV) recently issued. As of January 2008, there is yet another immunization update for adolescent children. The American Academy of Pediatrics and American Academy of Family Physicians jointly released recommendations to add the meningococcal vaccine to the recommended immunization schedule.

Meningococcal vaccine is now advised for routine vaccination of children 11-12 years of age and adolescents 13-18 years of age who have not been previously vaccinated. It is also recommended for other people at increased risk of the disease including college freshmen living in dorms and military recruits.

Meningococcal disease is caused by bacteria. It is the leading cause of bacterial meningitis in children 2 to 19 years of age. Meningitis is an infection of the fluid surrounding the brain and spinal cord. Meningococcal disease can be fatal in 5 to 10 percent of the people who get it. In other persons it can result in the loss of arms or legs or lead to other severe disabilities such as deafness, seizures or strokes. Approximately 76 percent of the cases of meningococcal disease among 11-19 year olds are vaccine preventable.

These vaccines have the ability to prevent severe disability and possibly death. I encourage you to discuss the new vaccine recommendations with your health care provider. As always, if you have any questions, please contact me at 419-473-8447 or 419-473-8424.

Fitness Center Named For Michael W. Carmean

The Board of Education held a ceremony on Friday, January 25th, between the JV and varsity boys' basketball games, to name Whitmer's new fitness center in honor of Michael W. Carmean, who retired as superintendent on July 31, 2007.

Library News

Fourth Annual Washington Local Warms up With Good Books!

Washington Local School Libraries will be celebrating Reading Month on **Thursday, February 28th,** by presenting the fourth annual: "Washington Local Warms up With Good Books".

Our theme this year is "Wild About Books" which will center on animals. This event will be held from 6:30 p.m. to 8:00 p.m. at Whitmer High School. Featured will be guest readers from the community and school. The **Toledo Area Humane Society** will give a presentation about animal care and a Poetry Slam for Jr. and Senior High School students will be held in the Whitmer cafeteria. Students may sign-up in the library if they are interested in participating in the Poetry Slam.

Mark your calendars and plan to join us for "Washington Local Warms up With Good Books" and "Get Wild About Books"!

Parent Club Meetings

**Thursdays
February 7 & March 13
In the Library
7-8 PM**

From the Counselors

February is a busy month for your eighth grader! On February 15th, the high school counselors will be visiting social studies classes to give all students registration materials for high school. Counselors will explain the registration process. Ask your student about the materials he or she received. In the materials, you will find a curriculum guide; the booklet that lists all of the courses available to choose from at Whitmer High School. All of the courses are described in detail. During social studies on February 26 and 27 students will meet with the high school counselors briefly here at Washington to discuss course options for 9th grade and submit schedule requests. Please take some time between February 15th and February 26th to help your student map out class choices.

To help you with this process, Whitmer High School has scheduled a **Question & Answer Night,** specifically for parents of incoming Freshmen. You are encouraged to attend, especially if you have not had a child attend high school already! High school counselors, administrators, and staff members will be on hand to answer your specific questions about Whitmer High School.

**Question & Answer Night at Whitmer
Thursday, February 21, 2008
7:00 PM
Whitmer Auditorium**

We welcome your calls and concerns,
Washington Counselors
Sharon Sheline 419-473-8350
Karen Yockey 419-473-8363

National Junior Honor Society

In the last two months the members of the National Junior Honor Society have been very busy. With one of the pillars of our organization being **Service** we are very proud to share that at this time we have more and more members surpassing their required number of five service hours. The variety of organizations receiving volunteer hours from our students keeps growing and growing and the follow up reflection writing the students complete truly provides evidence that they are gaining not monetarily but in so many other ways from their service time. At a young age these students are reaching out to our community, lending a helping hand and making a difference! **Video projects** explaining all five pillars were produced by our students and will be shown to the entire school during the morning announcements. We feel this will explain to other students at Washington the importance of NJHS and encourage them to meet the requirements to join later this year or when they are high school students. A sincere thank you to Mr. Lauber for his guidance with the video projects. February 14th may be Valentine's Day but it will also be the date of the **NJHS Valentine Dance**. For those parents that have volunteered to send in snack items and/or chaperone you will be contacted previous to the dance to remind you of the evening. And as always your assistance is greatly appreciated because without your help this evening would not be possible.

Co-Advisors: Mrs. Holly Farthing and Mrs. Lori Bosch

(Continued)

(Continued)

Language Arts

The teachers in the WJHS Language Arts Department would like to congratulate LaVelle Ridley, Nathan Ricker, Cierra Semelka, and Tyler Rooks. These four 8th grade students after two rounds of competition proved to be our top spellers out of 565 for the 2007 – 2008 school year. Upon earning this title all four also earned the right to participate in the 2008 Lucas County Area Spelling Bee held in the evening of February 19th at The Maumee Indoor Theater. This evening always proves to be interesting and exciting with spellers coming from across Lucas County. Adding to the evening is the chance to see news anchor Diane Larsen in person acting as the moderator and of course, possibly earning the right to head to the Blade Championship Bee in March. Good Luck to all Four!!

With the holiday break behind them the students in **Mrs. Bosch's** Language Arts classes began a unit focusing on Disability Awareness. Both nonfiction and fiction literary pieces from our anthology, several magazines, and The Toledo Blade were studied. This is just one unit out of several presented this year that will not only be a source of quality literature but provide a topic that the students can relate to their real life and take away a better understanding of others from it.

February will begin a new focus and a continued study of the essential skills to bring successful scores on the OAT Reading test that will be administered on April 28, 2008.

Your continued support of our LA class by providing the proper supplies, checks on homework, and making sure assignments from missed days are completed in a timely manner is appreciated tremendously.

The students in **Mrs. Farthing's** language arts classes just finished a unit on disability. During the month of February, students will be focusing on their next essay which is persuasive with research. In preparation for their essay, students will be looking at a couple of topics in which they will be debating as a class. Students will be looking at the pros and cons of the topic. Time will be given in class to conduct research, draft, revise, edit, and type their final copy.

Once students finish with their persuasive essay with research, they will be looking at poetry in more depth. We will be looking at poems and identifying the common characteristics of poems. Student will also have the opportunity to write their own poems.

Once again, if you have any questions or concerns, please feel free to contact me via e-mail at hfarthin@washloc.k12.oh.us or by phone at 419-473-8383 ext. 7708.

Math

Every year, Washington's math department involves students in a regional mathematics contest called "Promoting Excellence in Mathematics," which is sponsored by the Greater Toledo Council of Teachers of Mathematics (GTCTM). The contest is in two parts: a "Preliminary" and a "Final." In both cases, each test consists of a multiple-choice portion (20-30 questions) and an extended response question. Out of the 485 students who took preliminary math test, a total of forty-seven Washington students qualified to attend the final contest! In mid-February, these 47 students will be handed an admission ticket, instructions, and directions to the event to take the GTCTM final test. Every student receiving a ticket is strongly encouraged to attend. The final contest will be held on Saturday, March 1st at the University of Toledo Scott Park campus with certificates, cash awards, and plaques given to the top scorers. The math department congratulates all of the students who have qualified, and hopes that all show up to represent Washington at the final GTCTM at UT on Saturday, March 1st.

GREAT MATH RESOURCE!

The student edition of our 8th grade math textbook is provided on-line, and includes links to interactive activities, instant access to Web resources, and easy-to-use search functions. All the answers to the odd numbered problems found in the math textbook, as well as a description of how problems are solved are found on-line. You will not need a password to use the tutorial, but you will need the username and password to access the on-line student text and odd numbered answers. You MUST use both upper and lower case letters for the username and password.
Username: PREALG05OH
Password: vludlu75iA

The math department is offering a wonderful opportunity for all Washington students who need extra help in mathematics. This program is called After School Math Tutoring and is offered every Tuesday and Thursday from 3:00 to 3:45 pm. During these tutoring sessions, a certified teacher will assist students who are in need of improving their math skills and will oversee students who are retaking a math test or quiz. Any student who receives less than a 76% on a math test is permitted to retake the test for a better grade, but must show up to after school math tutoring to do so. All math teachers offer this opportunity to students who are in danger of failing 8th grade math, but it is up to the student to make the time to attend these sessions. A late bus will provide transportation home or students can arrange a ride home with a parent or guardian. For more information about After School Math Tutoring, please call Mr. Michaelis, Mathematics Facilitator, at 419-473-8383 Ext. 7732.

Science

Science students in **Mrs. Fortney's** class are now working under the Ohio State Science Standard for Earth Science. We started off with an understanding of structure of Earth, building on previous knowledge and exploring new areas of knowledge. One of the topics covered thus far was, The Rock Cycle. We learned that rocks make up the Earth are constantly being recycled. One form of rock is often broken down and changed into another. In lab we simulated changing sedimentary, metamorphic and igneous rocks. We used weathering and erosion, heat and pressure and melting and cooling to facilitate the changes. We have learned about the theory of plate tectonics and transfer of energy through waves. Now, we are applying that knowledge to our understanding of mountain building, seafloor spreading, earthquakes, volcanoes and hotspots. Students recently completed a layered curriculum activity in which the did power points, wrote eye witness accounts, wrote songs (and sang them), made books and joined in on other creative forms of expression to share their knowledge about earthquakes and volcanoes with their class mates. From now until spring break we will continue to meet the Earth Science Standards. To keep abreast of what is happening in our science classes please listen to the homework hotline and check your student's agenda book frequently.

Scientists in **Mr. Jacobs'** class will be studying how the interior structure of the Earth and the Earths' crust is divided into tectonic plates that are riding on top of the slow moving currents of magma in the mantle. Other processes that contribute to the continuous changing of the Earths' surface include Earthquakes and Volcanoes. All of these areas are directly related to the drifting of the continents and the plate tectonics theory. Students will complete a major project the first and second week of February when they choose an Earthquake from the past and research it. They will then create an informative pamphlet about that particular quake complete with statistics, facts and pictures.

As we begin the second semester, **Mr. Toney's** science classes are focusing on Earth science / geology. Our current textbook, *Inside the Restless Earth* students are studying the Theory of Plate Tectonics and the effect it has on planet Earth. The goal upon completion of this unit, is for students to master the following state indicators related to <u>Earth Systems</u>:

- Describe the interior structure of Earth and Earth's crust as divided into tectonic plates riding on top of the slow moving currents of magma in the mantle.
- Explain that most major geological events (e.g., earthquakes, volcanic eruptions, hot spots and mountain building) result from plate motion.
- Use models to analyze the size and shape of Earth, its surface and its interior (e.g., globes, topographic maps, satellite images).
- Explain that some processes involved in the rock cycle are directly related to thermal energy and forces in the mantle that drive plate motions.
- Describe how landforms are created through a combination of destructive (e.g., weathering and erosion) and constructive processes (e.g., crustal deformation, volcanic eruptions and deposition of sediment).
- Explain that folding, faulting and uplifting can rearrange the rock layers so the youngest is not always found on top.
- Illustrate how the three primary types of plate boundaries (transform, divergent and convergent) cause different landforms (e.g., mountains, volcanoes, ocean trenches).

American History

In **Mr. Durham's** Social Studies class, students will be learning about the Constitution and the formation of the new government in the United States. George Washington and his Presidency will be studied along with Thomas Jefferson, the Louisiana Purchase, the War of 1812, and the Industrial Revolution. It is very important for all students to bring necessary supplies to class on a daily basis.

Mrs. Leutz's American History students have been very busy since returning from the winter break. Having finished The Confederation Era; we are studying the creation of The Constitution: The Seven Principals, The Articles, The Bill of Rights, and The Amendments. Citizenship responsibilities will be discussed as well. After this, we will learn about George Washington's Presidency and the challenge faced creating a new nation. We will also study The Jefferson Era (including the War of 1812), and the Lewis and Clark expedition. For Lewis & Clark, journals will be created and presented to the class (each student will assume the identity of one of the members of The Corps of Discovery). Finally, we will learn about The Industrial Revolution and The Age of Jackson. We recognize February as "Black History Month" and have completed a packet about Rosa Parks and The Civil Rights Movement. We also continue to utilize *The Toledo Blade* once a month in our quest to report on current events.

(Continued)

PUBLICATIONS/ELECTRONIC COMMUNICATION

(Continued)

Reminders for Students...

Lost and Found
If you find something that does not belong to you, please give the item to one of your teachers. Lost and found items are kept in the main office. To help eliminate this situation, please write your name on your things, including notebooks, coats, etc., in pen or permanent marker.

Periodically, items that have been unclaimed for several weeks will be donated to charity. An announcement will be made during the week prior to the time when we would give items away.

Medication
Medication must be brought to school by a parent. It can only be administered with a medication form completed and signed by both a parent/guardian and doctor. This form can be obtained in the main office. Staff is not permitted to give any type of medication (even Tylenol or aspirin) without this form.

Phone Use
Students are allowed to use the office phones for *emergency reasons only* during the school day. All outside/after school activities/transportation need to be arranged beforehand. All other calls need to be made after 3:00 p.m. from the pay phone. The pay phone cost is 35¢.

How can we help you?

If you have visited our school during school hours you have probably noticed that the main doors are locked. We are keeping our building secure as a part of a continuing effort to provide our students with a safe learning environment.

Though the doors may be locked, please feel free to ring the bell and we will let you in and direct you one of the offices. Mrs. Merritt and Mrs. Laser will be happy to help you with whatever you may need:

In the principal's office, Mrs. Merritt can help with the following:
- Sign in for parent/teacher meetings
- Paying student fees/fines
- Dropping off medication (see sidebar for procedure)
- Dropping off something for a staff member

In the attendance/dean's/associate principal's office, Mrs. Laser can help you with the following:
- Picking up a student
- Drop something off for a student
- Students arriving late
- Disciplinary issues
- Updating student records

Conferences

Our second round of conferences is coming up at the end of February. These conferences will be by appointment only – as scheduled by the teachers – with priority given to those students who are in danger of being retained in the 8th grade. . If you would like to schedule a conference with your child's teachers at this time – or at any time during the year – please contact your child's counselor or homeroom teacher.

Karen Yockey *(419-473-8363)*

Sharon Sheline *(419-473-8350)*

Please note: there will be no school for students on Friday, February 22nd, due to parent/teacher conferences.

3rd quarter grade cards will be mailed home the week of April 14th.

If there is an outstanding fee/fine in your student's name, the grade card will be held. Most student fees can be paid in the main office. Library fines need to be paid in the library and cafeteria charges need to be paid in the cafeteria.

Source: Washington Junior High School, Washington Local School District; 5700 Whitmer Drive, Toledo, OH 43613; 419-473-8449.

Pre-AP

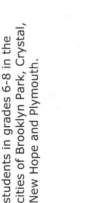

Pre-Advanced Placement at Plymouth Middle School

offers challenge and enthusiasm for learning during the middle school years and prepares students for the rigor of the Advanced Placement classes at the high school level.

Pre-AP classes are based on two important premises:

- Students can perform at rigorous academic levels.
- Middle school can prepare students for higher intellectual engagement by starting the development of advanced skills and knowledge as early as possible.

These expectations are reflected in curriculum and instruction throughout the school. Students are consistently challenged to expand their knowledge and skills to the next level.

Course Offerings

Pre-AP offers choice. Sixth, 7th and 8th grade students may take Pre-AP classes in English, social studies, and science at PMS. A student may apply in any grade for any or all of the Pre-AP classes offered.

Accelerated math is also available at Plymouth Middle School and will lead to AP math in high school.

Plymouth Middle School

Plymouth Middle School serves approximately 1,100 students in grades 6-8 in the cities of Brooklyn Park, Crystal, New Hope and Plymouth.

Plymouth Middle School
10011 36th Avenue North
Plymouth, MN 55441
763-504-7100
http://www.rdale.k12.mn.us/pms

Welcome to Plymouth Middle School

We are a learning community where students are supported and encouraged to reach their fullest potential.

(Continued)

(Continued)

Academics

At Plymouth Middle School, we recognize the unique needs of our students as they experience profound changes emotionally, socially, physically and intellectually. We emphasize the fostering of academic excellence in a safe and orderly environment while keeping in mind the fragile self-concept of the middle school student.

Students at PMS are on teams. Teams are the heart of the Plymouth program by providing a small learning community and a way for teachers and students to know each other well. Teams provide an excellent transition from elementary to middle school.

At Plymouth our teams consists of five core teachers who meet to plan curriculum and discuss student and program concerns. CORE subjects are:

- Language Arts (grade 6)
- English (grades 7/8)
- Social Studies/Social Sciences
- Math
- Science
- Reading
- Health
- Global Language—French or Spanish (grade 8)

Music/Fine Arts

Robbinsdale Area Schools maintains an award-winning tradition of outstanding performances in the arts. We give students of all ages a rich experience by teaching a variety of fine and performing arts.

Through these opportunities, students pursue special interests, develop talents, improve skills and reach their full potential. Education in the arts is a tool for critical thinking, effective communication and the creative demonstration of ideas. The arts actively engage our students in history and inspire a greater understanding of our world today.

Allied Art subjects offered to all grades at Plymouth Middle School are:

- Visual Arts
- Band
- Choir
- Computer Applications
- Family and Consumer Science (FACS)
- Physical Education
- Orchestra
- Technology Education

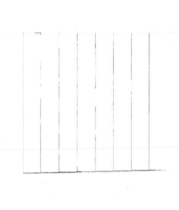

Program Enhancements

Home-base Program at Plymouth Middle School provides students with an opportunity to meet regularly with a teacher or advisor, giving students a sense of connection with that teacher/advisor. Home-base will focus on assisting students with improving skills as well as adjusting to the middle school and a more secondary focused format.

Students at PMS have many different opportunities for enrichment and extra help in their academic pursuits. Students who qualify may join the National Junior Honor Society as well as Accelerated Math classes. Homework Help nights, Targeted Services, tutoring and Special Education Services provide additional support for students.

When students achieve success in school, they are recognized and rewarded for their achievement. PMS recognizes students' achievements with these awards:

- Student of the Month
- Perfect Attendance
- High Honors and Honor Roll
- Art Awards
- Citizenship Award
- Positive Hallway Behavior Award
- GPA Improvement Award
- Panther Award

Source: From Plymouth Middle School and Robbinsdale Area Schools. Used with permission of Robbinsdale Area Schools.

PVHS
WEEK IN REVIEW FORM

Every week one I.D. team is chosen to help keep the administration informed of what's going on in our school. Please answer these questions as briefly and honestly as you can. You do not have to identify yourself. Please return to Mr. Damore's office on Monday. Thank you for your time and help.

1. What went RIGHT this week?

2. What went WRONG this week?

3. What would FIX #2?

4. Did you use any INSTRUCTIONAL STRATEGIES that you are excited about?

5. Do you have any IDEAS that would help us be a better school?

6. Nominee for RANDOM ACTS OF KINDNESS.

Source: Paradise Valley High School, Phoenix, Arizona.

OWEN J. ROBERTS WEEKLY CALENDAR

Filter the calendar by | All OJR Events | ▼ |

Select a date to view | 8/18/2008 | Go |

next week »

Event	Date and Time		Location
Special School Board Meeting	8/18/2008	6:00 PM	Admin. Building— Board Room
Middle School Marching Unit Band Camp	8/18/2008 8/21/2008	6:30 PM–8:00 PM	High School
New Family Orientation	8/19/2008	9:30 AM–10:30 AM	All Purpose Room
New Family Orientation	8/19/2008	9:30 AM–11:00 AM	Various Rooms
New Family Orientation	8/19/2008	9:30 AM–10:30 AM	

New Families to Owen J. Roberts are invited to attend the West Vincent New Family Orientation on Tuesday, August 19, at 9:30 AM. We will meet at the Henrietta Hankin Library on Route 401.

Source: Owen J. Roberts School District; Frank R. Scalise; 901 Ridge Road, Pottstown, PA 19465; 610-469-5100; http://www.ojrsd.com/events/index.asp?page=24.

ROBBINSDALE AREA SCHOOLS
ACTIVITIES CALENDAR

**Robbinsdale Area Schools
2008-09 Calendar
763-504-8000
www.rdale.k12.mn.us**

August 25–29	Teacher Workshop Week
September 1	Labor Day (Holiday)
September 2	First day of School
September 9	Primary Election
October 16-17	No School/Teacher's Convention
October 23 & 24	Half-Day Kindergarten Conferences
October 30	End of first quarter (Middle and High School)
October 31	No School—Staff Development
November 4	General Election*
November 26-28	No School—Thanksgiving (Holiday)
December 5	End of first trimester (Elementary)
December 22-January 2	No School—Winter Break
January 5	School Resumes
January 15	End of second quarter (Middle and High School)
January 16	No School—Staff Development
January 19	No School—Martin Luther King Jr's Birthday (Holiday)
February 5 & 6	Half-Day Kindergarten Conferences
February 16	No School—President's Day (Holiday)
March 13	End of second trimester (Elementary)
March 20	End of third quarter (Middle and High School)
March 23-27	No School—Spring Break
April 10	No School
April 13	No School
May 25	No School—Memorial Day (Holiday)
June 3	Last day of school for students
June 4	Commencement

JULY
Sun	Mon	Tue	Wed	Thu	Fri	Sat
		1	2	3	4	5
6	7	8	9	10	11	12
13	14	15	16	17	18	19
20	21	22	23	24	25	26
27	28	29	30	31		

AUGUST
Sun	Mon	Tue	Wed	Thu	Fri	Sat
					1	2
3	4	5	6	7	8	9
10	11	12	13	14	15	16
17	18	19	20	21	22	23
24	25	26	27	28	29	30

SEPTEMBER
Sun	Mon	Tue	Wed	Thu	Fri	Sat
31	1	2	3	4	5	6
7	8	9	10	11	12	13
14	15	16	17	18	19	20
21	22	23	24	25	26	27
28	29	30				

OCTOBER
Sun	Mon	Tue	Wed	Thu	Fri	Sat
			1	2	3	4
5	6	7	8	9	10	11
12	13	14	15	16	17	18
19	20	21	22	23	24	25
26	27	28	29	30	31	

NOVEMBER
Sun	Mon	Tue	Wed	Thu	Fri	Sat
						1
2	3	4	5	6	7	8
9	10	11	12	13	14	15
16	17	18	19	20	21	22
23	24	25	26	27	28	29
30						

DECEMBER
Sun	Mon	Tue	Wed	Thu	Fri	Sat
	1	2	3	4	5	6
7	8	9	10	11	12	13
14	15	16	17	18	19	20
21	22	23	24	25	26	27
28	29	30	31			

JANUARY
Sun	Mon	Tue	Wed	Thu	Fri	Sat
				1	2	3
4	5	6	7	8	9	10
11	12	13	14	15	16	17
18	19	20	21	22	23	24
25	26	27	28	29	30	31

FEBRUARY
Sun	Mon	Tue	Wed	Thu	Fri	Sat
1	2	3	4	5	6	7
8	9	10	11	12	13	14
15	16	17	18	19	20	21
22	23	24	25	26	27	28

MARCH
Sun	Mon	Tue	Wed	Thu	Fri	Sat
1	2	3	4	5	6	7
8	9	10	11	12	13	14
15	16	17	18	19	20	21
22	23	24	25	26	27	28
29	30	31				

APRIL
Sun	Mon	Tue	Wed	Thu	Fri	Sat
			1	2	3	4
5	6	7	8	9	10	11
12	13	14	15	16	17	18
19	20	21	22	23	24	25
26	27	28	29	30		

MAY
Sun	Mon	Tue	Wed	Thu	Fri	Sat
					1	2
3	4	5	6	7	8	9
10	11	12	13	14	15	16
17	18	19	20	21	22	23
24	25	26	27	28	29	30
31						

JUNE
Sun	Mon	Tue	Wed	Thu	Fri	Sat
	1	2	3	4	5	6
7	8	9	10	11	12	13
14	15	16	17	18	19	20
21	22	23	24	25	26	27
28	29	30				

*No school-sponsored events may be scheduled between 6-8 p.m.

- SCHOOL NOT IN SESSION
- STAFF PLANNING/DEVELOPMENT—NO SCHOOL
- HALF-DAY KINDERGARTEN PARENT/TEACHER CONFERENCES—NO SCHOOL FOR HALF-DAY K STUDENTS
- MID-QUARTER—SECONDARY
- LAST DAY OF QUARTER—SECONDARY
- LAST DAY OF TRIMESTER—K-5
- SUMMER BREAK/WEEKENDS

This calendar will be updated when parent information nights and mid-quarter dates are known.

Revised: January 2008

Source: Robbinsdale Area Schools.

5

Media Relations

"Reporters . . . a principal's best friends? Strange but true. Film at 10."

Even the most articulate educational leader, with the most carefully developed and implemented community assessment and communication strategies, may be painfully uncomfortable when dealing with the media. To educators, media coverage too often calls to mind memories of bad news reported or having been misquoted, misinterpreted, or accused of hiding the truth. To a certain degree, these perceptions stem from a general misconception of the media's role in covering education. It is easier to place blame than to face the fact that education advocates have not been proactive enough in getting their message out.

Educators have a lot to brag about, but they are usually too busy doing their jobs to spend time broadcasting their successes. But in this age of instant news, if you want to attract communitywide support and involvement, you can no longer afford to be modest about your school's accomplishments. The purpose of this chapter is to cast the idea net as widely as possible so that no matter where you are on the road of media relations, there will be something here that makes the trip a little quicker and the path a little smoother.

To begin, take a few minutes and conduct a simple analysis of one month's newspaper coverage of your school or district. Make a copy of everything that was printed: meeting announcements, letters to the editor, photos, news, feature stories—everything. Now rate each one as positive, negative, or neutral in content. Count the number in each category and compare this to the overall number of stories printed.

If you want to do a better job of managing the negative news, then you and your team must assume more responsibility for initiating positive stories. And you must assist the media in obtaining more complete information about those stories that are less than positive.

The dictionary describes news as "recent events and happenings, especially those that are unusual or notable." The three key words here are *recent*, *unusual*, and *notable*. An Arbor Day ceremony featuring the superintendent and governing board president turning the first shovel of dirt may be recent, but it is neither unusual nor notable. On the other hand, the fifth-grade field trip to the burned area of a state park to plant trees purchased with money earned from a recycling project is unusual and notable enough that it just might get sent out by a wire service. Remember, you are competing for news space and airtime with every other school and agency in town, as well as nationwide. If you want coverage, your story must stand out. News is the creation of the reporter, not the source. If a reporter doesn't see an event as newsworthy and doesn't report on it, it is, for all practical purposes, "non-news." However, if the reporter's attention is attracted to something unusual, whether good or bad by district standards, you better believe it will become news. As an educational leader, you want the public to know when students in your school are excited about learning and are succeeding in the classroom. But is it news? From a reporter's perspective, the school is just doing its job—and that is not news. In this context, think about what is being reported about education of late. People constantly hear that public education is in need of radical reform, that it is wasteful and ineffective, that students are not learning basic skills, that schools need to be run more like businesses, and so forth. In other words, it is when schools are not doing their job that education becomes newsworthy. Once you realize that it is the media's job to inform the community about what is happening, good or bad, and that the community expects to be so informed, then you can develop strategies to get school news covered in a positive manner.

BUILDING A WORKING RELATIONSHIP WITH REPORTERS

According to Margo Mateas, president of Public Relations Training Company, near San Jose, California (www.mediarelationsmaven.com), managers need to include PR staff in decisions. Practitioners must manage the truth, not bury it. To avoid being blindsided by the press or mishandling the message, PR staff need to be involved in problem solving and crisis communications from the beginning, not just told what to do after everyone else has met in a closed-door session. PR practitioners are the ones actually answering questions from journalists. They need to be equipped with information, messaging, and support to do their jobs. Working together on messaging will also keep everyone on the same page.

Ultimately, media relations is about relationships. Relationships have to be nurtured and developed with trust, with both sides keeping their word and maintaining integrity. When you're able to develop these kinds of relationships with reporters and PR people, the mutual benefit is overwhelming. Not only do you find suitable working relationships, but you may actually discover real friends that will last much longer than the current crisis you're facing. Contact and cooperation are the keys to building a successful relationship with news reporters. Respect the reporter's task of covering the story as thoroughly, accurately, responsibly, and objectively as possible. Remember that the reporter answers to an editor or news director. Let's hope that the reporter, in turn, respects your task of educating children with as few disruptions as possible and remembers that you answer to a superintendent, a board, and the public as well. When reporters and educators deal honestly, openly, and fairly with each other, the news reported will reflect that.

A reporter is a person with a job to do, just like you. Most reporters are trying conscientiously to do the best job they can, just like you. It is fascinating to hear educational leaders talk about "cutting the reporters out of the story" or making access to information difficult for them. Then, these same leaders wonder why they get such lousy coverage. You don't appreciate someone who makes your job or life more difficult. Why should they?

There is an old journalism saying: "Never argue with anyone who buys ink by the barrel and paper by the ton." To that admonition, add, "or who controls 3 hours of prime-time TV every night." Much of the negative media coverage generated about local schools can be traced back to some action or remark made by somebody in a school district who forgot these basic truths.

The most effective way of getting positive news coverage is to cooperate with the media. Treat them courteously and provide information about problems. Don't withhold it in the mistaken belief that they might not find out or will drop the subject and just go away. If you accommodate them on the negative stories, they will usually accommodate you when you want the positive stories run as well.

Principal John Baldwin of Shreveport, Louisiana, offers some excellent advice on how to deal with reporters: "I have cultivated personal relationships with key reporters by being completely candid with them, even when it was painful to do so. This has paid rich dividends when I needed them. I also try to be sensitive to the media's interest in innovation and controversy."

"Establishing up-front relationships with the media, be it television, print, or radio can be especially challenging with current media practices," explained Superintendent Dr. Paul Kinder of Blue Spring, Missouri. "Community organizations such as school districts have become the target of media hype to raise ratings for local news. News reporting has taken over more hours of channel programming than ever. Honesty is still the best and most effective way to deal with the media. The sensationalism of current television media often overshadows the details in events that would portray them fairly. In addition, being responsive and available also works to our advantage. Our public relations office has a mobile messenger, and this includes a cell phone that is on 24/7. Avoiding the press is seldom beneficial. When calls are not returned, reporters often just appear in person and they may believe we have something to hide. Finally, our responsibility is first and foremost to our students and their families. We can utilize the media to get a message out, but we must also work hard to protect our students and families from undue, harsh criticism."

Tips for Working With Reporters

- Get to know the reporters in your community! Get to know the reporters in your community! Meet with them face-to-face. Invite them into your schools, to community events. This bears repeating a third time: Get to know the reporters in your community! Pay attention to bylines in the newspapers and familiarize yourself with the writing style of the reporters who cover education. Most large daily papers have a writer assigned to the education beat. On smaller dailies, this reporter may have other coverage duties in addition to education. Watch the local television news shows and note the kinds of stories individual reporters are assigned to cover. When the reporter known for handling investigative assignments calls you, you'll know it's not for information about the annual school carnival—unless someone has accused a committee member of embezzling funds. Be knowledgeable about your state's open records laws and your school district's policies on the release of information. Determine up front what is public information about students and employees and what is not. Make sure your staff members know what information is restricted.

- Find out the filing deadlines for newspapers and television and radio stations in your community. You will get better coverage if you respect their time restrictions and plan to release your information accordingly.

- Your availability is a critical factor in getting good coverage. Respond to calls from reporters as promptly as possible. Reporters have relatively inflexible deadlines. If you cannot respond right away and no one else can handle the call, have your secretary phone to find out the reporter's deadline and let him or her know the approximate time you will be available. If you miss that deadline, you will miss the opportunity to get out your side of the story. You may also appear to be trying to hide something—never a good impression to leave with a reporter.

- Treat all reporters equally. Do not play favorites or allow one reporter to always scoop the others. However, if a reporter calls you and initiates a story, don't call all the others and share that reporter's story idea.

- Treat reporters as the professionals they are. Most go through the same amount of education and training as educators. Like educators, reporters work long hours and deserve respect.

- Treat reporters as you would any community member inquiring about your school. Take a personal interest in them; find out if they have children and where their children attend school.

- Don't tell a reporter how to do his or her job. Don't be like the administrator who handed a reporter a list of the questions he could ask the students, thus setting a negative tone for what should have been a positive story. You do not have the right to read or see a story before it is printed or broadcast. Once the story is underway, you have to trust the reporter's judgment and let him or her know that you are available to answer questions.

- Tell the truth. Understandably, you may want to give the school's or the district's perspective on the actions or events in question, but never lie. A false statement invariably comes to light, and the person who uttered it has damaged his or her personal credibility as well as that of the institution. Lying to a reporter will always come back to haunt you!

- Be prepared to be disappointed occasionally. The most interesting and photo-attractive event in school history will go uncovered, even when you've been told it will be covered, if a story of greater dramatic impact or news interest breaks at the same time. Be a good sport and let the reporter or editor know you understand.

- Remember that reporters don't write headlines. You may have thought you did a very positive interview, yet the headline was, or seemed to you to be, negative. Headlines are written to grab the casual reader's attention, so they must be short and "punchy." Don't blame the reporter.

- Reporters also don't write editorials. If there is a major story or incident involving your school or district that prompts an editorial, the editorial may have been based on the contents of a reporter's story, but, even in small newspapers, it would have been written by someone else.

- Avoid "no comment" replies. If you can't respond, explain why. Say, "I can't respond to that because it's a confidential personnel matter," or, "That matter is under investigation, and I'm not free to respond at this time," or whatever the truth is.

- Cultivate a working relationship with reporters during good times. Go out of your way to cooperate and provide information so that a mutual trust level is established. Then when a crisis hits, they will likely be willing to work with you to present a fair story. Dartmouth Middle School in Massachusetts has an ace in the hole: The editor of the local weekly is a former student who goes out of the way to cooperate with the school in getting the stories right. School officials have established a level of trust with that editor, and the school community is more likely to see factual, correct information printed in that local paper versus hearsay or rumors.

- Learn media terminology such as *press* versus *media, deadline, cutline, byline, off the record,* and *not for attribution.*
- Don't ever say anything "off the record"; even if a reporter reassures you that your comments are off the record, respond as if what you say is being taped, because ultimately, you have to take responsibility for everything you say. If you are not prepared to see your words in print or hear them on radio or television, don't say them. Remember, once you have spoken, you can never take back those words.
- Invite reporters to speak to student journalism classes and clubs and with the faculty or PTA/PTO about the news business. Give them a chance to talk about themselves and to share their experiences. Most reporters are intensely curious and are "people persons" who enjoy talking about what they do.
- Drop a note or pick up the phone once in a while to thank a reporter for a positive story about your school or district just to touch base.
- Keep a small, unobtrusive tape recorder at your side and record all interviews. Not only does this help you review and improve your media technique, it is also your insurance policy if you are seriously misquoted or if there is a substantial error in the resulting story. If you are talking to a newspaper reporter face-to-face, say, "I'm going to tape this if you don't mind." Many newspaper reporters now record interviews, in addition to using their traditional spiral notepads.
- Above all, be honest, fair, and courteous. In this relationship, as in all others, the Golden Rule really does apply.

GETTING YOUR STORY TO THE MEDIA

There are several ways to get your story out, but for most educational leaders, the easiest way is to call a reporter directly or prepare a news release. If you have already cultivated a relationship based on mutual trust, you won't have a problem getting through to the reporter or having him or her return your call.

If you plan to call a reporter with your story, be sure you call well before critical deadlines. If you are hoping for a photo, you will probably have to let the reporter know about the event at least 2 days in advance so a photographer can be scheduled. It is best to use the phone for unplanned stories or emergencies and then back up your call by sending a fax or e-mail with the same information. By handing the reporter a prepared news release when he or she arrives, you can be sure names are spelled correctly and other critical information is accurate. Reporters are busy people and don't always have time to take notes over the phone.

A fax machine and e-mail access are incredibly useful tools, especially if the story is breaking the same day. Along with a phone call, fax, or e-mail, provide complete information for the reporter and allow him or her to move swiftly on the story.

Another excellent tool, particularly in small communities with weekly newspapers, is the "tip sheet," described later in this chapter. This contains a schedule of upcoming events and is sent out on a regular basis to all the local media. Of course, a follow-up phone call is also a good idea.

Principal Nick Miller of Buffalo High School in Minnesota is a strong believer in aggressive publicity. His school averages about 10 articles in every issue of the local paper, and he encourages the editors to emphasize more than sports. The local Aurora,

Ohio, weekly newspaper has a mailbox in Aurora High School's mail room. A reporter stops by to pick up information on a regular basis. Many of the articles printed come from the school's monthly newsletter.

News conferences at the school-building level should be called only in very special circumstances or in extreme emergencies—and only if you are very confident in your media skills. A news conference is generally used in situations where you need to get important information to all the media at once. However, due to advanced technology, there are often faster and more reliable ways to communicate.

WRITING A NEWS RELEASE

The news release has long been a communications standard for getting information to all media sources in a timely fashion. But a vague, poorly written, uninteresting news release that fails to catch the reporter's eye most likely will end up in the "round file" next to the reporter's desk.

News releases should be used judiciously and written in a manner that simplifies follow-up for the reporter. Keep in mind that reporters are inundated with stacks of news releases every day from people like you competing for space or time. If yours does not stand out from the others, it is unlikely to be considered for that day's news mix.

Remember, a good news release deals with news. If something is not news, and if it is not of general interest to the reading or listening public at large, it does not belong in a news release. Avoid editorializing in your release. An opinion about the event (such as the administrator's comments in the examples provided by Paradise Valley Unified School District in Phoenix that appear at the end of this chapter) should be given in the form of a quotation by a cited source.

Another key to an effective news release is to make sure that it is timely. A release about a week-old event is history, not news. If you know the name of the reporter who covers education news, send the release to that person's attention. Otherwise, send it to the attention of the newspaper editor or radio/television news editor. When possible, send out your release 5 days to a week in advance. Then, call to check if the reporter received it.

Another effective way to disseminate the news from your school is to have all news releases handled by a particular staff member who is given time to work on this. Principal Gary Phillips at Fayette County High School in Georgia assigns this role to an English teacher. Not only does the teacher notify the media of upcoming events and awards received by students and teachers, but the teacher also welcomes members of the media to the school and attempts to smooth the way for public relations campaigns. Finally, don't be disappointed if all your news releases aren't used—neither are anybody else's. There is strong competition for news coverage, and education is not the only topic in which the public, or the media, is interested.

Content of a News Release

A good news release contains the following information:

- A *date* line, a *contact* line, and a *for release* line. Instructions on how to write these are included in the next section, "Guidelines for Preparing the News Release."
- An interesting lead sentence and paragraph. The questions the reporter will be thinking are, "Why should I care about this? What's the point?" State clearly up front what makes the story unique.

- Answers to the questions *who, what, where, when, why,* and *how.*
- If the story deals with a current hot topic, consider whether you need to include some background information. Cover the facts, but avoid editorializing—that is why news organizations have editors on staff.
- Reporters are always interested in money-related items and the *number* of people that the event/program/incident impacts.
- If there are several activities associated with an event, include a brief program outline and note the best times for photo opportunities.
- Check and double-check that your information is accurate, that names are spelled correctly, and that addresses and times are correct. Most errors in news stories can be traced back to the source.

A sample news release is inserted at chapter's end. Also included is the Media Contact Form from the Washington Elementary School District in Phoenix, Arizona, used to keep school and district administrators informed when another member of the staff has media contact. This contact is often unplanned, but it is a good idea for staff to inform you and for you to keep a record of it.

Guidelines for Preparing the News Release

- The key is to present information in a clear, concise, easy-to-read, professional format.
- Always use the same format for your releases—the same heading, paragraph indentations, and margins so that your style will look professional and be easily recognizable. Simplify punctuation and adhere to the same spelling and capitalization style. Get a copy of the *Associated Press Stylebook* and use it as a guide.
- The *date* line states the date the news release is issued by the school.
- The *contact* line gives the name and telephone number of a contact person who can provide additional information about the event (usually whoever generates the release) and, if appropriate, the names and phone numbers of others who are knowledgeable about the story and who are willing to be interviewed.
- The *for release* line announces the date you wish the news media (whether newspaper, radio, or television) to print or broadcast the information. In the example at chapter's end, the *for release* date states "immediate" because the event has just occurred and there is no need or reason to hold back the announcement. *Immediate* means the media is free to use the release upon receiving it. Some news items may need to be sent to the media prior to the date you want the item announced—for instance, the announcement of a special award or the appointment of a new principal. In this case, the *for release* line should read something like "Hold until Thursday, Jan. 24."
- If at all possible, news releases should be kept to one page. If the story is of such importance or demands such detail that more than one page is needed, put "—More—" at the bottom of the first page, indicating that the item continues to another page. At the top of the second page, put "Page Two," the date, and the title line of your release, followed by "(Continued)." Drop down two or three line spaces and continue with your copy.

One way to avoid writing a longer news release is to put "Editor Note" at the end of the release indicating that more information is attached. As in the case of the sample release, the editor can lengthen the story with the names of the students and other details about the event, including a picture if space permits.

Don't make the mistake of thinking you can trick the editors into printing more of your story than they wish by writing a longer news release. If your release is so long that there is not enough space for it, it might not get used at all. Or if the release has to be edited to fit the space available, key points might end up being left out.

PREPARING A MEDIA TIP SHEET

The "tip sheet" is a weekly or biweekly schedule of events and activities involving the school or district schools, such as "Around the XY District." It advises reporters and editors of a variety of possible story-generating items and allows them to pick and choose those they wish to cover depending on interest, space, and deadlines. The tip sheet can also be sent to the superintendent and governing board, and employee and parent organizations, and posted in the faculty/staff lounge to apprise everyone of upcoming events. A sample News Tip Form used by Washington School District is shown at the end of this chapter. The tip sheet could be sent by e-mail directly to your beat reporters, or posted on your Web sites, or e-mailed to all of your key communicators.

When you create a tip sheet, be sure to

- use a different masthead for the tip sheet than the one you use for news releases so that a reporter can easily distinguish between the two.
- list events and activities in calendar order. Each item is preceded by its day of the week, date, and time.
- write a brief description about the event or activity (using one or two lines), including location. Also include the name and phone number of a contact person for that event.
- make a note that the event is a good photo opportunity, if that is the case.
- list holiday and classroom activities that make good holiday features, such as kindergartners dressed as Pilgrims and Native Americans for a Thanksgiving feast, students operating mock voting booths on Election Day, Abe Lincoln visiting school on Presidents' Day, and students reciting appropriate speeches on Martin Luther King Jr. Day or on Cinco de Mayo. This makes great filler material that reporters know is always popular with the public.

WRITING A PUBLIC SERVICE ANNOUNCEMENT (PSA)

Television and radio stations are required by the Federal Communications Commission (FCC) to run a certain number of public service spots each week. These brief announcements are free of charge and are often overlooked as a way to get information to the public about education. You can use PSAs to highlight American Education Week or to announce a special event such as a community concert at your school or an annual PTA fundraiser. (A typical public service announcement is printed at the end of the chapter.)

- If your district or school has a special letterhead for issuing news releases, PSAs, and so on, use it. If not, regular district or school letterhead is perfectly acceptable. If you are using regular letterhead, be sure to put "Public Service Announcement" across the top of the page.
- The *date* line is for the date the PSA is sent out by the school.

- The *contact person* line should give the name of the person who can provide additional information about the event or who is authorized to speak for the district or school in commenting about the event, not simply the person in charge. A telephone number should always be included. Obviously, the person listed as the contact should be made aware in advance and be prepared to answer inquiries.
- The *topic* line should give the station editor a clear indication of the subject of the PSA.
- The *date of event* line is self-explanatory.
- The *requested air dates* means the date(s) you wish the radio or television station to broadcast your PSA. In the example, the dates indicate approximately a 2½-week period prior to the event. This tells the station that it has some latitude in airing the PSA. Obviously, you hope the station will air it more than once, but this may not happen. The greater the lead time and the longer the period of requested airdates you list, the better your chances of getting your PSA aired. Remember, the station must first record your PSA, then schedule a time to run it. A last-minute PSA is not likely to make it past the first person who reads it.
- Think of a PSA as a free commercial. But remember, because it is free, the station has no obligation to run your particular PSA. Unless the station's market is very small, it will likely have many more requests for PSA's than it has airtime to give away.
- The length of your PSA is very important. It must be 10, 30, or 60 seconds in length when read by an announcer. You want to get your story told in the shortest workable amount of time. Keep it clear and simple. Don't write a 60-second PSA for something that could be covered in 30 seconds.
- PSA copy should be very clear and precise about what you want someone to know or do. Write the announcement the way you would say it. Read the copy aloud and clearly—more than once—to make sure it is understandable and no longer than the length requested. Remember that what may make sense on paper does not always come across clearly when read aloud.

An announcer at the station is either going to record your PSA for later broadcast or read it over the air. Sometimes on television, PSA copy may be aired in written form, in a community bulletin board format, to be read by the viewer. This is especially likely in areas served by cable television companies. In any case, write the PSA exactly as it should be read and do not exceed the prescribed length. If it has to be edited by the station, it may not be used at all.

DEALING WITH NEWSPAPERS

Familiarize yourself with the various newspapers that serve your community. Many major dailies now publish zone editions that concentrate on local community news. Different reporters will cover these zone editions, so make sure you know who they are. This is where education stories of general local interest will usually be printed. If your paper publishes by zones, find out the deadline for your particular zone, as well as the deadline for the main edition. You also need to find out the paper's policy for printing stories in both the zone and the main edition. Most papers will run your story only once and will not look kindly on two reporters covering the same story—and neither will the reporters.

Learn the deadlines for special sections of the paper such as the community calendar. These sections usually have longer lead times because they are printed weekly, but they provide an excellent resource for notifying the community about upcoming school events.

If your paper has a regular education column, volunteer to write a guest editorial. Call the editor and ask what kind of education stories would be of interest to the paper and then submit feature story ideas on a regular basis. Although the majority of your ideas may not be used, the chances are that one or two will make an impression and find their way into print. Administrators have utilized this idea to their advantage at Sauk Rapids High School in Minnesota, and Meadowbrook Middle School in Poway, California. In Sauk Rapids, the administrative team writes a column for the two local newspapers. Many smaller newspapers also welcome articles written by students. If such a program doesn't exist, you may want to introduce it as a way to highlight student work and to generate publicity for your school or district at the same time.

Although large daily papers will generally assign a photographer if a photo is warranted, most weekly papers will accept good-quality black-and-white photos for publication. Find out their policies for accepting photographs and the standards they require. You might even get your photo printed with your own byline.

USING TELEVISION EFFECTIVELY

Competition for television airtime is very intense in a large market that contains more than one school district. A half-hour local news segment contains on the average only 11 minutes of actual news time, and this is split between local and state news and local tie-ins to national news. Your story must have strong community interest to get aired. If you are located in a small community where the school is the hub of activity for residents, you stand a better chance of getting regular, positive coverage of school programs.

There are several keys to using television effectively:

- Remember that television is a visual medium and is event oriented. When proposing stories, always suggest a visual angle. Don't waste time with nonvisual stories or boring ones (proclamations, presentations, and the like). Only one school's Arbor Day ceremony or food drive will be covered, so be first or have a different twist. All across the country, TV news stations report that research shows their viewers *do* want to see more positive news coverage, so opportunities are there if you present unique story ideas.
- Check out the lead time each station requires. Provide complete information about the story, including time, duration, specific location, directions, and contact person. Use the phone with discretion, as TV assignment-desk staff are busy people.
- Target daytime story coverage. Most television stations these days are on tight budgets and employ limited personnel. As a result, evening events are more difficult for them to cover and crews are generally sent to cover only the more dramatic stories, such as crisis situations or crime scenes. Exceptions to this are major sporting events at the high school level.
- If the station sends a cameraperson to your event without a reporter, be sure to give the cameraperson a copy of a news release containing the details of the event. This ensures your story will run with complete and accurate information. Be nice to the camera operator. He or she can make you look really good—or really dumb!
- Unlike newspapers, television stations generally don't assign a specific reporter to cover education. You need to know who the news directors and assignment editors

are at the local stations, because they are the ones you contact and the ones who decide which stories get covered. Find out if there are special types of education/ school stories in which they are interested.

- Take advantage of the station's community calendar and public service announcement options. Talk with the station's public service director about PSAs on issues of concern to the community, such as parental involvement in education, drug abuse, and dropout prevention. Use the community calendar for upcoming events that might not warrant special coverage (open house, kindergarten registrations). Community calendars are prevalent on local cable channels.
- Invite on-air personalities to be honorary spokespersons or guest celebrities for a community-oriented project or to speak to classes about their jobs (for example, invite the weatherperson to a science class). Often, such persons will bring a camera crew with them to record their station's community involvement, an important part of a station's advertising and promotional package.

Interviews: When It Is Your Turn on Camera

Television can be intimidating and uncomfortable when the lights are turned on you. Prior to your interview, anticipate questions and review your possible responses. Decide in advance the most important points you want to get across and try to focus on them throughout the interview. The key is to appear poised and competent. Often, the reporter will ask you the questions in an informal format before the cameras start to roll. Use your responses at that time to prepare for the real thing. One word of caution: remember that the camera is always "on"—you could be recorded without realizing it.

- Use concise answers no longer than 20 or 30 seconds. Avoid jargon.
- State the most important information first, and emphasize those points. Because only short segments of the interview will be used, use a headline approach: "The most critical issue here is . . ."
- Rephrase long or loaded queries into questions you can or want to answer. Give positive responses.
- Think before you speak. Unless you are on a live show, you can take as much time as you need because the tape will be edited before airing.
- If you wish to drop the subject, build in a cutoff with your answer. (For example, say that is all the information you have to give at this time, bridge back to your original message, and thank the reporter.)
- Discuss only those activities and policies within your area of responsibility.
- If you don't know the answer, say so. If you can't respond, explain why and bridge into an area you want to discuss.
- Be consistent. Give the same answers to repeated questions. Repetition helps make your point.
- Avoid answering "what-if" questions. Stick to the facts.
- Don't be guilty of a quick retort that you may regret later. Avoid sarcasm or attempts at humorous references. Be straightforward and professional.
- Avoid distracting mannerisms. Don't rock in your chair, pull at jewelry, say "er" or "uh," or cross your arms. Keep your face open and pleasant, make eye contact with the reporter, and use appropriate, but restrained, gestures.
- Stay relaxed, smiling, and positive.

WORKING WITH RADIO

The key to effective radio coverage is to get your message aired at the right time. Because radio stations broadcast 24 hours a day and include news coverage almost hourly, stories have a very limited life span. This also means that radio deadlines are tighter than those of television and newspapers. Millard South High School in Omaha, Nebraska, has found that, for immediate purposes, radio is the most effective media resource. Radio also can be especially effective in small communities with few schools or school districts in the broadcast area.

Use the same techniques with radio reporters that you would use with television or newspaper folks. Just remember, you will hear the results a lot faster, so be prepared to deal with issues and questions raised by the radio broadcast right away.

No one will see your face when you are on the radio, so be sure to speak clearly and distinctly. Stop talking after you have made your point or answered the question. Even if you are doing a radio interview by telephone, speak as if the reporter were in the room; it helps to make eye contact with something or someone while you are speaking.

There is a specialized radio format for just about every kind of listener, from classical to country music to the increasingly popular talk radio. Some markets are now experimenting with "kids' radio," which could provide an excellent media opportunity for schools. Listen to the various stations in your area and note those that carry community-related information. Try pitching your story ideas to them first.

Here are some ways that you can use radio to tell your story:

- Announce emergencies concerning school openings, closings, and evacuations.
- Compile public service announcements about special events, programs, or issues of concern to the community.
- List community calendar events.
- Submit a topic and volunteer to be interviewed for an in-depth, half-hour public service program. (Stations are required to do a certain number of these.)
- Sell the station on the idea of a monthly "Kids' Show" featuring students.
- Volunteer to be on a call-in talk show dealing with an educational subject.
- Negotiate your own weekly or monthly radio program, if you live in a small or rural community.
- Offer to present a guest editorial on the air.
- Don't forget to invite radio reporters to special school events. If you have a guest speaker or a choral event, the reporter may be able to record portions of the program to use on the air.
- Let the news director know that you are available to respond to educational issues in your community.

TIPS FOR TALKING TO THE MEDIA

As an educational leader, you may find yourself in a position of having to talk to a reporter when you are least prepared. When that happens, don't panic and don't answer immediately. Take time to stop and think first. If you are still uncomfortable with the question, say, "I don't have that information right now, but I'll check to see if I can get it for you."

Following are some remarks prepared by Judi Willis, APR, Paradise Valley Unified District (Arizona) Community Relations Director, that you might use as starting points for your comments when talking to the media:

- I'm not at liberty to discuss that topic at this time because it is a/an . . . (executive session matter, personnel matter, parent/student privacy issue, and so on), but I'll be happy to supply the information when it can be made public.
- I don't have all the information on this subject. I recommend you contact the . . . (superintendent, board president, community relations director). If he or she can't help you, please give me a call back.
- We will follow our governing board's policies and take appropriate action after we have concluded our investigation.
- Because this is a personnel matter, I'm not at liberty to talk about every aspect of the situation.

After a crisis, Willis suggests the following:

- We don't allow reporters on the campus to film or talk to our students about this situation. We have trained professionals talking with the students who are having problems. We believe it is in the best interests of our students to resume their normal routine as soon as possible.
- Although we feel badly about the students' education being interrupted, we won't tolerate this type of behavior (exhibited by a few students, which interrupts the education of their classmates) in our schools.
- We share the community's concern over this, and will review our procedures to see how we can keep it from happening again.

Bill of Rights for the Radio/Television Interviewee

In interviews of a spontaneous nature, you have the right

- to know who is interviewing you, and who he or she represents.
- to have total agreement on the ground rules by both parties, no matter how hastily arranged.
- to be treated courteously. The questions can be tough, but the reporter's demeanor should not be abusive.
- to have off-the-record comments, if previously stated, honored. (As a rule, never say anything off the record unless you know and trust the reporter completely.)
- to not be physically threatened or impaired by lights held too close or microphones shoved in your face.
- to break off the interview after a reasonable amount of time, but only after important questions have been answered.

In *prearranged* interviews, you have the right

- to all of the previously mentioned items.
- to know the general content, subject, and thrust of the interview, so you have time to research the appropriate information.

- to know approximately how long the interview will last.
- to know if there are other guests appearing with you on a talk or panel show, and what their roles will be.
- to have a public relations or other school representative present.
- to make your own audio- or videotape of the interview or to be able to obtain a complete tape from the radio/TV station.
- to make sure that no material is recorded by the reporter on audio- or videotape unless you are told you are being recorded. (The preinterview discussion, conversation between commercials, or after-show chitchat cannot be used on the air unless you approve.)
- to be allowed to answer without constant interruptions (assuming your answers are brief and to the point).
- to ignore editorial comments or pejorative asides by reporters or panelists.
- to have an accurate on-air introduction that will put the interview in the proper perspective.
- to have the basic intent and flavor of your answers come across accurately in the edited version of the film or tape.
- to have time to get some of your points across in the interview, and not be expected only to answer the reporter's questions.

When Answering Questions, Do . . .

- be relaxed, confident, and honest.
- maintain a neutral attitude.
- use pitch and rate changes for vocal variety.
- build in a cutoff with your answer if you wish to drop the subject.
- discuss only those activities and policies within the purview of your area of responsibility.
- admit you don't know an answer if that's the case. You can promise to get back with the answer; just be sure to deliver when you promise information.
- tape the interview yourself if the situation permits.
- use visual aids if you absolutely have to, but make sure they are simple, readable, uncluttered, and relevant to the subject.
- give positive answers.
- practice beforehand!

Don't . . .

- use jargon, acronyms, or technical terms.
- use "hesitation devices" such as "er" and "uh."
- be curt, even when answering the dumbest question.
- answer more than one question at a time.
- restate the question.
- begin with gratuitous phrases such as, "I'm glad you asked me that."
- give a "no comment" response—if you are unsure of the answer or can't discuss it, say so.
- get into a verbal fencing match if it is classified information; just indicate that it is classified and move on.
- volunteer information unless it supports a positive point you want to make.
- be defensive.

- ever assume anything is off the record—there is no such thing unless you are absolutely certain the reporter will honor the agreement.
- let anyone put words in your mouth. Agree only if the facts and figures are the truth.
- lie. Answer as honestly and completely as you can—your school and district's reputations rest on their spokespersons' veracity.

SUGGESTED READINGS

National School Public Relations Association. (1999). *School public relations: Building confidence in education.* Rockville, MD: Author.

Ordovensky, P., & Marx, G. (1993). *Working with the news media.* Arlington, VA: American Association of School Administrators.

Public Relations Society of America, Phoenix Chapter. (1990). Perfect pitch. *Communicator, 5*(8). (Newsletter available from PRSA, Phoenix, AZ)

[Use school letterhead, unless a special letterhead is used for news releases]

News Release

DATE:	MARCH 21, 2000
FOR RELEASE:	IMMEDIATE
CONTACT:	BILL TRAVIS, PRINCIPAL
	MOUNT VERNON HIGH SCHOOL
	537–5555

"MOUNT VERNON HIGH TAKES U.I.L. DISTRICT SWEEPSTAKES"

Students from Mount Vernon High School recently took first place in the District 14AAA University Interscholastic League competitions, held on March 19–20 at Winnsboro High School. Mount Vernon won the district "Sweepstakes" trophy by accumulating a total of 943 points in 15 events. This marks the sixth time in the past 8 years that Mount Vernon has won the overall trophy.

According to Superintendent Mike Harper, 21 students, representing all four grades, participated in the contests, which measure academic skills in a wide variety of competitive events. "We are extremely proud of our 'Academic Tigers' for their fine performances again this year. This 'Sweepstakes' win is a tribute not only to the hard work of the young people, but [also] to the dedication of the teachers who served as their coaches. A lot of hard work by the entire team went into this victory."

Twelve students from Mount Vernon will now compete in various contests at the regional level. Regional competition will be held at East Texas State University the first week in May.

—End—

(Editor Note: Attached are (a) a group photo of students and (b) names of competing students, their events, and the overall student, school, and district scores.)

Source: Corporate Education Consulting, Inc., Phoenix, AZ.

Chicago Public Schools

———————————————————————— *News Release*

For more information contact:
Celeste Garrett
CPS Office of Communications
Phone: 773-553-1620
Fax: 773-553-1622
Website: http://www.cps.k12.il.us

FOR IMMEDIATE RELEASE:
Thursday, Jan. 24, 2008

New Plan Includes Record Number of School Turnarounds

Students in four high schools, four elementary schools would stay,
new leadership, new teachers would move in under Renaissance 2010

Chicago Public Schools officials today, citing a sense of urgency, unveiled a series of proposals to address under-enrollment in 11 elementary schools, while addressing low performance in eight other schools that would undergo a "turnaround" if the plan is approved.

The plan also introduces a brand new Renaissance 2010 strategy: turning around several elementary schools that feed into a high school that would be turned around at the same time.

"The need for change in these schools is urgent," said CPS Chief Executive Officer Arne Duncan. "We can't wait to provide better education options for our children. We have to find a way to do it now."

The proposed strategies for each of the schools will be provided today to members of the Chicago Board of Education, which is scheduled to vote on the proposals at February's meeting. Over the next several weeks, school officials will hold public hearings to get community input on the plan.

The plan includes five different major strategies. In addition to the record number of school turnarounds, the proposed plan includes school relocations, phase-outs, consolidations, and closings. Also included is a proposal that would turn one high school, once split into three smaller schools, back into one large high school that would be turned around into a teacher training academy. If approved, these strategies would take effect in the fall.

"In searching for ways to address issues of under-enrollment and chronic under-performance, we had to look at all possibilities," Duncan said. "Each one of these schools has a different situation and different dynamics that called for different and creative solutions. We think we have been very thoughtful in this process, wanting first to cause the least amount of disruption in the lives of our children, but at the same time, address the needs of the community and the district."

The recommendations collectively would require fewer than 1,500 children to move, Duncan added.

--more--

Office of Communications · 125 South Clark Street · Chicago, IL 60603 · (773) 553-1620 · FAX: (773) 553-1621

Chicago Public Schools - Press Release

- **Andersen Elementary,** 1148 N. Honore Street, with about 580 pre-kindergarten through eighth grade students, would be phased out. New students who would have attended this school will attend Pritzker Elementary, 2009 W. Schiller Street, a few blocks away.

- **Midway Academy,** 5434 S. Lockwood Ave., a second- through eighth-grade school, with an enrollment of 90, would close to allow children to attend their neighborhood schools.

- **Carver Middle School**, 801 E. 133rd Pl., a fifth- through eighth-grade school with an enrollment of 244, would consolidate with its feeder school, Carver Primary, 901 E. 133rd Place, which is next door.

- **De La Cruz,** 2317 W. 23rd Pl., a middle school with 102 seventh- and eighth-graders, would be consolidated with Finkl Elementary, 2332 S. Western Ave., about two blocks away.

- **Abbott Elementary**, 3630 S. Wells St., which has only 99 students in grades kindergarten through eighth, would be consolidated with Graham Elementary, 4436 S. Union Ave., which is less than two miles away.

- **Irving Park Middle School,** 3815 N. Kedvale Ave., which has 348 students in grades seven and eight, would be phased out. New students who would have attended this school will attend Marshall Middle School, 3900 N. Lawndale Ave.

- **Edison Regional Gifted Center,** 6220 N. Olcott Ave., which serves 274 students in grades kindergarten through eighth, would be relocated to and share a building with the Albany Park Multicultural Academy, at 4929 N. Sawyer Ave. Edison would remain a Regional Gifted Center at the new location and both schools would retain their own identities.

- **Roque DeDuprey Elementary**, 1405 N. Washtenaw Ave., with an enrollment of 235 in grades first through eighth, would be relocated to Von Humboldt Elementary, 2620 W. Hirsch, which is one block away. Both schools would retain their separate identities.

Attached is a list of public hearings scheduled for parents and community members to voice opinions about the plan. District leaders will take all comments into consideration before presenting their final proposals to the board on Feb. 27, when board members are expected to vote on the matter.

The Chicago Public Schools is the nation's third-largest school system. It includes more than 600 schools and about 409,000 students.

Office of Communications · 125 South Clark Street · Chicago, IL 60603 · (773) 553-1620 · FAX: (773) 553-1621

Source: Chicago Public Schools, Chicago, IL.

**Washington School
District Media
Contact Form**

Name _____   Date _____

School/Department _____

Media Contacted (list station or paper & contact person): _____

_____

_____

_____

What's Happening:

 Why:

Who's Involved:

When:

Where:

Source: Washington School District, Phoenix, AZ.

News Tip Form

We want to keep the Washington School District community and our employees well informed of events and activities in the district. We know that there are LOTS of great things going on out there, but we need your help to find out the WHO, WHAT, WHEN, WHERE, and WHY!

Help us spread some good news. Fill out the form below when you hear of an event, a special project, a technique that works, or any newsworthy item in your school. Send it to Karen H. Kleinz, director of community relations, at the administrative center.

For best results on upcoming events, please give at least two weeks notice.

_____   _____   _____
            Name   School or Department   Date

Who: (People, titles, grade(s), etc.) _____

_____

_____

What: (Event, award, project, etc.) _____

_____

_____

When: (Dates and times) _____

Where: (Place) _____

Why or how: (Reason for award, event, etc.) _____

_____

_____

_____

_____

If this is a future event, is it open to the public?   ❏ Yes   ❏ No

Source: Washington School District, Phoenix, AZ.

[Use school letterhead, unless a special letterhead is used for news releases.]

Public Service Announcement

DATE:	May 1, 2000
CONTACT PERSON:	Bill Travis, Principal
	Mount Vernon High School
	537–5555
TOPIC:	Mount Vernon High School 2000 Athletic Banquet
DATE OF EVENT:	Thursday, May 18, 2000
REQUESTED AIRING DATES:	Weeks of May 1–7; May 8–14; May 15–18.
LENGTH:	30 seconds

THE STUDENT ATHLETES OF MOUNT VERNON HIGH SCHOOL INVITE ALL INTERESTED TIGER FANS TO ATTEND THE 2000 ATHLETIC BANQUET.

THE BANQUET WILL BE HELD ON THURSDAY, MAY 22ND, AT 6:30 PM, IN THE SCHOOL CAFETERIA.

ADMISSION IS ONLY FIVE DOLLARS, AND INCLUDES A DELICIOUS CATERED BARBECUE DINNER.

TICKETS MAY BE PURCHASED AT THE SCHOOL DISTRICT OFFICE, ON HIGHWAY 37 SOUTH.

FOR MORE INFORMATION, CALL MOUNT VERNON HIGH SCHOOL AT 537–5555.

Source: Corporate Education Consulting, Inc., Phoenix, AZ.

PART II

Building and Strengthening Partnerships

6

Building Your Team

"Building a better school is a team effort. If you're the only player on the field, don't expect to win."

One of the driving forces behind the move for education reform is the concept of shared decision making. A by-product of the national focus on educational improvement is a renewed interest in participating in the educational process by the various constituencies of a school.

- Staff members are no longer content with the traditional top-down management structure and are demanding the opportunity to have a voice in designing the system within which they work.
- The business community has recognized that if it wishes to impact outcomes of education and the quality of workers available to operate its enterprises, then it must take an active role in the schools where those outcomes are developed.
- Parents desire input into their children's instructional program so that it reflects their family philosophy and values, as well as the academic ambitions they have for their children.

To operate effectively within this new school reform/improvement environment, staff, parents, and community members all must have the opportunity for meaningful input into the educational process. Many of the methods schools have long used to communicate with their publics are no longer sufficient to meet today's needs. If these publics are to have valid input and involvement in school and district decisions, they must be informed about the critical issues facing their schools.

Educators face an enormous challenge in changing from a traditional authoritative, top-down management style that controls decision making to one in which all those affected by decisions share in the decision-making process. Shared decision making is not easy. It takes careful planning, strong communications skills, patience, and long-term commitment.

In setting goals and determining school agendas, the successful schools in the new century will be those that include all of their publics, not just those designated as professional educators. By involving all those in the community who have a vested interest in successful educational outcomes, you will be able to tap into many more areas of expertise and create a tremendous resource base to assist your school in preparing students to become productive citizens.

WHO MAKES UP THE TEAM?

Wise educational leaders have long used faculty advisory committees to provide feedback and assist in developing new programs. The advent of effective schools research has led to the formation of school improvement teams with increased responsibilities and a membership expanded to include parents and community members. A significant outgrowth of expanded responsibility at the building level is the formation of school site councils that seek to empower these team members by increasing their involvement in decision-making activities involving such critical areas as budgeting, staffing, and curriculum development—areas long thought to be the exclusive province of professional educators.

There are numerous ways to structure your team. It should be large enough to provide appropriate representation of all groups, yet not so large as to hamper communication and the cultivation of collegiality among its members. Several examples illustrate the wide range of options available:

1. Many districts around the country have created school advisory site councils, which are typically composed of five teachers, one support staff employee, and four parents/patrons. The principal serves as the chairperson and ex officio member. Members apply for the councils and are appointed by the superintendent's administrative council. Appointments are carefully considered to provide a balance of grade-level representation as well as demographic and philosophical orientation, thus ensuring that the council accurately reflects the interests of the local school community.

2. Magic City Campus High School in Minot, North Dakota, has emphasized teaming and collaboration through its 2000 Committee, which is working to improve the teaching/learning process and guide the school toward the 21st century. The committee is composed of three principals, three counselors, four teachers, three parents, and one media specialist.

3. Mt. Edgecumbe High School, a residential school in Sitka, Alaska, is using the Total Quality Management (TQM) teachings of W. Edwards Deming. Applying the TQM model, the students, staff, and administrators worked together to develop a consensus about the purposes of the school. Their 15-point model, Modified Deming Points for Continuous Improvement of Education, is at chapter's end.

4. The Faculty Advisory Council at East Burke Middle School in Icard, North Carolina, is composed of the head custodian, cafeteria manager, military reserve officer,

PTA president, four team leaders, special education team leader, guidance representative, principal, and assistant principal. This team meets for a full day in July, setting goals based on the mission statement, previous goals, and teacher expectations. During the school year, it meets weekly and covers "concerns" first and then the principal's agenda.

5. The School Council, made up of the principal, three teachers, four parents, two students, and two community representatives, has a major role at Swampscott High School in Massachusetts. This council conducts an annual needs assessment, identifies the educational needs of students, reviews the annual budget, and develops an annual School Improvement Plan.

6. Thornridge High School in Dolton, Illinois, takes a different route utilizing the team concept. Principal Gwendolyn Lee created a Principal's Cabinet, which consists of students representing every club in the school. This provides a broader base for student input than relying on the regular student government groups.

Regardless of the structure used, the key is to allow for representation by all interested segments of your school community. Your collaborative efforts will be successful only if you allow for a diversity of opinions and remain open to new ideas and new approaches to problem solving. The most successful teams are able to find common ground and arrive at decisions through consensus building, thus ensuring the continued interest and involvement of team members. Remember, the operative word is *inclusion*.

SUCCESSFUL TEAMS COMMUNICATE WELL

No group of people can function as a team unless there is complete and open communication among its members. Effective teams have developed intensive communications systems, both formal and informal—and ongoing.

Clearly, two-way communication builds trust among team members by providing the information that they want and need on a timely basis. It allows for feedback and inspires respect, pride, and cooperation among members. When team members are well-informed and understand their responsibility for the decisions that lead to change, they are then able to help others in the school community improve student attitude and learning by understanding and adapting successfully to proposed changes.

For the members of your school's team to communicate well, they also need to understand how they communicate with each other. As the leader, you should be sure to periodically make time at meetings to discuss communication techniques and talk about the process of communication used by the team.

You might consider videotaping one of your meetings and analyzing the effectiveness of the team's communication skills. Can you identify the interactions that block progress and those that move the team ahead? Is the atmosphere nonthreatening? Is it supportive? Can you tell from the conversation whether team members have a clear understanding of their goals and what is expected of them, or does there appear to be no direction to the discussion?

People work together best when they understand how their skills and personal needs interrelate with those of other team members and the goals of the school. Once committed to the team concept, members should be able to create a partnership that functions to resolve real issues and provides a sense of accountability for outcomes. It's pretty basic: buy-in equals ownership.

THE LEADER AS FACILITATOR

Even the most dedicated team will fail without a skilled leader to guide it. This leader can no longer be concerned with managing people—giving them specific orders and directions and dictating the course and focus of their efforts. You must instead begin leading your team by creating a shared vision that encourages innovation, creativity, responsibility, and accountability. Along with developing this shared sense of purpose, good leaders also treat team members as valued professionals who have important contributions to make.

Instead of managing and supervising, educational leaders must be coaches and facilitators while at the same time overseeing the planning and implementation of the team's projects. An Implementation/Monitoring Plan chart to help you get organized and keep on track can be found at chapter's end. Leaders recognize that true change must be generated from within the school system, and that the best ideas must come up from the classroom rather than being handed down from the administration. Leaders strive to create a feeling of ownership of both achievements and problems, as well as a sense of belonging and community.

As a leader, you have the task to help others become comfortable with change and realize their own potential. Learn to identify and cultivate other leaders within your school to assist in mobilizing your community to restructure for the future. True leaders carry a vision that looks beyond the immediate to the future, beyond the probable to the possible.

The late Larrae Rocheleau, former superintendent of Mt. Edgecumbe High School in Sitka, Alaska, admitted that, after over 30 years in education, only a few years ago did he come to clearly and fully understand the difference between a manager and a leader: "A manager works in a system; a leader not only works *in* the system but also *on* the system."

DEFINING THE TASK

For teams to be effective, they must first be knowledgeable about their purpose and then have confidence in their ability to accomplish their task. Once teams realize that things can no longer be accomplished in the same old ways, they become more open to the ideas of others—be they superintendents or bus drivers. Today's economy asks that everyone be willing to consider doing more with less, to create new solutions to accomplish both present and future goals.

According to the National School Public Relations Association, successful practitioners of school-level management team building have identified nine challenges to creating successful teams that the educational leader must work to resolve. These are as follows:

1. Differences of experience and education

2. Value conflicts

3. Diverse reasons for joining the team

4. Members with single-item agendas

5. Lack of trust

6. Fear of failure and rejection

7. Communication blockers

8. Purposeful disruption of team efforts

9. Incorporating new members into the team without a clear rationale for their participation

GETTING TO WORK

Once you have assembled your team and agreed on your purpose, it is time to go to work. According to school public relations practitioners, seven key elements, when followed in sequence, offer the best chance for success. You are basically replicating, in microcosm, the strategic planning process of developing a marketing plan (Chapter 2).

1. *Conduct a needs assessment.* To identify your primary goals, you must first assess your needs so that you can plan appropriately. Collect and analyze your data, paying special attention to the differences between current practices and the ideal outcomes desired.

2. *Set your goals.* Make sure all goals are clear and understood by everyone on the team. Determine the measurable indicators of success for each goal.

3. *Develop your improvement plan.* Identify the objectives needed to reach each goal and develop action steps for each. Designate areas of responsibility for team members and develop timelines for the various parts of the plan. Provide training as needed on an ongoing basis.

4. *Implement the improvement plan.* Each team member should be involved in and accountable for his or her assigned responsibilities.

5. *Reflect and adjust.* Review progress and reflect on the outcomes on a regular basis to determine the effectiveness of the plan. Adjust your strategy as necessary to maintain the focus of your efforts and stay on track to your goal.

6. *Evaluate.* Based on your identified indicators of success, did you meet your goals? Use your evaluation to begin the planning cycle again.

7. *Communicate.* Throughout the entire planning process, it is important to communicate not only with the team but with the rest of your staff and community as well. Build support for your efforts by sharing information about the process and the results.

Teams that both understand what they have been empowered to do and know that they have the commitment and administrative support necessary to accomplish their goals will be successful, not only in that task but also in establishing the type of community involvement needed to create true educational change—and reform—from within the school, not imposed on it.

SUGGESTED READINGS

Bennis, W. (1997). *Managing people is like herding cats.* Provo, UT: Executive Excellence.

Covey, S. (1994). *First things first.* Salt Lake City, UT: Covey Institute.

Edwards, M. E. (1990). School community relations for the 21st century. *Journal of Educational Public Relations,* 13(3), 4–7.

Gardner, H. (1995). *Leading minds: An anatomy of leadership.* New York: Basic Books.

Lambert, L. (1998). *Building leadership capacity in schools.* Alexandria, VA: Association for Supervision and Curriculum Development.

National School Public Relations Association. (1991). *Team building 2000* (Pocket folder). Rockville, MD: Author.

National School Public Relations Association. (1993, January). *School-based management: Communication is the key. It starts in the classroom.* Rockville, MD: Author. (Newsletter available from publisher)

Odden, A. (1997). *A policymaker's guide to incentives for students, teachers, and schools.* Denver, CO: Education Commission of the States.

Rubin, H. (1998). *Collaboration skills for educators and nonprofit leaders.* Chicago: Lyceum Books.

Modified Deming Points for Continuous Improvement of Education

1. Create constancy of purpose toward improvement of students and service. Aim to create the best quality students, capable of improving all forms of processes and entering meaningful positions in society.

2. Adopt the new philosophy. Educational management must awaken to the challenge, must learn their responsibilities, and must take on leadership for change.

3. Work to abolish grading and the harmful effects of rating people.

4. Cease dependence on testing to achieve quality. Eliminate the need for inspections on a mass basis (standardized achievement tests, minimum graduation exams, etc.) by providing learning experiences which create quality performance.

5. Work with the educational institutions from which students come. Minimize total cost of education by improving the relationship with student sources and helping to improve the quality of students coming into your system. A single source of students coming into a system such as junior high students moving into a high school is an opportunity to build long-term relationships of loyalty and trust for the benefit of students.

6. Improve constantly and forever the system of student involvement and service, to improve quality and productivity.

7. Institute education and training on the job for students, teachers, classified staff, and administrators.

8. Institute leadership. The aim of supervision should be to help people use machines, gadgets, and materials to do a better job.

9. Drive out fear, so that everyone may work effectively for the school system. Create an environment which encourages people to speak freely.

10. Break down barriers between departments. People in teaching, special education, accounting, food service, administration, curriculum development and research, etc. must work as a team. Develop strategies for increasing the cooperation among groups and individual people.

11. Eliminate slogans, exhortations, and targets for teachers and students asking for perfect performance and new levels of productivity. Exhortations create adversarial relationships. The bulk of the causes of low quality and low productivity belong to the system and thus lie beyond the control of teachers and students.

12. Eliminate work standards (quotas) on teachers and students (e.g., raise test scores by 10% and lower drop-out rates by 15%). Substitute leadership.

13. Remove barriers that rob students, teachers, and management (principals, superintendents, and central office support staff) of their right to pride and joy of workmanship. This means, inter alia, abolition of the annual or merit rating and of management by objective. The responsibility of all educational managers must be changed from quantity to quality.

14. Institute a vigorous program of education and self-improvement for everyone.

15. Put everybody in the school to work to accomplish the transformation. The transformation is everybody's job.

Source: Mt. Edgecumbe High School, Sitka, AK.

Implementation/Monitoring Plan

Implementation				*Monitoring*					
What Needs to Be Done	*Who Will Do It*	*With What Resources*	*When*	*Who Monitors*	*A or NA* Date*	*Keep*	*Stop*	*Revise*	*Comments*

Evaluation Plan				
Design				*Results*
		Data Collection		
Evaluation Design Instruments		*Who*	*When*	*A or NA* Date*	*Evidence*

* A = achieved; NA = not achieved.

Source: Mt. Edgecumbe High School, Sitka, AK.

7

Involving Parents in School

"Not every teacher is a parent, but every parent is a teacher."

One of the most valuable things a parent can teach a child is the importance of education. When parents exhibit interest in their child's school, the child gets a sense that school is important.

Schools clearly work best when parents take an active interest in their children's schooling and encourage them to do well. Research has demonstrated over and over that parent involvement is a critical component of the learning process. The evidence has shown that programs designed for strong parent involvement and schools that relate well to their communities have students who outperform other schools. Children whose parents help them at home score higher on aptitude tests than those whose parents don't help. Schools in which children are failing have been found to improve dramatically when parents become involved.

In *The Evidence Continues to Grow: Parent Involvement Improves Student Achievement*, Ann Henderson (1987) summed up the research as follows:

- The family provides the primary educational environment.
- Involving parents in their children's education improves student achievement.
- Parent involvement is most effective when it is comprehensive, long lasting, and well planned.
- The benefits are not confined to early childhood or the elementary level; there are strong effects from involving parents continuously through high school.
- Involving parents in their own children's education at home is not enough. To ensure the quality of schools as institutions serving the community, parents must be involved at all levels in the school.

- Children from low-income and minority families have the most to gain when schools involve parents. Parents do not have to be well educated to help.
- You cannot look at the school and home in isolation from one another; you must understand how they interconnect.

EFFECTIVE EDUCATORS SEEK PARENT SUPPORT

Because parent involvement starts at the building level, it is up to the educational leader to help bridge the home–school gap and make involvement a reality in every community. In a study of six New Jersey counties, the education researcher Benjamin Bloom (1976) identified five factors that were found in successful parent involvement programs:

1. *Climate.* Successful programs exuded a warm, caring environment and made parents feel like important members of the school team.

2. *Relevance.* The programs were based on what parents cared about. Concerns were identified by surveying parents.

3. *Convenience.* Successful programs made it easy for parents to get involved. They provided transportation, child care, and so forth, to encourage participation.

4. *Publicity.* The programs used several mediums to reach parents, such as newsletters, flyers, public service announcements, and local media. Parents were personally invited to participate. Schools with large non–English-speaking populations communicated in whatever languages were required to reach parents.

5. *Commitment.* The staff made parent involvement a goal and demonstrated their commitment.

In their book *Parents on Your Side*, Lee and Marlene Canter (1991) describe the four qualities shared by teachers who have been successful in involving parents in the educational process:

1. Effective teachers know they must have the support of parents.

2. In every interaction with parents, effective teachers demonstrate their concern for the child.

3. In all situations, effective teachers treat parents the way they would want to be treated.

4. In every interaction with parents, effective teachers demonstrate professionalism and confidence.

The same qualities obviously apply to principals and staff. Educators, as a team, must work together with parents to build support for the school's program and activities. Educators need to provide multiple ways for parents to participate so that they can begin at their own individual comfort level. Educators must help parents improve their skills so that they can better respond to the school's request for assistance.

WAYS TO INVOLVE PARENTS

Volunteer Programs. Many parents want to be involved in their child's school on a more active level than just encouraging excellence or helping with homework. There must be activities available in which they can participate. Educators must see that these opportunities exist and must be open to projects that parents initiate. Whether it is participating in PTA, raising money for the school band, helping in the library, tutoring, or assisting the school nurse with eye tests, parents can be a tremendous asset to schools that lack the personnel, resources, and time to organize and carry out the "extras" that add to a school's effectiveness. If someone on staff can encourage and coordinate volunteer activities, that's great; if not, perhaps a trusted, energetic volunteer will take on the job.

At South Park Middle School in Corpus Christi, Texas, parents headed up the production of the school's first-ever yearbook. When parents act as chaperones at school dances and on bus trips, or as monitors at athletic events, less rowdiness and fewer disciplinary problems occur. It is vitally important that parents who volunteer as chaperones be apprised of school procedures on how to handle problems as they arise. For busy parents to volunteer, they have to feel needed and wanted. So it is up to you or your volunteer coordinator to get the word out that your school welcomes volunteers.

Early Parent Involvement. Missouri's Blue Springs School District has a rich tradition of parental involvement in its schools. For many generations, Blue Springs parents have become active members in the learning community. This begins as early as a child's birth. The district has offered the Parents as Teachers Program since 1985, and what began with only 13 families has grown as of 2007–2008 to more than 4,000 families of children ages birth to 5 years. Certified professionals go into homes and share developmentally appropriate learning activities for the child that will enhance their developmental progress. These parents become part of the learning community and emerge as partners in the education of their child. The parents that participate in the Parents as Teachers Program are also more likely to remain involved in their child's formal education.

Student Recognition. Parents have a great sense of pride when their children are recognized. It is no secret that the best-attended events on campus are those at which children perform. Create as many ways as possible to reward and recognize students. In designing awards, you are limited only by your imagination in what can be recognized. Let students create peer recognition awards as well. Recognition helps students build pride in themselves, their work, and their school. Praising students for their contributions to the school team and recognizing group efforts will foster a positive school family that supports learning achievements. There are several examples of student recognition certificates at the end of this chapter, as well as an in-house form for positive phone calls to parents. To recognize students and their parents, Patrick Savini, director of the Sussex County Vocational-Technical School in Georgetown, Delaware, hosts an Honor Roll Breakfast. It is an extremely popular and well-attended event.

Parent Workshops. Offer a daylong workshop for parents that provides a variety of sessions focusing on parenting skills. Use the expertise of your own staff, as well as invite speakers from community social service agencies. Sessions can cover a broad spectrum of topics, from discipline to stress reduction. At Meadowbrook Middle School in Poway,

California, refresher classes in math for parents have been very successful. Parents preview a month in advance the concepts that staff members will be presenting to their children in pre-algebra and algebra. To better facilitate planning for these events, survey parents in advance to determine their interests.

Grade-Level Curriculum Handbook. Create a handbook for parents that explains the curriculum and skills that students are expected to learn at each grade level. If possible, include a calendar of studies so parents know at what time of year their children will be studying certain topics. Provide a list of supplemental activities that parents can do with their children to reinforce skills.

Home Visits. Encourage teachers to make home visits prior to the first day of school. Personal contact maintained year-round facilitates parent involvement by building a personal relationship and providing a sense that parents are part of the school family. Sussex County Vocational-Technical School in Georgetown, Delaware, with a student population of about 1,100, has a home visitation program for parents of all incoming ninth-grade students.

School Visits/Calls. Is your school open to visitors? Are your teachers open to inquiry from parents? Develop a process that parents will feel comfortable using, a process that announces that your school is willing, even enthusiastic, about receiving communication from parents—and this includes visits. Of course, there will be times when a visit is inconvenient and a parent can't sit down with a child's teacher or administrator. But if the response to parents' overtures is always positive, they will not feel rebuffed and will sense that the school is interested in their children's welfare and progress.

Open House. Although having an open house a few weeks after school opens is the traditional way, experiment with a schoolwide open house during the first week of school. Parents are eager to meet teachers and to experience their children's school environment. There may not be a lot of the children's work to display, but there won't be many complaints to hear, either.

Sharon Lewis, a fifth-grade teacher at Simpson Elementary School in Phoenix, Arizona, holds her open house the week before school starts from 4 to 6 in the afternoon. She mails invitations and then follows up with a phone call. That extra phone call is what really brings in the majority of the parents. She invites the principal and any special teachers who will be involved with her students. Over the years, she has discovered that the attendance is much better than for the schoolwide open house held later in the fall.

Take-Home Resource Materials. Make supplementary study materials and videotapes available for parents to check out and use with their children at home. Include study guides to assist parents. Some districts now have programs that allow parents to check out computers.

Parent Room on Campus. If there is an extra room in your building, create a place where parents can review resource materials, watch educational videos, and network with each other.

Meetings in Parents' Homes. Don't always ask parents to come to the school to meet with you. Invite parents to host small-group meetings on single topics in their homes. Changing the territory can often facilitate more open communication.

ESL for Parents. Offer English-as-a-second-language (ESL) classes in the evening for parents. Provide child care during this time. Blue Springs Schools in Missouri have made this a very successful program:

> Educating the child alone does not meet all of the needs of these families so we also provide opportunities for our limited English proficient parents to learn skills that will assist them to become more fluent in English. Evening classes are held for any adult that is in need of assistance in learning English and child care is provided so they may attend classes. This is a free service for our community and has resulted in many families being better acclimated into our neighborhoods and town.

Friday Folder. Send all papers home in a special folder once a week. Include a sign-off sheet for parents to verify that they received the information.

Notes and Cards Mailed Home. New Castle (Indiana) Middle School sends congratulatory notes to honor students and Students of the Week for perfect attendance or for special accomplishments. Cards are given out for birthdays, and condolence cards are mailed home when a death in the family occurs.

Coffee With the Principal. Hold a regular coffee klatch and invite parents to drop by and chat. Consider finding a neutral site off campus, such as a nearby fast-food restaurant or a favorite community meeting place.

Doughnuts for Dads. Hold an early morning doughnuts and coffee get-together to catch dads on their way to work. Create a Fathers Club or Mothers Club to take on special projects. Principal Andrea Martin has added "Muffins for Mom" to her outreach program for parents at Winnfield Kindergarten School in Winnfield, Louisiana.

Church Support. Work with local clergy to set up alternate ways to reach the community regarding the importance of family involvement in schools. Some churches allow their parishioners to set up tables for petition signing or for bond election handouts. This is usually done just outside the church entrance or during coffee time after services.

Parent Committees. Offer parents the opportunity to serve on curriculum committees or ad hoc project committees. Consider implementing a parent–teacher forum as Principal Peter Sack did at Swampscott High School in Massachusetts. A nonprofit educational foundation was founded by the educators and parents of Custer County High School in Miles City, Montana, to raise money to provide scholarships for graduating seniors. Principal Fred Anderson says that it has grown from awarding 1 scholarship in 1992 to awarding 41 scholarships last year. Booster clubs for athletic teams, band, drama, and so on are a wonderful way to unify school, parents, and community. The Fayette County High School Athletic Booster Club in Fayetteville, Georgia, supports a variety of activities and pulls in business support from around the city. In the planning stage is an Academic Booster Club.

Career Day. Hold a career day and invite parents to talk about their jobs—or do the reverse and have students shadow parents at work.

College Preview Night. Invite parents to hear from representatives of local colleges and universities. Provide scholarship information.

Parent Talents. For a change, invite parents to showcase their talents and perform for the students. Or your school might prefer a parent/faculty/staff talent show with students serving as judges. Parents can also be effective in reinforcing skills being taught in the classroom. During a unit on persuasive writing, the owner of an advertising agency in Sedalia, Missouri, who was the father of a middle school student, came to class and instructed students on the steps needed to write an effective advertisement.

Athletic Competitions. Seek parent volunteers to participate in a basketball or volleyball game (or league) between parents and teachers or parents and students. Open Gym one or two nights a week reserved for students, parents, and staff fosters camaraderie among that group.

Social Services Referral. Be prepared to assist parents who need support from social service agencies by providing them with referral information.

Families' '50s Dance. Greenacres Junior High in Washington holds a PTA-sponsored "'50s" dance the first Friday in May each year. The idea originated several years ago after two suicides had occurred. The school wanted to find a way for families to come together in the school setting and have fun. It has grown through the years and now attracts over 450 people dressed up and dancing to 1950s music. Principal Sharon Jayne says that Elvis drops by each year.

Family Fun Night. Host an evening for families to play games or watch a movie together, to swim, or to check out sites on the Internet in the computer lab.

Parent Buddies. Involve the PTA or other parent volunteers in being buddies to new parents at the school. Parents are more likely to get involved if they are made to feel welcome immediately and helped to get oriented.

Grandparents' Day. Sunnyslope Elementary School in Port Orchard, Washington, has a special day for grandparents to visit the school. It's quite popular with both students and grandparents, and many grandparents come from quite a distance to be there for this special occasion.

Monthly Parent Activity. Offer a regular activity focused on ways parents can assist their child in school. One session might focus on homework, one on self-esteem, and so forth. This is a wonderful way for parents to emphasize group awareness of a problem and to work together and support each other in developing parenting skills. "ParenTalks" are held monthly at Cascade Middle School in Bend, Oregon. Principal Marion Morehouse feels that it is important to introduce parents to current educational research and issues. The interaction of these groups (parents with the school, or with each other) provides administrators with an outstanding opportunity for parental feedback.

CHANGING DEMOGRAPHICS OF THE AMERICAN FAMILY

To excel, children need support and reinforcement at home—the place where they spend the bulk of their time. Researcher Benjamin Bloom has observed that the home environment is a major factor in whether children are motivated to learn, whether they achieve academic success, and the number of years of schooling they complete.

But in too many instances, the home environment is the least supportive of students or the least encouraging of learning. Today, it seems that society has determined that it is up to educators to take the lead in creating a nurturing, supportive, responsible learning environment for students.

Principals and teachers must not only educate and inform parents about the importance of their role, they must also provide training and resources so that parents can be successful in that role. True educators feel a responsibility to motivate parents to motivate their children.

One of the greatest challenges facing education today arises from the demographic changes that encompass culture, race, age, and socioeconomic status—in short, just about every aspect of American society. A very real gap exists between schools and those they serve, and that gap is slowly widening to become education's version of the Grand Canyon. If schools are to bridge that gap, school leaders must design new and effective ways to communicate with the changing population that schools serve. Some facts about today's families include the following:

- In 1955, an estimated 60 percent of households consisted of a working father, a homemaker mother, and two or more school-age children. That family now represents less than 10 percent of households.
- About one in four school children now lives in a one-parent family.
- Children in single-parent homes are about five times more likely to live in poverty than children with both parents at home.

A study conducted by the Knowledge Network for All Americans (Lloyd, Ramsey, & Groennings, 1992) found that most families are inadequately preparing children for the demands of today's world. The following are some of the survey's findings:

- Many children in America are not born healthy, do not receive adequate nutrition, do not live in safe homes and neighborhoods, and do not get preventive health care, thereby experiencing impaired educational development.
- Many parents are not providing their children with character education that encourages responsible, constructive behavior.
- Far too many children enter school unprepared to learn, and leave high school without the basic knowledge and skills to get decent jobs or to enter college.
- Most self-reliant, academically achieving, well-rounded, and healthy children have parents who have created a stable, supportive family.

These findings concerning American families come as no surprise to any experienced or observant educational leader. But along with changing family structure, schools must also be prepared to deal with racial and cultural differences that may lead to negative interaction and conflict if not handled appropriately. Not only are today's families structured differently, they look and think differently as well.

- Fifteen percent of students entering public school today speak a language other than English, and this figure is expected to increase.
- More than half of all students in public and private schools in 53 of the largest U.S. cities are from ethnic minority groups. In many schools, the minority is the majority.
- The 1990 U.S. Census showed that the African American population in the United States had increased by 13 percent, the Hispanic population by 53 percent, and the Asian population by 108 percent. In contrast, the Caucasian population increased by only 6 percent.
- According to the U.S. Census Bureau's estimation for 2005, approximately 45 percent of American children under the age of 5 were minorities. The total minority population in the United States that year was 98.3 million. In 2006, the nation's minority population reached 100.7 million. Hispanics accounted for almost half (1.4 million) of the national population growth of 2.9 million between July 1, 2005, and July 1, 2006. In 35 of the country's 50 largest cities, white people are or soon will be in the minority.

HARD-TO-REACH PARENTS

A study conducted by Don Davies (1988) of the Institute for Responsive Education examined relationships between hard-to-reach parents and the school. The conclusion was that most of the parents in the study were, in fact, reachable, but that schools were either not really trying to involve them or not knowledgeable about or sensitive enough to overcome cultural and social-class barriers. The six primary barriers that limited school involvement for the hard-to-reach parents were identified as follows:

1. Children from families not conforming to middle-class norms are often seen by school officials as those who will have trouble in school.

2. Communication between schools and poor families is mostly negative. Most of these parents are contacted only when their children are in trouble.

3. Teachers and administrators appear to think of these families as being deficient, and they concentrate on the families' problems rather than on their strengths.

4. School staff tend to believe that the problems of parents who are hard to reach are the fault of parents, not the schools.

5. Many poverty-level families have a low assessment of themselves in their abilities to be involved in their children's schooling.

6. Most parents from all groups studied expressed a strong desire to be involved in their children's schooling.

Educators must be especially careful not to further alienate parents by labeling them as hard to reach. Instead, take a look at your own attitudes and the methods you and your staff are using to communicate. Educators must assure all parents that they have a part to play in their child's education.

An important area to consider in trying to involve parents is communicating in the appropriate language. You need to make an extra effort to include non–English-speaking parents in your programs, as the language barrier may be all that is keeping them from participating. These parents are often some of the most supportive toward schools and, once welcomed, will give unselfishly of their time.

From The Parent Institute (1992) comes 10 ideas for involving hard-to-reach parents:

1. *Commitment.* The school must want to involve parents and be willing to work hard to get them involved. You must personally reflect this commitment.

2. *Strong personal outreach.* If parents have had a negative experience in their own schooling, they may hesitate to get involved. Personal contact by someone at your school can often bridge the gap.

3. *Nonjudgmental attitude.* Research shows that low-income parents (like most parents) want to help their children and will implement suggestions offered by teachers—if they really understand what is being asked. When teachers reach out, these parents will help.

4. *Creativity.* Traditional methods of parent involvement often do not work. Creative approaches are more likely to work, such as an ice cream social on a Sunday afternoon.

5. *Informal workshops that solve parents' problems.* Formal meetings are often unsuccessful with hard-to-reach parents. They may prefer interacting with their children at "make and take" workshops or working on community projects. Helpful social, economic, or medical advice could also be provided in conjunction with the event.

6. *Flexibility.* Holding meetings at times and places convenient to parents—not educators—is essential.

7. *Child care.* The number one reason mothers do not attend evening meetings is that they have no one to care for their other children. Providing child care will assure a higher attendance rate from moms.

8. *Support from the top.* Make sure you stand at the door to greet every parent who attends.

9. *Parent volunteers.* Parents will always have more credibility with their friends and neighbors in the community than anyone from the school. Encourage parents to ask those they know to take part in school activities.

10. *Follow-up.* Telephone parents the day after a meeting to thank them for attending. If they don't have a telephone, write a note. Be sure to follow up with some form of thank-you to every parent who helped.

PARENTS NEEDED FOR POLITICAL AND ECONOMIC SUPPORT

To further persuade you that parents are essential to the well-being of your school, just remind yourself that only one-fourth of American households have a school-age child in them. This means that the families who consider themselves to have a strong stake in the quality of your school are vastly outnumbered by those who may not care one way or another. What's more, some of these households without children may consider tax-supported expenditures for schools for other people's children to be a waste of money.

When it comes time to seek out community support for a bond or budget election, to whom do you turn for political support (that is, for votes)? Parents who identify with their child's school are more likely to turn out to vote for school issues—and to vote affirmatively. They are also a potential advocacy group for encouraging others to vote for educational needs. Schools need political support to thrive and survive, which means parents are more important than ever before. In that same context, the fewer parents there are, the more important they are to the schools.

REFERENCES AND SUGGESTED READINGS

Bloom, B. S. (1976). *Human characteristics and school learning.* New York: McGraw-Hill.

Canter, L., & Canter, M. (1991). *Parents on your side.* Santa Monica, CA: Lee Canter & Associates.

Corner, J. P. (1989). Is "parenting" necessary to better teaching? *Journal of Educational Public Relations, 12*(1), 22–27.

Davies, D. (1988). Benefits of and barriers to parent involvement. *Community Education Research Digest, 2*(2), 11–19.

Dill, V. S. (1998). *A peaceable school.* Bloomington, IN: Phi Delta Kappa International.

Henderson, A. T. (1987). *The evidence continues to grow: Parent involvement improves student achievement.* Columbia, MD: National Committee for Citizens in Education.

Holliday, A. E. (1990). A model policy for a district's school–community relations program. *Journal of Educational Public Relations, 13*(1), 4–7.

Leibowitz, G. R. (1991). Who is responsible for student success? *Journal of Educational Public Relations, 14*(3), 6–8.

Lloyd, K., Ramsey, D., & Groennings, S. (1992). *Knowledge revolution for all Americans: Empowering public schools.* Arlington, VA: Knowledge Network for All Americans.

National School Public Relations Association. (1988). *Helping parents help their kids kit* (Pocket folder). Rockville, MD: Author.

Parent Institute, The. (1992). *What's working in parent involvement, 2*(4), 2(7), 3(2). (Monthly newsletter available from The Parent Institute, Fairfax Station, VA)

EAST IRONDEQUOIT CENTRAL SCHOOL DISTRICT

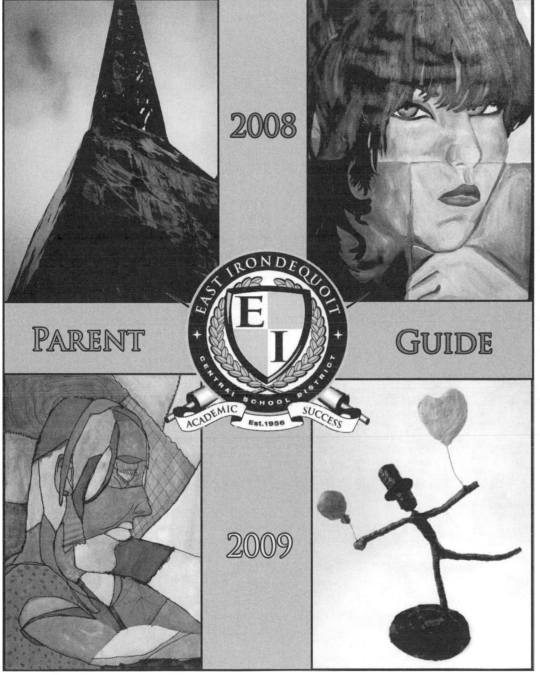

BUILDING A FUTURE . . . ONE STUDENT AT A TIME

News...Notes...Notices

Thank you to the following students for the artwork shown on the Parent Guide cover: (clockwise from top right) Virginia Griepp, grade 9; Caitlyn Garofolo, grade 7; Marcus Gaudio, Jr., grade 8; and Ashley Sykes, grade 12.

Nomination forms for the 2008 Eastridge Alumni Hall of Fame are available at the Eastridge High School main office, 2350 East Ridge Road and at the East Irondequoit Administrative Offices, 600 Pardee Road. Alumni who graduated in 1993 or earlier are eligible for nomination. The nomination deadline is January 19, 2009.

EI Lancer Band Rainbow of Stars Field Band Competition

For Ticket Information: Jim Marasco 266-3352

7:00 p.m. Saturday, September 6 Eastridge Field

East Irondequoit Athletic Department
'Meet the Coaches Night'
6:30 p.m.
Wednesday
September 17
East Irondequoit Middle School
Required meeting for *ALL athletes* on *FALL* Modified B sports teams *AND their parents.*
(Academic Eligibility Handbook will be reviewed)

Eastridge Homecoming / Spirit Week

Monday, September 8		Spirit Week begins
Friday, September 12	6:30 p.m.	Homecoming Float Parade
	7:00 p.m.	Homecoming Football Game
Saturday, September 13	8:00 p.m.	Homecoming Dance, Ninth Grade Academy Gym

Homecoming events are planned throughout Spirit Week for fall sports teams.

**East Irondequoit Athletic Association
2008-09 Parent Information Meeting
7 p.m. September 24   Eastridge High School
All parents are welcome**

2   *Visit our website ~ eicsd.k12.ny.us*

Source: East Irondequoit Central School District. Cover design by Danielle Gorevski.

ORANGE COUNTY PUBLIC SCHOOLS
PARENT INVOLVEMENT SURVEY

Blue Ribbon Panel on EDUCATION

Parental Involvement Survey 2005

❖ **If you have already completed the online survey in January, please do not complete again, you are already counted!**

Dear Parent or Legal Guardian:

The Blue Ribbon Panel on Education Taskforce understands that parental and community involvement is crucial in supporting our schools as they meet student needs. Therefore, we invite you to participate by completing a parent involvement survey. The responses that you provide to this survey are anonymous and will be used to identify and support the Parental Involvement and Community Support Committee's recommendations to Orange County Public Schools. The results of this survey and recommendations will be available to you on the Orange County Public Schools' Community Resources website (https://volunteer.ocps.net/Surveys.asp) in May.

For your survey to be counted, you may submit a paper form or the online form. ALL forms must be in by March 25, 2005.

▲ To submit the online survey, go to: (https://volunteer.ocps.net/Surveys.asp)
▲ To submit the paper survey, return to Community Resources, 445 West Amelia Street, Orlando, FL 32801 or your child's school.

PARENT INFORMATION (To answer the questions, place an "X" next to the response.)

1. Age
   ☐ Less than 20   ☐ 21-35   ☐ 36-50   ☐ 51and older

2. Race
   ☐ American Indian/American Eskimo   ☐ White, Non-Hispanic
   ☐ Asian; Pacific Islander   ☐ Multi-Racial
   ☐ Black, Non-Hispanic   ☐ Other _____
   ☐ Hispanic

3. Gender
   ☐ Female   ☐ Male

4. Marital Status
   ☐ Single   ☐ Married   ☐ Divorced

5. Combined Income
   ☐ less than $21,000   ☐ $50,001 - $75,000
   ☐ $21,001 - $50,000   ☐ $75,001and more

6. Highest Education Completed
   ☐ High School Diploma/GED   ☐ Bachelors Degree
   ☐ Technical/Vocational License   ☐ Masters Degree
   ☐ Associates Degree   ☐ Doctorate Degree

7. School Location (Select the school your child attends)
   ☐ Arbor Ridge School   ☐ Lake Eola Charter   ☐ Rolling Hills Elementary
   ☐ Bay Meadows Elementary   ☐ Memorial Middle   ☐ Southwest Middle
   ☐ Blankner School   ☐ Maxey Elementary   ☐ Tangelo Park Elementary
   ☐ Carver Middle   ☐ Nap Ford Charter   ☐ Ventura Elementary
   ☐ Fern Creek Elementary   ☐ Orlo Vista Elementary   ☐ Winter Park High
   ☐ Jones High   ☐ Richmond Heights Elementary

(Continued)

(Continued)

Place an "X" in the box that indicates your response: Strongly Disagree, Disagree, Neutral, Agree or Strongly Agree.

Questions 8 through 15 *Parent feelings, attitudes and beliefs about themselves, administrators, faculty and the school in general.*	Strongly Agree	Agree	Neutral	Disagree	Strongly Disagree
8. I feel welcomed and appreciated when I come to the school.					
9. I believe there are things I can do to help at my child's school.					
10. I am clear about how I can be involved at the school in ways that would help my child.					
11. I am comfortable in communicating with the school administrators (principal, assistant principal, dean).					
12. I am comfortable talking with my child's teacher.					
13. I feel that what I contribute to the school is valued.					
14. Do you know how to be involved with your child's education away from the school campus?					
15. Any additional comments:					

Questions 16 through 22 *Barriers that affect a parent's participation at school.*	Strongly Agree	Agree	Neutral	Disagree	Strongly Disagree
16. It is difficult for me to participate in parent-teacher conferences and/or other school activities.					
17. I have difficulties because of time constraints (job/other responsibilities).					
18. I have difficulties participating in school activities because of childcare (other small children).					
19. I have difficulties participating in school activities because of transportation.					
20. I have difficulties participating in school activities because of other matters.					
21. There are language/cultural barriers that interfere with my participation at my child's school.					
22. Any additional comments:					

Questions 23 through 27 *Parent's knowledge of the school district's structure and organization.*	*Strongly Agree*	*Agree*	*Neutral*	*Disagree*	*Strongly Disagree*
23. I would like to better understand the way the school system works.					
24. I know how to contact the administrators at my school.					
25. I know that the district is divided into five Learning Communities with an area superintendent supervising the schools in the different Learning Communities?					
26. I am involved in my child's education.					
27. Any additional comments:					

Source: Orange County Public Schools.

Fall Mountain Regional High School

Wildcat Winners Club

_____   _____

Name   Class

Has made the following positive accomplishment:

_____

_____

_____

_____

_____

_____

_____

_____

Pride is a personal commitment.   Congratulations to you and
It is an attitude which separates   your son/daughter
   excellence from mediocrity.

                                        _____

                                                   Teacher

Office of the Principal
Fall Mountain Regional High School

Dear _____

It gives me great pleasure to inform you that

_____

Has made an excellent scholastic record for the last marking period and is to be highly commended. It is a pleasure to recognize this achievement and to express to you our appreciation for your fine cooperation in making this record possible.

_____   _____

Date   ALAN CHMIEL,
                                                              PRINCIPAL

Principal's Positive Phone Call
Fall Mountain Regional High School

STUDENT'S NAME: _____

TEACHER: _____

SUBJECT: _____

PARENT'S NAME (IF DIFFERENT FROM STUDENT'S): _____

HOME PHONE: _____

WHAT'S POSITIVE: _____

DATE OF CONTACT: _____

TIME OF CONTACT: _____

PARENT CONSULTED: _____

NATIONAL ASSOCIATION OF ELEMENTARY SCHOOL PRINCIPALS' REPORT TO PARENTS—SAMPLE PAGES

RP 25:3

Attendance

It's really pretty simple: The more school a child misses, the more likely he or she is to fall behind academically. Although most teachers allow students to make up the work they missed, nothing can make up for losing a valuable day of instruction. Therefore, it's your responsibility, as parents and caregivers, to minimize the number of days your child misses school. Here are some tips that can help:

When They Don't Want to Go to School

Virtually every parent has heard, "I just don't want to go to school today." If your child says this occasionally, firmly insist that attending school is a responsibility and that he or she must go. If complaints become more frequent, you need to discover the cause. One or more of the following situations may apply:

• *"The dog ate my homework."* Many times children will resist going to school if they have neglected to study for a test, complete homework, or finish a project. First, explain to them that staying home won't solve the problem. Then, working with your child, set up a system to keep track of tests and assignments.

• *Fear of bullies.* If your child actually seems afraid to go to school, encourage him or her to open up and share why they are scared. Tell your child that you will get help and immediately notify the principal, the child's teacher, and a counselor.

• *Falling behind.* Sometimes, children don't want to go to school because they feel "stupid." Meet with the teacher to find out how your child is doing. If necessary, explore tests your child can take to track his or her learning and ask about special help that may be available.

• *"My teacher hates me."* In this situation, it's best to overcome your reluctance and schedule a conference with the teacher. The key is to have an open and honest discussion of the reasons for the child's feelings, and ways to improve the teacher-child relationship.

• *Set a good example.* Parents who are habitually late to work, or take "sick days" when they aren't really sick, set a wrong example for their children.

When It's Your Fault

Whether it's to avoid crowds, get cheaper airfares, or coattail on a parent's business trip, a disturbing number of families take their children out of school to go on vacations. It's a trend that is very disruptive to their children's education. If possible, try to schedule vacations, doctors' appointments, and other commitments during school breaks. If you must pull your kids out of class, do the following:

• *Give plenty of notice.* It's difficult, and sometimes impossible, for a teacher to prepare assignments and make-up work on short notice. Let the teacher know at least two weeks in advance if your child will be missing class.

• *Take responsibility.* Simply having the assignments isn't good enough. Make sure your child thoroughly completes the assignments instead of rushing through them at the last minute.

• *Don't do the work.* While it may be tempting to "help" your child with his or her assignments, make sure that the work they turn in is their own.

Attendance is an extremely important part of your child's education. By minimizing the instruction your child misses, you can ensure that he or she gets the most out of school.

(Continued)

(Continued)

 # INFORME POR LOS PADRES

RP 25:3

Asistencia Escolar

Es simple: Mientras más días escolares pierde el niño, está más propenso a retrasarse academicamente. Aunque la mayoría de los maestros permiten que los niños recuperen el trabajo que perdieron, nada puede reemplazar un día de instrucción valiosa. Por lo tanto, es su responsabilidad, como padre, minimizar el número de días que su niño pierde de ir a la escuela. Los siguientes son algunos consejos para ayudarlo:

Cuando No Quieren Ir a la Escuela

Casi todos los padres han escuchado, "No quiero ir a la escuela hoy." Insiste que es su responsabilidad asistir a la escuela y debe ir. Si oye las quejas frecuentemente, usted necesita descubrir la razon verdadera. Una o más de las siguientes situaciones podrían aplicarse:

• *"El perro se comió mi tarea escolar."* A veces el niño resiste ir a la escuela si no ha estudiado para un examen, o si no ha completado la tarea o un proyecto. Primero, explíquele que quedarse en casa no resolverá el problema. Entonces, trabaje junto con su niño para establecer un sistema de control para las pruebas y asignaciones.

• *Temor a la intimidación.* Si su niño realmente siente temor de ir a la escuela, anímelo a compartir las razones por las cuales siente temor. Dígale a su niño que usted buscará ayuda y hágalo inmediatamente por medio de comunicarse con el maestro y asesor.

• *Quedarse atrás.* A veces los niños no quieren ir a la escuela porque se sienten "tontos." Reúnase con el maestro para averiguar cómo le va a su niño. Si es necesario, explore pruebas que su niño puede tomar para controlar su aprendizaje, pregunte sobre ayuda especial que puede estar disponible.

• *"El maestro me odia."* En esta situación, es mejor reunirse con el maestro. Lo que siente su niño y maneras de mejorar la relación entre su niño

y el maestro. La clave es mantener comunicaciones abiertas y honestas con la escuela.

• *Establecer un buen ejemplo:* Los padres que habitualmente llegan atrasados al trabajo o toman "días de enfermedad" cuando no están enfermos establecen un mal ejemplo para sus niños.

Cuando es Su Idea

Ya sea para evitar los gentíos, lograr tarifas más económicas, o para acompañar al padre en un viaje de negocios, un alarmante número de familias sacan sus hijos de la escuela para ir de vacaciones. Es una tendencia altamente desanimada porque interrumpe la educación de su niño. Si es posible, trate de planear las vacaciones, visitas médicas, y otras obligaciones durante las vacaciones escolares, días feriados, o medios días de clases. Si sus niños deben perder clases, considere las siguientes:

• *Avise con anticipación.* Es difícil y a veces imposible para el maestro preparar asignaciones de recuperación y trabajo escolar al no recibir aviso oportuno. Dé a saber al maestro por lo menos dos semanas antes si su niño deberé dejar de ir a la escuela.

• *Tome responsabilidad.* Simplemente tener las asignaciones no es suficiente. Asegúrese de que su niño complete bien las asignaciones en lugar de hacerlas con prisa al último minuto.

• *No haga el trabajo.* Aunque pueda se tentador "ayudarle" a su niño con sus areas, asegúrese de que el trabajo sea de ellos.

La asistencia escolar es una parte muy importante de la educación de su niño. Si usted puede disminuir la cantidad de instrucción que pierde su niño, puede asegurarse de que su niño aproveche de obtener el máximo beneficio de la escuela.

 *Informe por los Padres,* fue escrita por los directores escolores y los miembros de NAESP pueden reproducirlo sin permiso. Los últimos números de éste año son asequible en la sección por los miembros del www.naesp.org.

REPORT TO PARENTS

RP 25:6

Field Trips

Field trips are a wonderful way for teachers to enhance what their students are learning in the classroom. They also provide parents an opportunity to be directly involved in their child's education. Here are some tips to help you, and your child, get the most out of field trips:

Volunteer if you can: Taking a day off from work to chaperone a field trip is a great way to see what your child is learning and what your child and his/her friends are really like at school. Research shows that children whose parents are involved in school do better than those whose parents are not. So, if you can, take the time to chaperone a field trip

Save conferences for later: Avoid the temptation to discuss your child's progress with the teacher during a field trip. As a chaperone, you have responsibilities and the teacher needs to stay focused on the details of the field trip. Schedule another time where both you and the teacher can focus on your child.

Leave the siblings at home: Field trips are designed to reinforce what the students have been studying in class. Therefore, the field trip won't be as meaningful to younger siblings. Besides, other children could distract you from your role as chaperone. If the destination is truly wonderful, plan a second trip, with the whole family, later.

Be a model: How students behave is a reflection on the school. Therefore, principals and teachers expect students' behavior to be exemplary. Chaperones should model good behavior by listening to and following the rules laid out by the teacher. Let the students see you paying attention when the teacher, principal, or featured speaker is talking. If you're driving, obey the speed limit, wear your seat belt, and please don't smoke around the children.

Be in charge: As a chaperone, you're not along to be the students' buddy. You're the boss. Enforce the rules consistently, right from the beginning. Be stern, if necessary, and make sure the students understand the consequences for any misbehavior.

Be discreet: The teacher may need to divulge private information to you about one of the students (*e.g.,* medical condition), or you may overhear private conversations among the students. In either case, keep the information to yourself unless there's an emergency.

Keep to the schedule: Field trips are carefully orchestrated, with set times for arrival, departure, lunch, and events. It's important that all the chaperones follow the schedule precisely and keep the kids on time all day long.

Focus on the children: Although chaperoning may be a good opportunity to meet other parents, you need to stay focused on keeping your group of students together and on task. If you want to meet other parents, organize a get-together or attend a PTA meeting.

Be honest with the teacher: Don't wait until the end of the field trip to "vent" serious frustrations. Immediately report to the teacher if the children in your group behave in an unsafe or disrespectful manner.

Pass along compliments: Let the teacher know if you get compliments about your group's or the school's behavior while on the trip. Congratulate the children, as well, for being excellent ambassadors for the school.

One last thought—if you're not one of the "official" chaperones, please don't be an "unofficial" one. When other parents show up at field trip destinations, it causes problems for the teacher and school. Remind yourself that the field trip is a learning opportunity for the class, not a family outing. The best thing non-chaperone parents can do is to be eager listeners when their children return from the field trip.

 *Report to Parents,* written to serve elementary and middle school principals, may be reproduced by National Association of Elementary School Principals members without permission. Current year back issues are available in the Members Only section of www.naesp.org.

(Continued)

(Continued)

RP 25:6

Los Viajes de Estudios Escolares

Los viajes de estudios presentan maravillosas oportunidades para que los maestros realcen los estudios que están aprendiendo los alumnos en la sala de clases. Estos proporcionan también para los padres oportunidades para participar directamente en la educación de su niño. Las siguientes son algunas sugerencias para ayudarle a usted y a su niño sacar mejor provecho de los viajes de estudio:

Servir como voluntario: Tomar un día libre para acompañar a su niño en un viaje de estudio es una buena forma de ver lo que su niño está aprendiendo y cómo es su niño y sus amigos en la escuela. Según las investigaciones, los niños cuyos padres participan en la escuela rinden mejor académicamente que los niños cuyos padres no participan. Por esta razón, si usted puede, tome el tiempo para servir como acompañante un viaje de estudio.

Dejar las conferencias para más tarde: Evite la tentación de discutir el progreso de su niño con el maestro durante un viaje de estudio. Como acompañante, usted tiene responsabilidades y el maestro debe mantenerse enfocado en los detalles del viaje de estudio. Busque otra ocasión para que usted y el maestro puedan concentrarse en su niño.

Dejar en casa a sus otros niños menores: La mayoría de los viajes de estudios están diseñados para reforzar lo que los alumnos han estado estudiando en la clase. Por lo tanto, el viaje de estudio no será tan significativo para sus otros niños menores. Además, los otros niños le podrían distraer de su papel como acompañante. Si el destino es realmente maravilloso, planifique un segundo viaje para más tarde, en el cual podrá llevar a la familia entera.

Servir como modelo: La conducta de los alumnos es una reflección de la escuela. Por lo tanto, los directores y maestros esperan que la conducta de los alumnos sea ejemplar. Los acompañantes deben modelar la buena conducta por medio de escuchar y seguir las reglas establecidas por el maestro. Deje que los alumnos vean que usted está poniendo atención mientras el maestro, director, o lector hablen. Si usted está conduciendo, siga los límites de velocidad, use el cinturón de seguridad, y por favor no fume alrededor de los niños.

Estar encargado del grupo: Como acompañante, usted no está allí para ser el mejor amigo de los alumnos. Usted es el jefe. Debe asegurar el cumplimiento de las reglas de una manera consistente, desde el comienzo. Si es necesario, sea rígido y asegure que los estudiantes comprendan las consecuencias de la mala conducta.

Ser discreto. Es posible que el maestro tenga que divulgar información privada sobre uno de los alumnos (por ejemplo, una condición médica), o que usted escuche conversaciones privadas entre los alumnos. En cualquier caso, no comparta la información a menos que haya una emergencia.

Seguir el horario: Los viajes de estudios son cuidadosamente organizados, con horas establecidas para la llegada, la salida, el almuerzo, y los eventos. Es importante que todos los acompañantes sigan el horario de una forma precisa y que mantengan los niños a la hora todo el día.

Concentrarse en los niños: Aunque servir como acompañante puede presentar una buena oportunidad para conocer a los otros padres, usted debe mantenerse enfocado en mantener su grupo de alumnos juntos y asegurar que sigan el horario. Si usted desea conocer a los otros padres, organice una reunión o asista a una reunión del PTA.

Ser honesto con el maestro: No espere hasta el final del viaje de estudio para expresar serias frustraciones. Informe inmediatamente al maestro si los niños en su grupo se comportan mal o de una manera poco segura y sin respeto.

Expresar las felicitaciones: Dígale al maestro si usted recibe felicitaciones sobre la conducta de su grupo o de la escuela mientras están en el viaje de estudio. Felicite también a los niños por ser tan excelentes embajadores de la escuela.

Por último—si usted no es uno de los acompañantes "oficiales" por favor no sea uno "no oficial." Cuando otros padres se presentan en los destinos de los viajes de estudios, esto causa problemas para el maestro y la escuela. Recuerde que para la clase el viaje de estudio es una oportunidad para aprender, no una excursión familiar. Lo mejor que los padres que no son acompañantes pueden hacer es estar oyentes entusiasmados cuando sus niños regresan del viaje de estudio.

 *Informe por los Padres,* fue escrita por los directores escolares y los miembros de NAESP pueden reproducirlo sin permiso. Los últimos números de éste año son asequible en la sección por los miembros del www.naesp.org.

▲▲▲ REPORT TO PARENTS

RP 25:8

Managing Money

How much do your children understand about money? Do they know about budgeting? Is "gimme" one of their favorite phrases? Are they focused on having what others have? While many parents don't start discussing money management with their children until they're teenagers, it's smart to begin early—very early. Even children in kindergarten can understand that money can be earned, that it can be saved, and that it's important to think carefully about how it's spent.

Here are some suggestions to help you teach your children how to wisely handle money:

• **Don't keep the family finances a secret.** Include your children in discussions about the family's budget. Teach them that there is a set amount of money your family earns each year, and that it's important to budget what you spend to make sure you are not exceeding your earnings. You don't have to be specific about your actual income. The important thing is to talk about budget categories (*i.e.*, housing, car, insurance, clothing, food), and the importance of creating and sticking to a budget. Also, explain the strategies you use to meet long-term (*i.e.*, retirement, college) and short-term (*i.e.*, holidays, vacation) goals.

• **Give your children an allowance.** A weekly allowance is one of the best tools for teaching children about money management. Even a minimal allowance can help children understand spending and saving. If you decide to give an allowance, make sure you stick to it. Don't give your children more money if they quickly spend their allowance; teach them to wait until the next week. While some families allow children to earn extra money for doing individual chores, others disagree with the practice.

• **Show children the value of saving.** Talk to your children about the value of saving money by using these tips:

Talk about it. Discuss why saving money to buy something "big" is rewarding.

Open a savings account. With the help of bank personnel, explain how banks operate, show your children how to read a bank statement, and talk about the interest they will receive.

Set goals. Help your children set a savings goal and then chart the weekly savings progress. Praise them for making progress toward their goal.

Discourage frivolous spending: Encourage your children to think about what they want before they buy it. Discourage impulse buying.

Discuss options. When your children have saved enough money, discuss investment options. Consider having them buy a savings bond. Bonds help children understand the pay-off of saving and give them something to "hold" for the future.

• **Make sure children learn to stay within their limits.** Beware of the lure of credit and debit cards. Credit is a difficult concept to teach and it's very easy for children to spend above their resources. Put a limit on how much your children may spend without parental approval.

• **Check the Web.** There are lots of excellent Web sites designed specifically to help parents teach their children money management skills. Among the best are: **www.jumpstart.org, www.makingallowances.com, www.investoreducation.org, www.nefe.org, www.ntrbonline.org**, and **www.themint.org**.

(Continued)

(Continued)

INFORME POR LOS PADRES

RP 25:8

La Administración del Dinero

Cuánto comprenden sus niños sobre el dinero? ¿Saben lo que es hacer un presupuesto? ¿Es la palabra "dámelo" una de sus frases favoritas? ¿Se encuentran enfocados en tener lo que los demás tienen? Aunque muchos padres no comiencen a discutir la administración del dinero con sus niños hasta que éstos sean adolescentes, es importante comenzar temprano—muy temprano. Aún los niños en el jardín de la infancia pueden comprender que el dinero se gana, se puede ahorrar, y que es importante pensar cuidadosamente sobre cómo se gasta.

Aquí hay algunas sugerencias para ayudarle a enseñarle a sus niños cómo tratar sabiamente el dinero

• No mantenga secretas las finanzas familiares.

Incluya a sus niños en discusiones sobre el presupuesto familiar. Enséñeles que hay una cantidad de dinero establecida que su familia gana al año y que es importante hacer un presupuesto de lo que gasta para asegurarse de no sobrepasar los ingresos. No es necesario dar información específica sobre sus ingresos. Lo importante es hablar sobre categorías de presupuesto (por ejemplo, la vivienda, automóvil, seguro, ropa, comida), y la importancia de crear y seguir un presupuesto. Explique también las estrategias que usted usará para lograr metas de largo plazo (por ejemplo, la jubilación, estudios universitarios) y de corto plazo (por ejemplo, los feriados, vacaciones).

• Déle a sus niños una subvención. Una
subvención es una de las mejores herramientas para enseñarle a los niños sobre la administración del dinero. Aún una subvención mínima puede ayudar a los niños a comprender lo que significa gastar y ahorrar. Si usted decide darles una subvención, asegúrese de mantenerse firme. No le entregue más dinero a sus niños si gastan la mesada; enséñeles a esperar hasta el mes siguiente. Mientras que algunas familias permiten que sus niños ganen dinero extra haciendo tareas individuales, otras no están deacuerdo con esta práctica.

• Enséñele a los niños el valor de ahorrar. Hable con ellos sobre el valor de ahorrar dinero por medio de usar las siguientes sugerencias:

Discuta con sus niños la importancia de los ahorros. Explique por qué es remunerativo ahorrar dinero para comprar algo "grande."

Abra una cuenta de ahorros. Con ayuda del personal del banco, explique cómo operan los bancos, enséñele a sus hijos cómo leer el estado de la cuenta del banco, y hable sobre los intereses que recibirán.

Establezca metas. Ayude a sus niños a establecer una meta para ahorros y controle el progreso de los Elogielos por su progreso.

Trate de disuador los gastos frivolos. Anime a sus niños a pensar sobre lo que desean antes de comprarlo. Trate de disuadir las compras impulsivas.

Discuta las opciones. Cuando sus niños hayan ahorrado suficiente dinero, discuta las opciones de inversión. Considere hacerlos comprar un bono de ahorros. Los bonos ayudan a los niños a comprender la remuneración de los ahorros y les proporciona algo para "mantener" para el futuro.

• Asegúrese que los niños aprendan a mantenerse dentro de sus límites. Tenga cuidado con las atracciones de las tarjetas de crédito y débito. El crédito es un concepto difícil de enseñar y es muy fácil para los niños gastar más de sus recursos. Limite la cantidad de dinero que sus niños pueden gastar sin permiso.

• Visite el Web. Hay muchos sitios del Web excelentes que han sido diseñados específicamente para ayudar a los padres a enseñarle a sus niños sobre las destrezaspara la administración de dinero. Entre las mejores están: **www.jumpstart.org, www.makingallowances.com, www.investoreducation.org, www.nefe.org, www.ntrbonline.org**, y **www.themint.org**.

Informe por los Padres, fue escrita por los directors escolores y los miembros de NAESP pueden reproducirlo sin permiso. Los últimos números de éste año son asequible en la sección por los miembros del www.naesp.org.

8

Community Outreach

It takes an entire village to educate a single child.

—African proverb

The American school system is the institution responsible for teaching children the history and ideals of the culture and the language and thinking skills that will allow them to become productive members of society. In earlier days, children were expected to learn hands-on applications under the guidance and tutelage of family members and friends, or they were apprenticed to local crafts workers. Moral instruction was provided by home and church. The entire community assumed a share of the responsibility for educating its children. Townsfolk joined together to build and care for the school building, search for a teacher, and protect the school environment from harm. The teacher was held in high esteem within the community and was often provided housing as well as a salary.

Communities are still responsible through their tax dollars for building and maintaining public schools and paying the salaries of educators who teach and care for children. But, unfortunately, many of today's taxpayers believe their responsibility to the school ends there and are loath to contribute additional resources once their own children are grown. Teachers are expected to be skilled professionals who continually work on their professional growth, yet they are often paid less than hourly laborers who dropped out of high school.

Still, it is essential for educators to remember that the financial support for public schools is community based; that is, the voters or their elected representatives determine the future tax dollars that provide the resources for schools. If the community believes that its schools and the professionals who work there are dedicated to their task, then the community will support school efforts and will contribute the resources necessary to get the job done. However, if the community believes otherwise, it will withhold critical financial support. There is little in the way of alternative means of support when a community loses faith in its schools. But when a community believes in its schools, almost nothing will be impossible for you and your team.

In recent decades, the nation has shifted away from the concept of the local school being the focal point of a community of responsibility to the concept that (a) schools are just another consumer service, or (b) schools are essentially charged with relieving the community and parents of the collective burdens that once were shared by all. No longer perceived as a responsibility shared by the community, the well-being of children has become almost solely the province of parents and schools.

With the growth of the concept of site-based management and other forms of decentralized decision making, education may now be in the early stages of coming full circle. To meet the needs of students in the 21st century, it is imperative that schools take the lead in reinitiating community involvement and support. Thus, educational leaders must encourage all members of the community—parents, other adults, the elderly, and business, civic, and religious groups—to once again make educating children a priority. Schools must form alliances and coalitions to provide the social services needed by children and must work collectively with the community as a whole for economic progress through better education. A major trend for strengthening community involvement and support is community schools. Gerald Tirozzi, executive director of the National Association of Secondary School Principals, states that "The community school concept—keeping the school open in the late afternoons, weekends, and summer months—enhances the potential for parents and the community to engage in a broad range of school-based programs and activities."

If there is to be true educational reform, schools must be willing to change, and the community must also be committed to providing the resources and support to sustain the change process and usher in a new era of improved education. As an educational leader, you must inspire your community to renew guardianship of its schools—and its children—in order to guarantee the nation's future.

GETTING THE COMMUNITY INVOLVED

Communicating with your constituencies is important, but communicating is merely the first step in getting people involved. There are infinite numbers of ways to interest your community in its school. The only limitation is your imagination and resourcefulness. It is vital that educators be open to all options. Don't focus just on fiscal resources, but seek out in-kind services and mutually beneficial personnel resources. Create programs that give the community a vested interest in education—and in the local school.

Most adults like to be around happy, energetic, positive youngsters, so encourage student programs that interact with the community as much as possible. The Ninilchik, Alaska, schools post notices of all school events at local businesses, which sends a solid "everybody is welcome" message.

Tutoring. Research has proven that one-on-one tutoring has a major impact on at-risk students. Most people who volunteer in schools do so because they have a desire to positively influence a child's life. Tutoring programs that are structured so that the tutors are able to build a relationship with a student, serve as a role model, and observe a child's progress on a regular basis are the most successful at recruiting and retaining volunteers. Elderly and retired persons constitute a superb talent bank. In addition, companies that might not financially support a special project may be more than willing to offer employees release time each week for tutoring students. Everyone wins in this kind of program because of the valuable service provided and the goodwill generated.

Mentoring. Afterschool programs provide excellent mentoring opportunities. City agencies, such as police and fire departments, often encourage their officers to get involved in school and community programs, and these officers make outstanding role models for students. A nearby military base is another good source of mentors. These groups are sometimes overlooked when recruiting mentors because it is assumed that they are too busy, yet they often have flexible schedules that allow time for working with students. Mentors can participate in athletic activities or provide homework assistance, as well as just be there to listen, to be a friend, and to take an interest in individual students.

Flowing Wells Unified School District in Tucson, Arizona, used community partnerships to build a comprehensive afterschool student mentoring program. "NCWM," or No Child Without a Mentor, is the program's motto.

Planning, process, and partnerships ensure that the afterschool programs in the Flowing Wells District truly benefit students and the community. Planning starts with a commitment from the Governing Board to have a "24/7" school in a community where "all of our people take care of all of our students," explains Superintendent Dr. Nicholas Clement. Transforming words into actions is based on clear guidelines for programs, from requiring that service learning projects fit into the curriculum and include reflection activities, to a maximum requirement of $1 per student for celebration food and drinks.

Partnerships are the foundation for all of the district's afterschool programs. Community partners work with students and teachers to define their service learning projects. Partnerships include Big Brothers Big Sisters—Project MAX (Mentoring Academic Experience); IBM Exite (Exploring Interest in Technology and Engineering); Learn and Serve, Girls 2 Girls mentoring; 21st Century Community Learning Centers; TestGear; and YES (Youth Enrichment Services).

School–Business Partnerships. Now one of the most prevalent forms of community involvement, school–business partnerships are an important part of many school programs. These can take several different forms, but basically, an individual school is matched with a business or civic organization.

Successful partnerships have specific goals and objectives, and both parties have a clear understanding of their roles and responsibilities. The key is that the partnerships are cooperative and provide positive experiences for both parties.

According to Bret Lovejoy, former executive director of the Association for Career and Technical Education, "Businesses are in desperate need of highly educated and skilled employees, and they are eager to involve themselves in school activities if it means better prepared graduates to help local businesses compete." Like members of every other interest group, business leaders have to believe they are going to benefit from their efforts. They have to understand that schools are serious about delivering on their promises. They have to know that if they are solicited for support, they will be able to have a say in how that support is directed. If educational leaders are creative in their approach and honest in their purpose, the private sector is poised to be the greatest supporter in America of a reformed and improved school system. A sample of the Minot, North Dakota, School District's resolution advocating Education–Business Partnerships is included at chapter's end.

For schools with vocational/technical programs, school–business partnerships are a natural. Don Bosco Technical High School in Boston, Massachusetts, has long had a number of successful intern and apprentice programs in place. The experiences of Golightly Vocational/Technical Center in Detroit, Michigan, indicate that programs involving business and community leaders as advisors, consultants, and mentors for programs and students are the most effective in developing and maintaining partnerships.

Mountain View Elementary School in Phoenix, Arizona, has a partnership with a branch of a local bank whereby the bank provides a computer and assists the school in setting up a simulated bank where students apply their math skills.

John Jacobs Elementary School, also in Phoenix, has a partnership with a nearby resort hotel. Several mornings each week, the ESL teacher and her aide go to the hotel before work to teach a class for the non–English-speaking housekeeping staff. The principal gives leadership and team-building workshops for the hotel's management. In return, the hotel provides meeting rooms for school inservice meetings, student self-esteem training, and special events, and gives free dinner certificates for staff recognition drawings.

Cooperative school–business programs might offer internships, shadowing, guest speakers, and hands-on experiences. South Park Middle School in Corpus Christi, Texas, has had a great deal of success with its "Adopt-a-School" program. Another successful program has been established at Swampscott High School in Massachusetts. An extensive internship program and a second semester senior release program places students on a volunteer basis in a variety of business and social service agencies.

Elections. "The Blue Springs School District has passed 23 consecutive bond elections because of the outstanding support we are fortunate to have in our community," says Dr. Paul Kinder, superintendent of the Blue Springs School District in Blue Springs, Missouri. "These bond campaigns are conducted with many of the same components of 20 years ago, while other portions have been modified to meet the changing information-gathering style of our constituents. Each bond election includes first prioritizing the possible facility issues from our CAC (Citizen's Advisory Committee), and then our Board of Education makes the final decision to place the issue on the ballot. We conduct studies about our voting public and target our message to those voters. We spend a great deal of time analyzing our public and assessing our voters' responses.

"Our last bond election in 2005 included an informational DVD created by the communications department in our district. This DVD assured that consistency of the message, in its entirety, was shared. It gave our patrons a visual image of the needs in our district and an auditory connection to add to their schema."

Coalitions. If schools are to better serve student needs, they must look at building coalitions with various community groups. Coalitions can identify and target community objectives and assist in finding appropriate support for school projects. These can include both curriculum and facility needs. Creative educators need to work with community leaders to determine ways in which the mission, activities, resources, and employees/ members of various organizations can assist in supporting the schools. The Corporate Academy was established at Thornton High School in Colorado. Students interested in an internship are paired with companies such as EchoStar to learn all aspects of the business.

A Wellness Fair is an example of such a coalition. Work with local health care professionals and hospitals to host a Wellness Fair on campus. If you hold it on a school day, it will give you an opportunity to provide school tours for community members when they have finished their wellness evaluation.

Join with local emergency and public service agencies to sponsor a community Safe Kid Day. Have safety vehicles and equipment on display, give lessons in cardiopulmonary resuscitation (CPR), hold a bicycle rodeo, give search and rescue demonstrations, and show safety videos. If there is a local canine unit at a state or federal agency, call on its services; demonstrations by narcotics "sniffer" dogs are always popular. Recruit a local business or the PTA to donate a bike and other gifts for a giveaway drawing as an incentive for attendance.

Cooperative Events. Holding joint events in conjunction with another organization or business can bring the entire community together in positive interaction. Workplace Orientation is a program for ninth and tenth graders at Angola High School in Indiana. Students are bused for one hour every day to business classrooms in the community. Another successful school–business event is held in the Spokane Valley in Washington State. Tidyman's Foods, a grocery store chain headquartered in Spokane, partners with Greenacres Junior High School to sponsor a three-day Freshman Business Conference for selected students at a local hotel. Businesses as well as other groups can join with schools to foster meaningful interaction.

Sunnyslope Elementary School and the Phoenix Symphony held a special outdoor spring concert for the local community. Members of the student strings group (stringed instrument players) performed with the symphony in a program that was memorable for all involved. Consider other fine arts groups that might be willing to collaborate with your students, such as opera companies, dancers, artists, poets, vocal performers, and puppeteers. The Northern Lights, a vocal group from the Music Department at North High School in Sheboygan, Wisconsin, presents 30 to 40 concerts a year for community organizations.

In addition, North High athletes serve as outstanding school ambassadors by speaking to students in lower grades about study habits, drug use, and alcohol consumption. These young men and women seem to get this type of message across better than adults.

Benefits. Reverse the usual trend and have your school hold a special carnival or fair or "whatever-a-thon" to raise money for a local charity rather than for a school project. Sponsor a "Clean Up the Community" day for students, staff, and parents to pick up trash and to repair and spruce up joint use areas.

Publications. Bonanza High School in Las Vegas, Nevada, puts all of its school publications— community and athletic newsletters, announcement bulletins, brag sheets, special announcement flyers, various pamphlets and handouts—in the lobby so that any person who walks through the door, day or night, can pick them up. Kent County High School in Worton, Maryland, puts the school newspaper and yearbook in local doctor and dentist offices. Belleville West High School in Belleville, Illinois, has produced a school video that communicates a positive image of excellence to anyone who wishes to view it.

Speakers Bureau. Tap into the knowledge, experience, talents, abilities, and skills of staff members who would be willing to speak to groups and organizations on subjects of community interest in which the staff member is expert.

Don't forget to include yourself in this speakers bureau, but only if you feel comfortable in front of an audience. Most educational leaders have a great deal of platform experience, but if you don't, consider joining Toastmasters or another similar speech improvement organization that will give you the experience and know-how you need. In fact, you might want to survey your staff to determine if they are interested in starting such a group on campus.

Principal Richard Olthoff has compiled a summary of the Major Magic City Campus Teaching-Learning Programs that his school, in Minot, North Dakota, has developed and implemented over the years. It is included at chapter's end. When preparing a speech to give about the school, it is a handy reference guide. When answering questions from the audience, he is able to recall programs that might otherwise be forgotten at that moment. A word to the wise: The best impromptu speeches are those written well in advance.

Foundations. A school foundation generally raises funds to provide scholarships, grants, and incentive awards for students and staff. Alumni are excellent resource people to involve in establishing a foundation to benefit your school. These are most often found at the district level, but there is no inherent reason a foundation could not exist at the building level. At East Burke Middle School in Icard, North Carolina, a tax-exempt, nonprofit, business partners' association, Partners for Progress, has been established.

Holiday Activities. Schools can play an active role in the community during the holidays by holding food and clothing drives, offering the talents of art classes in decorating businesses and storefronts, and supplying musical groups for business or organization functions.

School Facilities. Make your building available for civic theater, basketball leagues, community group meetings, dance recitals, arts fairs, adult night classes, and so on.

Personal Contacts. Network! Get actively involved in leadership positions in the community, join a local service club, serve on the boards of local charities or youth organizations, have breakfast with members of the Chamber of Commerce, keep local legislators informed of your needs. Encourage, by word and example, your staff members to do the same. Don't neglect to continue to cultivate these resources after the initial contact is made.

Customer Service

Another key component to community outreach is customer service. While some of what has been previously mentioned fits in this category, different districts take different approaches to what works.

Here is a snapshot from Mount Vernon City Schools in Illinois.

Horace Mann once said, "The public school is the greatest discovery made by man. . . . Education is best provided in school embracing children of all religious, social and ethnic backgrounds." The public schools have a civic mission to perpetuate community values, beliefs, and customs and to promote the democratic society and American way of life. The employees, students, and schools of District 80 fulfill our civic mission in several ways. The superintendent's appointed term from the governor on the Illinois Commission on Volunteerism and Community Service just recently expired. A concerted effort has been made to instill a sense of responsibility to students and staff to volunteer in our community and to provide community service. This not only allows the district to keep the community informed about what is happening in the schools, but also shows that District 80 is a key player in the community. Several examples of certified and classified staff fulfilling their civic mission follow:

- All administrators belong to a civic or community organization and attend the meetings. (i.e., Rotary, Kiwanis, Chamber of Commerce, United Way, Health Board, Hospital Board, various churches, Minority Affairs and Human Relations Commission, Red Cross Board, YMCA, Cedarhurst Center for the Arts, Boy Scouts).
- The teacher union annually raises funds to send students to summer camps. Last summer, 43 different students were granted "scholarships" to attend camps.
- Each school annually participates in the citywide cleanup day to help beautify the city.
- Groups of students visit nursing homes and businesses during the school year to do band or orchestra performances, paint seasonal scenes on windows, read reports, and do art work.
- Teams of staff members play in golf scramble fundraisers for the United Way, KARE foundation, cancer, and other community causes.
- District 80 staff collects the gate receipts for the annual Cedarhurst Craft Fair, which attracts over 15,000 attendees. Many also volunteer with civic groups in the food court.
- Students and staff help collect funds for the KARE Foundation (Kids At Risk Educationally), and take over 100 students Christmas shopping for clothes.
- The Early Childhood and Middle School staff participate in the community Children's Health Fair.
- The competitive sports program provides entertainment for community members.
- The music department has an annual "Night on Broadway" or theatrical performance to provide entertainment for the community.
- The music department provides numerous concerts for the parents and community.
- Patriotic events to honor 9/11, American veterans, and the history of the Star Spangled Banner have been held.
- Coin drives are held annually to raise money for charitable events.

In addition to individual school employees' commitment to the Mount Vernon community, the district officially encourages community collaborations and community use of the school facilities. One of the beliefs listed in the Strategic Plan for the Mount Vernon City Schools states, "Quality education results from a partnership that is shared among the home, school, and community and that the school should operate as a member of the community." Some examples of formal partnerships that have been created to illustrate this belief follow:

- A Learn and Serve Grant with Casey Middle School and the United Way where agency representatives discuss their mission and Middle School students decide which agency they will collaborate with in service learning projects
- A formal agreement with the YMCA where they use the Primary Center for their after-school day care program. District 80 provides the site, healthy snacks, and use of computer lab, media center, and material free of charge to keep the cost to parents at a minimum.
- A formal agreement with the YMCA and Jefferson County Sports Authority to use the gymnasiums free of charge for evening sports programs
- Formal agreements with community groups to use the District 80 facilities on an as-needed basis free of charge for activities or fundraisers (Red Cross, Rotary, Children's Health Fair, Hospitals)
- The buildings are used for neighborhood watch meetings.
- The buildings are used for community meetings for the County Board and City of Mount Vernon.
- The Central Office is a polling place.
- A Pre-school for All Grant has allowed District 80 to formally collaborate with St. Mary School and Southtown Youth Programs and house our state Pre-K program in their sites.

The best way to garner parent and community support is to involve them with the schools. Schools must find ways to create customer awareness and serve them however they can. Because this is a priority in District 80, we enjoy an excellent relationship and support from local government and community organizations.

SUGGESTED READINGS

Funk, D. L. (1991). Strong education is strong business. *Journal of Educational Public Relations, 14*(2), 18–23.

Guttmann, R. C. (1993). Community relations: Guidepoints to improving and keeping them strong. In J. L. & J. J. Herman (Eds.), *People and education: Vol. 1. The human side of school* (pp. 105–120). Newbury Park, CA: Corwin.

Hopkins, B. J., & Wendel, F. C. *(1997). Creating school-community-business partnerships.* Bloomington, IN: Phi Delta Kappa International.

Lloyd, K., Ramsey, D., & Groennings, S. (1992). *Knowledge revolution for all Americans: Empowering public schools.* Arlington, VA: Knowledge Network for All Americans.

National School Public Relations Association. (1999). *School public relations: Building confidence in education,* Rockville, MD: Author.

Otterbourg, S. D. (1986). *School partnership handbook.* Englewood Cliffs, NJ: Prentice Hall.

Shelton, C. W. (1987). *Doable dozen: A checklist of practical ideas for school business partnerships.* Fairfax, VA: National Community Education Association.

Minot Public School District
Resolution
Education/Business Partnerships

WHEREAS partnerships are an opportunity for education and business to band together and make an important investment in the future of our city, state, and nation, and

WHEREAS education/business partnerships foster working together to integrate technology, new directions of teaching and learning, and structural changes that can bridge educational experiences with work experiences, and

WHEREAS experience confirms that both education and business come out as winners when they collaboratively share their unique skills, competencies, and diverse perspectives to meet common needs, and

WHEREAS education/business partnerships foster the belief that our students' ability to compete in the global information economy is inextricably linked to our success in providing appropriate teaching/learning opportunities, and

WHEREAS education/business partnerships are a key to reaching the shared goals of finding new ways to prepare a workforce for the 21st century, and

WHEREAS education/business partnerships address the educational reform theme of encouraging lifelong learning skills (inquiry, analysis, problem solving, collaborative learning, and decision making), and

WHEREAS education/business partnerships are one of the major themes in both state and national educational reform models,

NOW THEREFORE BE IT RESOLVED that the Minot Public School District Board of Education endorses the following two points: (1) the development of partnership agreements between businesses in Minot and the Minot Public School District; and (2) business use of school district facilities, equipment, and people as an inducement for entering the partnership agreement.

Source: Minot Public School District Board of Education, Minot, ND.

Major Magic City Campus Teaching-Learning Programs

Program	Purpose
Implemented a research-based program entitled "Enhancing Student Communication Skills Across the Curriculum"	Teacher Effectiveness Student Learning
Implemented a research-based program entitled "Enhancing Student Writing Skills Across the Curriculum"	Teacher Effectiveness Student Learning
Implemented a research-based program entitled "Enhancing Student Reading Skills Across the Curriculum"	Teacher Effectiveness Student Learning
Implemented a research-based program entitled "Enhancing Student Speaking Skills Across the Curriculum"	Teacher Effectiveness Student Learning
Implemented a research-based program entitled "Enhancing Student Listening Skills Across the Curriculum"	Teacher Effectiveness Student Learning
Proposed and implemented the school board–approved policy increasing the minimum student load from four to five academic courses and increasing the minimum graduation credits from 19 to 20	Student Learning
Implemented a research-based program entitled "Questions—Discussion Teaching Skills"	Teacher Effectiveness Student Learning
Implemented a research-based program entitled "Enhancing Teacher Questioning Skills"	Teacher Effectiveness Student Learning
Proposed and implemented the school board–approved "MCC Attendance System," following two years of research	Student Learning
Implemented the "NCA Outcomes Accreditation" 3-year cycle process	Student Learning
Implemented a research-based, student teacher program encompassing the following topics: Introduction to MCC, Mastery Learning, Student Teacher Handbook, Lesson Design, Planning and Organization, and Special Services Familiarization	Teacher Effectiveness Student Learning
Implemented the "Outcomes-Based Curriculum Development" process	Teacher Effectiveness Student Learning

Major Magic City Campus Teaching-Learning Programs

Program	Purpose
Implemented a reseach-based program entitled "Enhancing Lesson Design"	Teacher Effectiveness Student Learning
Implemented a computer lab of IBM machines to enhance business student skills	Student Learning
Implemented a research-based program entitled "Teaching-Learning Cycle, Time-on-Task, Classroom Organization Management, Principles of Learning"	Teacher Effectiveness Student Learning
Implemented the "Intercom Silence" policy to safeguard academic time-on-task and create a more positive school climate	Teacher Effectiveness Student Learning
Implemented a research-based program entitled "A Review of Higher Order Questioning"	Teacher Effectiveness Student Learning
Implemented two computer labs: Macintosh lab for English writing classes (to enhance student writing skills) and Apple 2GS lab for general student use	Student Learning
Implemented "Outcomes-Based Education" forums	Teacher Effectiveness
Implemented a research-based program entitled "Enhancing Student Study Skills"	Teacher Effectiveness Student Learning
Implemented a research-based program entitled "Motivation Theory Revisited"	Teacher Effectiveness Student Learning
Implemented a research-based program of "In-Depth Teacher Supervision"	Teacher Effectiveness
Implemented "Educational Reform" forums	Teacher Effectiveness Student Learning
Implemented "Parent/School Partnership" plan	Teacher Effectiveness Student Learning
Implemented "Authentic Achievement" staff development program	Teacher Effectiveness Student Learning
Implemented the "MCC 2000 Committee"	Teacher Effectiveness Student Learning

Source: Magic City Campus High School, Minot, ND.

9

Rallying Support for Public Education

At a time like this, the real failure of education becomes apparent.
Education has failed to educate about education.

—Norman Cousins

When you say "public education," it does not simply refer to "reading, writing, and 'rithmetic." It encompasses a broad expanse of learning opportunities. It doesn't always mean sitting in a classroom behind a desk. It doesn't always mean what is learned from a textbook. Public education has morphed many times over in the last century. No longer are students walking through the front door of a school mainly intent on academic success leading to a 4-year university degree. There are students who want to enter the work force and be trained in fields as diverse as fire science or culinary arts, auto mechanics or video game design and computer programming.

It is critical that educators champion their programs and make the public aware of the diversity of today's public education. More and more, with competition from private schools and pressure from the business community, public education is in the spotlight to produce members of a workforce who are skilled for today's "global economy," whether that be students who continue to higher education, or those who become a part of today's labor workforce.

One example of business–education partnerships and programs that are found throughout the nation, but are not necessarily as well publicized as basic academics, are career and vocational-technical courses and avenues for students to find their niche in society.

CAREER AND VOCATIONAL-TECHNICAL EDUCATION

Some of the nation's greatest chefs, artisans, craftspersons, trades people, and technical engineers, too numerous to name them all, have come out of Career and Technical Education programs in public schools across the country.

The Web site of the Vermont Career Development Center in Bennington (www.svcdc .org) captures the essence of why public schools offer career and technical education:

> In the past, people thought of vocational education as a pathway for people who would enter a narrowly defined workforce directly after high school graduation. Today, technical education is so much more. As our economy and our communities grow increasingly complex, the need of our students to have diverse, rich educational experiences is increasing. Technical education is uniquely prepared to provide students with this richness by connecting them with state-of-the-art resources and experts from a variety of [professional] fields.

> . . . . In technical education, students learn by doing. They develop and work through projects, gathering related theoretical understanding and academic skills along the way. They come to see the skills that they are developing as critical to the success of their endeavors. . . . Further, in modern technical education, there is great emphasis placed on the acquisition of transferable skills, as our students will go on to a great variety of continuing education and career experiences. Technical education, at its best, teaches success, encourages lifelong learning, and provides opportunities to go beyond one's academic training.

What is true for Vermont is true for essentially every other state in the nation. Strong career and (vocational) technical education (CTE) programs combine applied knowledge with strong academic rigor. There are no better ways to connect schools with communities than through building partnerships between employers and applicable CTE programs, and by showcasing the achievements of outstanding CTE students.

This is true for rural, urban, large, and small public school communities. For example, the Barre Regional Vocational-Technical Center in Barre, Vermont (a town with a population of 9,529 people; www.vita-learn.org/brvc/index.html), offers the following:

Automotive Technology

CAD/Engineering Design

Construction

Cosmetology

Culinary Arts

Graphic Arts

Health Careers

Heating, Ventilation, and AC

Human Services

Network Management

Pre-technical Exploratory

Programming

Pre-technical Foundational Combination (Arts, Information Technology, Engineering)

The Southwest Vermont Career Development Center (mentioned above) in Bennington (http://www.svcdc.org) is a regional technical center (in some states, these are called "Joint Technological Education Districts") that serves high school and adult students from the southwestern region of Vermont and adjacent New York and Massachusetts. It offers courses in

Automotive Technology

Business Administration Information Support

Business Financial Support Occupations

Business Management

CAD/Engineering Design

Communications Technology

Construction

Emergency and Fire Management

Forestry and Natural Resources

Health Careers

Horticulture

Human Services

Information Support and Maintenance

Law Enforcement

Legal Services

Marketing Education

Network Management

Performing Arts

Precision Machining Trades

Pre-technical Exploratory

Pre-technical Foundational Agriculture, Food, and Natural Resources

Pre-technical Foundational Architecture and Construction

Pre-technical Foundational Arts, A/V Technology, and Communications

Pre-technical Foundational Business Management and Administration

Pre-technical Foundational Combination (Construction; Engineering)

Pre-technical Foundational Combination (Health, Human Services)

Pre-technical Foundational Combination (Engineering, Manufacturing)

Pre-technical Foundational Information Technology

Pre-technical Foundational Law, Public Safety, and Security

Video Production

And let's not forget to mention careers in the health care field such as nursing, radiology, and lab technology, to name a few.

In some states, schools are joining together in coalitions to give a voice to public education through advertisements, by seeking out people's stories, highlighting what is really being done to educate students, and bringing a "face" to learning. An example from Arizona follows.

HOW STATE COALITION CAMPAIGNS ARE RAISING SUPPORT FOR PUBLIC EDUCATION

The discussion of the need for public education support has long been "preached to the choir" in education circles. In the past few years, many state business and education leaders have taken the initiative by forming "coalitions" of education, business, and community leaders, and by creating public information campaigns to rally support for public education funding and the institution itself.

Time and again, national surveys continue to show that less than half of the responders think we are doing a good job of educating our children, while more than 80 percent say that they support their local schools and believe that *they* are doing a good job of educating their children. A 2007 Phi Delta Kappa/Gallup poll showed that the public generally assigns high marks to its public schools, but gives the highest marks to those schools nearest to them. To be sure, a majority of those surveyed already have children in school, and thus, their information is gained firsthand. So how do we change the perceptions of the general public about public education?

One such effort is the "AZ Public Schools Making a Difference Every Day" campaign, which was publicly launched in March of 2008 after more than 3 years of strategic planning. In this effort, a group of Arizona's leading education organizations banded together with the business community to change the statewide dialogue about public education in Arizona. The aim of this joint nonpolitical, nonpartisan campaign was to shine a light on what's right with the state's public schools.

"All the groups came together because we felt the discussion about public education in Arizona was out of balance," said Panfilo H. Contreras, executive director of the Arizona School Boards Association, one of the organizations involved." The campaign's simple premise is this: Arizonans know and appreciate the good things happening at their children's schools or the school in their neighborhood, but many don't realize that Arizona public schools throughout the state are making a difference every day, positively impacting the lives of the state's 1.12 million public school children.

Participating organizations in the Arizona Public Schools Making a Difference Every Day campaign are the Arizona Education Association (AEA), Arizona Interscholastic

Association (AIA), Arizona PTA, Arizona Rural Schools Association (ARSA), Arizona School Administrators (ASA), Arizona Schools Boards Association (ASBA), Association of Arizona School Business Officials (AASBO), and the Greater Phoenix Education Management Council (GPEMC).

"Certainly there are issues that demand, and are getting our serious attention, but we felt we needed to stand up and level the playing field by honoring the good things that are happening in public schools throughout the state, too," Contreras added.

Stories about the good things happening in Arizona's public schools are waiting to be discovered on the campaign's Web site, www.azschoolsmakeadifference.org. Visitors can view good news stories about schools around the state, with a focus on "vast appeal." They can also sign up to receive a weekly e-mail newsletter highlighting the most recent good news stories.

Anyone from parents to teachers to public school supporters can submit good news stories about public education to the campaign by e-mail at info@azschoolsmakeadifference .org or by using the form on the campaign Web site at www.azschoolsmakeadifference .org/tellstory.asp. Following this is a one-page summary of the Arizona program.

www.azschoolsmakeadifference.org

Great things are happening in Arizona's public schools each and every day. Our teachers, students, and schools are making a difference today and for the future. Stay tuned to this site for inspiring stories and evidence of **Arizona's Public Schools Making a Difference Every Day!**

- Sign up to receive e-mail briefs and newsletters.
- Read more about the AZ Public Schools Making a Difference Every Day campaign.

Who We Are

You likely know that great things are happening in your child's school or your neighborhood school. But you may not be aware of the inspiring things happening in public schools throughout Arizona. In the coming months, we will showcase the success stories in public education across the state. And it all starts with you. Send us your stories and join the effort to demonstrate that **Arizona Public Schools Make a Difference Every Day!**

The AZ Public Schools Making a Difference Every Day campaign is a nonpolitical and nonpartisan effort brought to you in part by the Arizona School Boards Association (ASBA), the Arizona Interscholastic Association (AIA), the Arizona Rural Schools Association (ARSA), the Arizona School Administrators (ASA), the Association of Arizona School Business Officials (AASBO) the Greater Phoenix Education Management Council (GPEMC), and the Arizona Education Association (AEA).

Tell Us
Your Story...

Thank you for telling us how Arizona public schools are making a difference. Please explain the story you would like to share briefly in the space below [a Web form is presented at this point]. We will follow up with you in the near future for more information. Thank you!

Source: Arizona Public Schools.

10

Strengthening and Showcasing Instruction

"Showcasing instruction is empowering."

An often-missed opportunity for positive school promotion is showcasing what goes on in the classroom. This can be of an instructional nature or a celebration of accomplishments.

In the instructional sense, teachers are using strategies that were unheard of when parents of present-day students and the majority of community members were in school. Because citizens of our school districts tend to relate the total school experience to what they experienced as students, it is important they understand that profound changes have occurred in the way instruction is now delivered. The community also needs to have confidence that the way lessons are taught and the way knowledge is applied in this new century will meet future needs of students and the community as a whole. The only way complete confidence will occur is if the citizens see for themselves how these new instructional strategies are being used.

COOPERATIVE LEARNING

Cooperative instruction is not a new concept in education. In the United States, this was widely used in the one-room school. For instruction in a variety of subjects and at different levels to take place, students in the one-room school had to help each other. The current application of this concept takes its cues from business and from higher-level thinking skills.

Business and industry leaders have long been advocating teamwork. One hears of learning teams, discussion groups, forums, and focus groups in the workplace. Think of the effect of applying some of these strategies at "Back-to-School" nights and PTA meetings. Getting parents to talk with each other in a small group in a directed way and then reporting back to the whole group can show parents the depth of thinking and interaction skills that are encouraged in each child. Showing parents how a challenging concept can be taught and understood fully through a cooperative strategy can be very powerful. And using a "value-line" strategy, where parents stand in a spot on the line that reflects their thinking on an issue, points out one way valuing and respecting the opinions of others can be taught.

Cooperative strategies can also be an effective means of communication for school staff. Think of the empowerment of people when an administrator has certified and noncertified staff working together to solve problems and to enhance the learning opportunities of students. The value of using a team approach was brought out earlier in this book, but why not demonstrate the effectiveness and efficiency of cooperative instructional strategies with staff members? A rural district in Montana did this, and the administrators discovered points of view that people had been hesitant to state individually.

Robert Patton from Icard, North Carolina, and Thomas Blair from Sauk Rapids, Minnesota, are two principals who strongly believe in the benefits of having staff attend state and national education conferences. When teachers return to school, they bring with them new ideas, knowledge of the latest advances in educational technology, a renewed spirit from being with other enthusiastic educators, and increased professionalism, all of which enhance the learning environment and the credibility of their school. Cathy Watson, principal of Ravenel Elementary School in Seneca, South Carolina, encourages her teachers to share with peers and to invite visitors from other schools to come in and benefit from the knowledge and experience of Ravenel's outstanding teachers.

AUTHENTIC INSTRUCTION

"Why do I have to learn this? I'll never use this stuff." For too long, educators replied to this query with, "Because it's on the test . . . because it's the lesson for today . . . because it's required." The advent of authentic instruction in recent years is slowly eliminating that initial question from the mouths of our students. Parents and the community at large aren't privy to the day-to-day approaches to learning that are taking place in classrooms across the country. Only when a deadline must be met or a particular type of research must be completed do parents usually get involved with the instructional approach to learning (i.e., homework). Showcasing to parents and the community that what is being taught in the classroom is meaningful to students because it represents the real world provides a proactive statement that schools are doing the job they are supposed to do.

How can authentic instruction be showcased to the public? Do not overlook the traditional means of disseminating information: newsletters, radio, television, newspaper articles, PTA/PTO meetings, and the Internet. A fifth-grade class in a rural area made an award-winning video of a reenactment of a Civil War battle. The video was developed as a documentary, and students researched and explained orally and in writing the historical significance of the battle from the viewpoints of different people who were affected at that time. A television station 50 miles away came to tape the reenactment. Students and teachers were interviewed as to how this project was meaningful to them.

Newspapers are still a viable means to showcase authentic instruction. In urban areas, if the main newspaper will not devote space to an individual school, often the zone editions of metro dailies or regional weeklies are happy to do so. This occurred to a sixth-grade English teacher in a middle school in North Carolina. Ballad writing, a poetic form originating in medieval times to relate a sad story, was part of a thematic unit on the medieval period. After reading examples of ballads from that period and more recent ballads popular in the United States, students had the option of writing a ballad pertaining to knights and damsels or using a current topic from the news. The majority of students were more highly affected by current news stories and chose contemporary topics for their ballads. The regional weekly published on the front page not only this fact but also examples of the students' work.

Authentic instruction, making learning real, can also be celebrated using the Internet. School districts have access to a variety of high-quality software that allows for the creation of "community access" sites on a district's Web sites. One school district used such a site to showcase the skills that students had learned in their physics class. The PowerPoint presentation showed students actively engaged inside and outside the classroom designing a new baseball field for their school that took into consideration terrain configurations, lighting heights, fence requirements, and possible velocity and direction of balls hit.

Unless examples of authentic instruction are revealed to parents and the community, they will continue to think that instruction hasn't changed much from when they were in school.

PROBLEM-BASED LEARNING

Across the country, more schools, at all levels of instruction, are utilizing problem-based learning, service learning, project-based learning, and case studies as instructional avenues. What may seem commonplace to educators is a new way of doing things to the community at large. Parents of students are often involved in some way due to the active research required outside the classroom. The school benefits, and bond issues are easier to pass when parents and community are informed about the reasoning behind choosing different paths for instruction. Problem-based and project-based learning, service learning, and case studies not only provide authentic learning opportunities and higher-order, critical thinking situations for students, but the community also benefits from all these minds at work discovering how to make their life better.

Showcasing students doing something positive for themselves and the community and featuring teachers who are implementing these instructional strategies validates the strengths of the school, its programs, and the people making this happen.

INTERDISCIPLINARY UNITS

Interdisciplinary units have been a regular feature of elementary classrooms for years. Recently, such units are coming into their own more and more at the middle and high school levels as well. Brain research is telling us that patterns, connected learning, and application result in knowledge that is retained and usable for the long term. To create a meaningful, authentic, and content-rich interdisciplinary unit requires a lot of effort on the part of staff members and students. The community should be informed of these rich educational experiences. Two middle school teams in Missouri did just that, and their respective communities responded with accolades to the school and faculty.

The eighth-grade team at Holden Middle School in Missouri developed an interdisciplinary unit on the Oregon Trail. This was not just a series of "forced" activities; rather, it was meaningful instruction that incorporated state standards in science, math, language arts, social studies, art, music, and physical education. The 3-week unit was celebrated at the end with a special evening event for families and the community. Fifteen booths were set up with students demonstrating what they learned about life on the Oregon Trail—from cooking and geometric quilt patterns to societal configurations and geographical challenges. A program consisting of a drama in song, dance, and narrative told the story of the pioneers and their hardships and victories. At the end of the program, both students and teachers were astounded by the standing ovation and congratulations bestowed on them from the community.

To increase the students' knowledge of their community, the Dreamweavers sixth-grade team at Sedalia Middle School, also in Missouri, did a 3-month unit that focused on the students' own town. The unit, titled "Windows on Sedalia," was started in the language arts class with students choosing some aspect of Sedalia to pursue in their showcase portfolio. Once again, as at Holden, all instruction followed the benchmarks of the state standards in the various disciplines. One of the culminating activities involved a guided tour of the historical places in downtown Sedalia. To the surprise of all the adults involved, each student added tremendous background information during the tour. This event, as well as the exhibition of students' portfolios, resulted in a large, front-page article and photo in the local newspaper. Parents, relatives, and community members came and were fascinated by the quality of work that the students exhibited in their research and creative expression.

In both of these situations, celebrating the instruction that took place in the classroom affirmed and enhanced the respect the parents and the community had for the educational opportunities afforded the students.

INCORPORATING TECHNOLOGY

Schools everywhere are scrambling to integrate technology into the classroom. Once sufficient hardware is bought for the classroom and teachers are trained to use the software purchased to further instruction and assist with record keeping, integrating that technology into instructional strategies is of prime importance. Both the software used for student presentations or compositions as well as access to the Internet open the door to the world for students, no matter the size of the school, no matter how urban or rural the community.

How can parents know firsthand about the technological advances in the classroom? Again, through the availability of commercial software designed specifically for school use, various frameworks for online instruction can also be utilized via a school district's Web site to create platforms for online instruction. These online classroom can be accessed from school, home, office, libraries, or community centers, thus allowing adults to see firsthand how technology can help deliver instruction. Opening computer labs for family nights, with students demonstrating technological knowledge, is what some schools are doing. L'Ouverture Computer Technology Magnet School, the K–5 Wichita, Kansas, school mentioned in Chapter 2, holds a monthly Internet training session that is open to the community and staffed by third, fourth, and fifth graders.

Exciting learning is taking place in the educational setting when technology and the resources of the Internet are infused into the learning process. Parents and the community at large are eager for educators to provide the technological opportunities so necessary for students who are preparing to enter the world of work.

Although the World Wide Web is an amazing research tool, parents and educators are also concerned that students will be able to access material that is inappropriate. A curious student may try to search for inappropriate sites, or the naive surfer may stumble upon them. To protect against this, it has become commonplace for schools to put safety measures in place. They have filters installed on their computer systems or use site-blocking software to limit where students can "go" while working on a computer. One doesn't have to search very hard to find offensive material on the Internet. A chat room for conversations between strangers who share a common interest might not seem dangerous, but there is no way to know if the 14-year-old boy sending electronic mail to your 14-year-old daughter is really who he claims to be.

The best way for parents and educators to relieve their anxiety about the danger of Internet use by children is to know what they are doing online, who they are talking with, and what they are seeing. (See the i-SAFE resource at end of chapter, or view their Web site at www.isafe.org.)

MULTIPLE INTELLIGENCES

With increased knowledge of multiple intelligences, instruction in the classroom can look and feel considerably different today. As more and more teachers are revising instructional strategies to accommodate the different ways that students learn, parents need to be informed about the pedagogical reasoning behind these strategies. Without this background knowledge, parents will be confused when their child comes home with an assignment that combines different subject areas into one project.

To help parents understand why students were learning math in a different way, the principal and teachers of an elementary school in Pennsylvania organized a "Mathematics Multiple Intelligence Fair." Students and teachers from various grade levels highlighted one of the multiple intelligences in each booth and showed how math could be taught from different perspectives. The evening was well received by parents who acknowledged having a better understanding of their children's math homework assignments.

An award-winning program in a middle school in Phoenix, Arizona, on immigration evokes every one of the multiple intelligences: verbal/linguistic, body/kinesthetic, musical, visual/spatial, naturalistic, logical/mathematical, intrapersonal, and interpersonal. Community volunteers who assist with the program are repeatedly astounded by the depth of understanding, knowledge, and appreciation of our country's heritage that students obtain from this approach to instruction.

ASSESSMENT

Along with the infusion of multiple intelligences in the classroom is the role of assessment. Parents understand true-false, multiple-choice, or essay tests, "But what is this thing called a rubric?" they're asking. "What is going to happen to my child's portfolio, and how does this portfolio relate to my child's grade?"

As more and more state tests are focusing on performance-based assessment, the tools for measurement are changing in the classroom. To have access to "the final test" before instruction begins is contrary to the way parents were instructed years ago. Explaining to parents that the rubric provides the guide for students to achieve at the highest level, without guessing at what quality work means, creates fewer inquiry and complaint calls to the administrative office. Several schools feature a parent information component in their "Back-to-School" night. A quick explanation and demonstration of the use of rubrics and portfolios dispels the fear of the unknown "test."

Education is like a teeter-totter: it is either going up or going down. There is no stationary middle ground. As schools seek to improve what is happening in the classroom, change will occur. Statistics showing school improvement are always important factors to the public, but showcasing the actual instructional strategies does much for the school. Featuring these strategies validates the strength of the school and its programs, the teaching staff—both certified and noncertified—and the achievement of the students. The result is that parents and the community will be more supportive personally and financially when they have an understanding of what is actually taking place in the classroom.

SUGGESTED READINGS

Armstrong, T. (1994). *Multiple intelligences in the classroom.* Alexandria, VA: Association for Supervision and Curriculum Development.

Gardner, H. (1983). *Frames of mind: The theory of multiple intelligences.* New York: Basic Books.

Gardner, H. (1993). *Multiple intelligences: The theory in practice.* New York: Basic Books.

Garger, S., & Guild, P. B. (1998). *Marching to different drummers* (2nd ed.). Alexandria, VA: Association for Supervision and Curriculum Development.

Kagan, M., Kagan, S., & Robertson, L. (1995). *Cooperative learning structures for class building.* San Clemente, CA: Kagan Cooperative Learning.

Lazear, D. (1994). *Multiple approaches to assessment.* Tucson, AZ: Zephyr Press.

Mezich, J. (1993). *Using portfolios to strengthen student assessment in the language arts.* Bellevue, WA: Bureau of Education and Research.

Napolitano, J. (1999, August 26). Online world a danger for kids. *The Arizona Republic,* p. B7.

Sylwester, R. (1995). *A celebration of neurons: An educator's guide to the human brain.* Alexandria, VA: Association for Supervision and Curriculum Development.

i-SAFE Recognizes Hawaii's Commitment to e-Safety Education: 66,000 Hawaii Students Are Trained to Be Safe and Responsible Online (www.isafe.org)

According to an online news source (www.marketwire.com), i-SAFE is a nonprofit organization whose mission is to educate and empower students, parents, seniors, and community members on Internet safety. i-SAFE helps parents and students to recognize and avoid dangerous, destructive, or unlawful online behavior, and to respond appropriately. K–12 curriculum and community outreach programs for students, parents, law enforcement, and community leaders with e-Safety curriculum have been taught in 271 public and private Hawaiian schools, with a favorable impact on the online lives of students all across the Islands.

Over half of the students completing online surveys after i-SAFE lessons reported they would be less likely to meet an Internet acquaintance face-to-face. Nearly three-quarters (71%) agreed that they will now be more careful about where they go and what they'll do on the Internet. Fifty-two percent of students are now more careful about sharing personal information online. When it comes to music piracy, i-SAFE lessons have changed the minds of 52% of potential illegal "downloaders."

"We began our relationship with Hawaii educators five years ago," says Teri Schroeder, i-SAFE CEO and Program Director. "At that time, it took incredible foresight for them to see the need for e-Safety education; however, their leadership in raising awareness and educating their students has brought about these phenomenal results. I applaud our Hawaii partners at the Hawaii Department of Education (HDOE), Kamehameha schools, and the Hawaii Catholic School Department (HCSD)."

Interestingly, both houses of Hawaii's legislature are currently considering e-Safety bills (H.B. 2899 and S.B. 2106) requiring the HDOE to implement a comprehensive 3-year pilot project on Oahu that includes classroom-based education and community awareness—much like the i-SAFE program, which is already being implemented at no charge. "The pending legislation in regards to Internet safety just validates that the Hawaii Department of Education, in partnership with i-SAFE for five years already, is ahead of the curve in proactively ensuring the safety of our keiki [kids] online," says Stephen Kow, HDOE Educational Specialist for Educational Technology. "It's great when Hawaii shows the rest of our nation how things ought to be done right."

The i-SAFE Program (www.isafe.org) has now reached 4.2 million students across the United States. It blends classroom lessons with community outreach designed to foster active participation of students and their instructors, and empowers students to reach out to their peers through mentoring activities, as well as to their parents and community members. Strategic partnerships help i-SAFE raise awareness beyond the classroom in Hawaii.

Source: www.isafe.org. Teri Schroeder, CEO.

PART III

Acknowledging Change

11

Crisis Management

There can't be a crisis next week. My schedule is already full.

—Henry Kissinger

S ociety has always considered its schools to be safe havens for children, places where they can be free to learn in a protected environment. Unfortunately, the reality in today's world is that schools are no longer sacrosanct. They are no longer islands of safety within a community in turmoil, no longer immune from violence and the desperate acts of society. What a sad commentary it is that to be designated a "safe school" today, the school must have metal detectors, surveillance cameras, security guards, perimeter fences, "screamer boxes," and/or bar-coded photo IDs.

An educator must be prepared on a moment's notice to deal with a crisis situation involving the school. Most districts define a crisis as any situation that threatens the safety and well-being of the school, students, or staff, either physically or emotionally. Crises may range from natural disasters to bomb threats, from school violence to a gas leak, but all crises have one thing in common: They will likely involve the assistance of health or law enforcement agencies and, as a result, will attract the attention of the media. Thus, there is the need to be able to communicate with your constituencies in a timely and appropriate manner.

The U.S. Department of Education's Office of Safe and Drug-Free Schools produced the January 2007 *Practical Information on Crisis Planning: A Guide for Schools and Communities,* which offers this view of how a crisis could be interpreted: "Crises range in scope and intensity from incidents that directly or indirectly affect a single student to ones that impact the entire community." A crisis situation can happen before, during, or after school, and on or off school campuses. The definition of a crisis varies with the unique needs, resources and assets of a school and community. Staff and students may be severely affected by an incident in another city or state. The events at Columbine High

School, and those of September 11, 2001, for example, left the entire nation feeling vulnerable.

Judy Wall, Communications Director for Federal Way (Washington) School District, explains the challenge this way:

A crisis can impact a single building or the entire district depending on the nature of the crisis. The most important consideration when dealing with a crisis is the health, safety, and welfare of the students and staff—and prompt notification of parents. You have a greater chance of managing a crisis situation if you have a district-level plan, and an individual building plan that is based on the district plan.

Building-level crises can take many different forms. Some typical examples follow:

- Accident or injury on campus
- Transportation accident
- Arrests on campus
- Fire
- Bomb threat
- Individual medical emergency
- Weapons incident
- Suicide
- Child napping
- Assault
- Gang violence
- Racial or civic violence
- Chemical spill
- Power outage
- Food poisoning
- Vandalism
- Gas leak
- Robbery
- Drug or alcohol incident or overdose
- Sexual molestation (on or off campus)
- Armed intruder
- Hostage situation
- Natural disaster (earthquake, flood, hurricane)
- Shooting
- Unfounded rumor
- Infectious disease outbreak

The first order of business in any crisis is to take control of the situation and protect the welfare of students and staff. The next step is to communicate the situation to parents and the community. A well-executed crisis plan will make the job of communicating easier and could even contribute to a swifter, smoother resolution of the crisis.

Credibility is your most valuable communication asset in a crisis. You must be prepared to deal openly and honestly with the community and the media to explain the situation and the steps being taken to remedy it. By being above board with reporters and providing them with as many facts as possible, you add to your credibility and get your side of the story out. This is where a solid, day-to-day communication effort with the media pays off.

The choices schools face in crisis management are (a) to be caught without a plan, in which case you are forced to communicate in a defensive mode, or (b) to be prepared in advance by having a crisis plan in place that allows you to communicate proactively.

ORGANIZING A CRISIS PLANNING COMMITTEE

The most successful crisis plans are those that are developed through the participation of the people who will actually be involved in carrying them out. Although crisis plans contain the same basic elements, each plan will vary slightly due to the nature of the crisis, the unique needs of the school site, the makeup of the staff, and the resources available in the local community. The stronger your team's ownership of the plan, the more effective it will be in meeting the specific needs of your school.

Your district probably has a general crisis plan, and you will need to follow the guidelines set down there. However, that does not preclude the need for a building-level plan. You will need to tailor the district's standard format to your specific school site needs.

Nedda Shafir, Public Information Officer at Cave Creek Unified School District in Arizona, and a 30-year education veteran nationally recognized for crisis management planning and execution, notes in her article, "Recognizing the Critical Need for Emergency Notification in Today's Rapidly Changing World," that preplanning is a critical step. (See "Making Sure the Message Gets Through" at end of chapter.)

According to the Centers for Disease Control and Prevention (CDC) in Atlanta, Georgia (www.cdc.gov), "crisis and emergency risk communication is the attempt to provide information that allows an individual, stakeholders, or an entire community to make the best possible decisions about their well-being during a crisis." Often, this communication must be done within nearly impossible time constraints and requires public acceptance of the imperfect nature of the available choices for action. Successful crisis and emergency risk communication is achieved through the skillful use of risk communication theory and techniques. (See end of section for further online resources.)

Kevin Teale, Communications Director of the Iowa Department of Health, believes that "a lot of folks seem to think a crisis isn't going to happen to them and when it does happen, they don't have any plans in place to deal with it. So it's important that you put a plan together, even if the likelihood of something happening to you seems rather remote. If you have something put down on paper, when the unexpected happens, you can go to that plan and react appropriately."

The CDC recommends spending the most time on the pre-event phase, which is in many ways the most important phase. The research is clear: every day spent preparing is an investment in successful communication later on.

During preplanning, your organization needs to consider several factors to ensure it has the ability to communicate effectively during a crisis:

- What functions are you going to need in an emergency?
- What resources are available?
- Who are your partners and stakeholders?

Begin by forming a committee of staff members. Ask for volunteers first so that you will be working with people who have a genuine interest. This committee's charge is to study potential crisis situations that might take place at your school and to develop an action plan. It is important that your planning committee be representative of key staff positions such as nurses, teachers, counselors, secretaries, and custodians. Be sure to invite a representative from the district office, as the district will play a critical support role in any crisis situation that your school has. At the high school level, you may also wish to include one or more student representatives. The more people you can involve in studying and talking about possible crises and their impact on the school, the more prepared you will be when one actually hits.

Before you begin to write a plan, the crisis planning committee needs to analyze your school's crisis needs and gather supporting data and reference material.

- Brainstorm possible crisis situations. You should cover the gamut from a broken leg to food poisoning to a tornado or hurricane.
- Conduct an open-ended survey of staff members to determine their areas of concern. They may identify an emerging crisis or something the planning team overlooked. The survey may also indicate the most likely crisis situations to occur on your campus by the number of people concerned with a specific issue.
- Collect sample crisis plans from other schools and districts and from local businesses as well. Institutions such as hospitals often have plans that are excellent references for schools.
- Assemble all pertinent information about your campus. Include accurate maps of the building and extended campus; staff lists; special programs housed on site (disabled, preschool, self-contained, detention, and so on); building blueprints; and location of fire hydrants, power boxes, circuit breakers, gas and plumbing controls, telephones, and anything else that might be needed in a crisis. The Emergency Management Kit Checklist at the end of this chapter will help you assemble items needed for an emergency.
- Invite local emergency service agencies (fire and police departments, city or county disaster relief agencies, and the like) to speak to your team or perhaps even to the entire staff. Ultimately, your plan will be more effective if everyone's role is clearly understood.
- Gather historical data about crisis incidents that have occurred on your campus in the past and at other schools in your district. What happened? How was it handled? What was the outcome?
- Review state laws and regulations and district policies that apply to your emergency plan.
- Conduct a security audit of your campus. You may want to invite community agency representatives to assist with this effort.
- Once you have determined the various crisis situations your plan will address, divide your team into subcommittees and assign specific crisis topics to each (e.g., bomb threats, fire, natural disasters, accidents and medical emergencies, suicide, and so on).
- Decide on an appropriate format that each subcommittee will follow so that the action plan is presented in a consistent manner. A standardized three-ring notebook is the most flexible format because it allows you to update and make changes easily.
- Note: It is fine to have your Crisis Plan saved on your computer or network, but a power outage or computer crash renders such resources essentially useless. Always have a printed copy available for everyone in your school or district who would need it in a possible emergency. Many school districts have opted to create a "crisis communications kit."

Some related resources include the following:

- The American Schools Safety Crisis Response Kit, http://www.americanschoolsafety .com/crisis-response-kit.html
- The Emergency Preparedness Service, http://www.emprep.com

- Helpful Hints for School Emergency Management: Emergency "Go-Kits," a downloadable document, http://rems.ed.gov/views/documents/HH_GoKits.pdf

The following are further resources available on the Internet:

- "Crisis Management: An Opportunity Instead of a Threat," by Marie Yossava, http://www.bizcommunity.com/Article/196/18/2558.html
- Bernstein Crisis Management, Inc., http://www.bernsteincrisismanagement .com/nl/crisismgr000515.html

DEVELOPING A CRISIS PLAN

It is interesting to note that the Chinese symbol for crisis incorporates the symbols for danger and opportunity. A good crisis plan allows you to deal with the danger and provides you with the opportunity to communicate the situation effectively.

Your crisis plan should contain at least the following 10 sections:

1. List of crisis team members, their phone numbers, and the chain of command. The principal is normally designated as the person in charge. A chain of command is important in case the principal or other team members are absent or incapacitated. The next name down the chain can then immediately assume responsibility for managing the crisis.

2. Description of procedures for the person in charge.

3. Identification of school area that can be used as a crisis center. It should have access to a phone or radio and be the area where crisis team members can be found.

4. When an extreme situation warrants that the school be sealed from outsiders, it is often referred to as a "lockdown." Some schools prefer not to be subtle but rather will sound a siren, blow a whistle, or simply announce over the intercom, "This is a lockdown!" Two sample lockdown information sheets are provided at the end of the chapter. One shows the responsibilities and procedures for staff to follow. The other is a "what-to-do list" should a lockdown occur; it is in the form of a flyer that can be posted on campus.

5. Crisis assignments and descriptions of procedures for all personnel. Each crisis team member should be assigned specific tasks. Classroom teachers are responsible for their students and should remain with their class throughout the duration of the crisis. All other staff members should have specific assignments. Those not needed for duties such as handling phones, securing files, and taking care of the injured should be assigned to classrooms to assist teachers in caring for students. People are less likely to panic and will function more efficiently if they have a clear, advance understanding of the role they will play during a crisis situation. An example of a crisis assignment and checklist is provided at the end of the chapter.

6. Evacuation procedures. You will need several different evacuation plans in anticipation of possible hindrances that may block escape routes. You should also determine, in advance, an alternate off-campus site within walking distance to which students and staff can evacuate. This might be another school or a church or business that has agreed to offer shelter in an emergency. Evacuation by bus should also be addressed.

7. Communication procedures. This should include designating a spokesperson to communicate with parents, relatives of staff, the community, and the news media. Vallivue High School in Caldwell, Idaho, has organized a telephone calling tree to

keep staff members informed of what is happening. To update its staff, Georgetown High School in Texas uses a computer calling system that can telephone all staff with a recorded message. A sample Emergency Calling Tree is included at chapter's end.

8. Situation-specific procedures. The list of possible crisis situations listed earlier in this chapter and the list generated by your crisis planning committee will help you identify areas that need to be addressed in detail. Procedures will vary for each type of incident, but simple, clear guidelines will assist you through almost any crisis.

9. Training procedures and evaluation drills. Make sure that every staff member has a copy of his or her responsibilities and is completely familiar with the crisis plan. Conduct a training session at the start of each year and hold several refreshers during the year, much as you would do fire drills. Provide each member of the crisis team with a complete crisis procedure manual.

10. Provision for updating crisis plan at regular intervals.

SCHOOL CRISIS TEAM

The school crisis team should consist of people on your campus capable of assuming responsibility for managing components of the crisis, as well as other individuals as needed. These are the people who will initially be responsible for (a) responding to the immediate concerns, and (b) notifying the appropriate people. These first two action steps must occur rapidly and in as organized and controlled a manner as possible. You will want people who are able to remain cool and rational during the crisis, as well as people with specific skills that would be of benefit to those involved. Suggested school site crisis team members include the following:

- Principal
- Assistant principal
- Secretary
- Lead foreman or custodian
- School nurse
- Counselor or social worker
- Staff members not assigned to a homeroom (for example, P. E. teacher, librarian, art or music teacher)
- School District Public Information Officer

The principal should serve as the head of the team and be designated the person in charge. Included at the end of this chapter is a sheet, Crisis Procedures for Person in Charge, on which to list important telephone numbers that will be needed in an emergency. Keep those numbers close at hand.

MANAGING THE CRISIS

No matter what crisis occurs, the following action steps must be addressed for a successful resolution:

- Respond to the event by first meeting the needs of those involved and then containing the crisis.
- Notify the appropriate agencies and officials.
- Manage the crisis by following planned procedures until it is resolved.
- Communicate the situation to internal and external groups.

Once immediate needs have been addressed and the crisis is contained as much as possible, the crisis team should assemble to assess the facts of the situation. First, quickly determine how much time you have to plan your response, for you know that the media will soon be at your door demanding an explanation. Collect as much information as possible about what happened and assign someone to keep a written record. Make sure your team members all have the same facts about the crisis. In a crisis of long duration, the crisis team should meet at regular intervals for updates so that everyone continues to have the same information. (See "Guidelines for Handling Specific Varieties of Bad News" and "Threat Call Checklist" at end of chapter.)

COMMUNICATING THE SITUATION

Based on the information collected by the crisis team, determine what information is restricted and what your primary message should be. Analyze the possible outcomes and reactions of the public. Develop a response to the crisis and begin communicating. Don't shortchange yourself for time in reviewing and analyzing the situation, but it is important to get to this step as quickly as possible. All communication should be based on facts and should convey your concern about individual needs.

At this point, your spokesperson should take over. If you have a communications specialist for your district, let him or her handle the situation. If not, a previously selected designee from the crisis team should act as spokesperson. This should be someone other than the principal or person in charge because that person's attention should be focused on the well-being of students and staff and on managing and resolving the crisis itself.

Don't ever assume the media won't find out a crisis is underway! Media attention is just a cell phone photo, text message, or BlackBerry e-mail away! Often, a news reporter or TV camera crew will beat emergency crews to the scene. In certain circumstances, instead of waiting for the media to show up, you can better support your efforts by contacting them directly with the facts of the situation.

Instruct staff that all information is to be disseminated through the crisis spokesperson. No one should make any statement to the media without clearing it through the spokesperson or the person in charge. Any staff member approached by a member of the media should direct that individual to the spokesperson.

Following are some guidelines that the crisis spokesperson should keep in mind when dealing with the media:

- Your first priority is resolving the crisis.
- You have the right to set the ground rules in a crisis.
- Don't let reporters bully you into saying more than you should, or into speculating about "what-ifs."
- Stay calm and stick to your facts.
- Don't give more information than is necessary; it will only cloud the issue.
- Stay with your primary message—and keep repeating it.
- Don't attempt to conceal information that is a matter of public record.
- Be honest and explain the situation, along with the positive actions you have taken to resolve it.
- Don't be rude or discourteous to reporters or anyone else, even if they are rude to you.
- Never give a "no comment" reply.

If the spokesperson is unable to answer the questions asked, here are several optional answers that may be of help:

- "No information is available at this time, but I'll get back to you as soon as I know something."
- "I cannot release that information at this time, but I will be happy to discuss it with you when I can."
- "That is under investigation at the moment, so I'm not free to discuss it further."
- "I will try and get that information for you. I will call you back later when I have the facts at hand."
- "We will release that information just as soon as we have been cleared to do so."

Again, understand this is an age of instant communication; there may well be informal messages going out over which you have no control. Communicate by e-mail or phone message system to your key communicators list—parents, staff, community members—with your accurate messages and information.

Communicating With Staff and Parents

Keep school staff updated as often as feasible during the crisis. Your crisis plan should provide several alternative methods of communication, and the situation will determine the best one to use. Ken Cazier, principal at Star Valley Junior High School in Afton, Wyoming, makes absolutely sure that a copy of the school's crisis plan is readily available in each teacher's classroom and in the main office.

The media will be able to assist you in communicating with parents during the crisis. As mentioned in previous chapters, get to know your local media—establish good relationships with your beat reporters—before you "have to." They will help you get the accurate information out to the parents/community. If you have enough telephone lines, you may be able to set up a crisis hotline for parents to call, or perhaps school personnel can staff a phone bank. However, always keep one or two lines clear for emergency use.

Following the crisis, it is important that you communicate with parents as soon as possible, preferably the day of the incident. This is most easily accomplished by sending a letter home with students. You will have to move swiftly to prepare the letter and get it copied and distributed by the time students leave. The letter should briefly describe what happened and then focus on the steps you have taken to reestablish a safe environment and address the situation. Emphasize your concern and your commitment to attending to the health and safety of your students. Guidelines for Emergency Notification and Sample Letters to Students/Parents are included at chapter's end.

AFTER THE CRISIS

Once the crisis is resolved and you have communicated with the appropriate constituencies, you still have work to do. Be available to answer questions and address the concerns of staff and parents following the crisis. At the earliest possible time, bring the crisis team together for a debriefing. Review your written log of events and study the effectiveness of your responses. Note the things that could have been handled differently and revise your crisis plan as needed.

Determine what support services are needed to deal with the aftermath. Arrange for counseling and psychological services for as long as necessary. When appropriate, create support groups for students, families, and staff. Be as proactive as possible in meeting the personal needs of everyone involved in the crisis in order to bring the campus back to normal.

Project future consequences of the crisis. What ramifications will it have for your school next week, at graduation, and on the anniversary of the event? What student behavior problems might occur in response? Anticipate the possible postcrisis responses by students and community members, and prepare a plan to address them proactively.

It is important to remember that no two crises are the same and that no plan, no matter how well prepared, will address every aspect of the situation. Plans provide guidelines by which to operate, as well as give you a starting point for taking control of the crisis situation. A crisis may not be avoidable, but it can be managed if the right decisions are made and the right actions are taken early.

But, of course, many crises are avoidable. A crisis may be prevented by taking the time to identify potential problem situations and correcting them. Very few crises are surprises to everybody in the organization. The simple act of closing the gate on a construction area, removing broken playground equipment, or really listening to a student's concerns could mean the difference between an addressable situation and a full-blown crisis. As the old saying cautions, "An ounce of prevention is worth a pound of cure." Consider implementing a violence prevention program in your school. One such successful program used in Arkansas, Maryland, and Virginia is called, "Youth Links = Safe Schools." It was started by Betty Bumpers, the founder and president of Peace Links, a Washington, D.C.–based international women's organization seeking alternatives to global violence. Youth Links is based on the assumption that students are not necessarily the problem when there is violence in a school, and that young people have within them the seeds of solutions. The Youth Links violence prevention program, called "Listen-Up," gathers together students, school officials, and community leaders in a listening forum to bring about positive change. In school after school, when changes suggested by the students have been made, that assumption has been right on target.

A PRIVATE CRISIS

There is another type of crisis that educators face. It is not big or noisy and the media won't come. But it is a real problem and a situation that sometimes only a teacher is in a position to notice: child abuse. This is always a delicate situation, and often, the child will initially deny being abused. Teachers and administrators dread making a false accusation, but if a child is in danger, it is better to err on the side of protecting the child—and you may well be the child's only protector. Schools and districts must report any abuse, according to the law. It may be uncomfortable, but it is not optional. It is advisable to communicate with district legal counsel in any situation involving students and adults, and to follow board policy. Included at the end of the chapter are several guidelines for obtaining necessary information prior to reporting your concern to the authorities.

REFERENCES AND SUGGESTED READINGS

Baldwin, H. A. (1990). *Planning for disaster: A guide for school administrators.* Bloomington, IN: Phi Delta Kappa Educational Foundation.

Dill, V. S. (1997). *A peaceable school.* Bloomington, IN: Phi Delta Kappa International.

Lukaszewski, J. E. (1987). Anatomy of a crisis response. *Public Relations Journal, 43*(1), 45–47.

National School Public Relations Association. (1986). *School public relations: The complete book.* Rockville, MD: Author.

Peters, T., & Waterman, R. H., Jr. (1982). *In search of excellence: Lessons from America's best-run companies.* New York: Warner Books.

Shafir, N. (2006, June). Recognizing the critical need for emergency notification in today's rapidly changing world. *School Business Affairs, 72*(6), 6–10.

U.S. Department of Education, Office of Safe and Drug-Free Schools. (2007, January). *Practical information on crisis planning: A guide for schools and communities.* Washington, DC: Author.

Walling, D. R. (Ed.). (1997). *Hot buttons.* Bloomington, IN: Phi Delta Kappa International.

MAKING SURE THE MESSAGE GETS THROUGH—CREATING AN EFFECTIVE MESSAGE

Even though the focus is usually on getting the message out, of equal importance is making sure the message gets through. Warnings are effective only if they are accurate and result in appropriate action. The human components of effective warning systems have been described at length in the social and behavioral sciences literature since the 1950s and more recently in the public health and epidemiological literature (e.g., Mileti & Sorensen, 1990).

Although both disciplines have used empirical research, the approaches are different. The former addresses the conceptualization of the social-psychological process from the time of first warning to the time of response. The latter addresses health-related outcomes—such as deaths, injuries, or illnesses in the population exposed to the hazardous event, and identifies and quantifies the predictors of the risks for those outcomes.

The warning response process is categorized into the following components:

1. Perceiving the warning (hear, see, feel).

2. Understanding the warning.

3. Believing that the warning is real and that the contents are accurate.

4. Confirming the warning from other sources or people.

5. Personalizing the warning.

6. Deciding on a course of action.

7. Acting on that decision.

Further, a distinction is made between sender and receiver characteristics for each of the components (Nigg, 1995).
Sender characteristics focus on

1. The nature of the warning messages (content and style).

2. The channels through which the messages are given (type and number).

3. The frequency by which the messages are broadcast (number and pattern).

4. The persons or organizations receiving the message (officialness, credibility, and familiarity).

Receiver characteristics are primarily

1. Environmental (cues, proximity).

2. Social (network, resources, role, culture, activity).

3. Psychological (knowledge, cognition, experience).

4. Physiological (disabilities).

Principal conclusions that influence the effectiveness of warnings are [as follows]:

1. Warnings are most effective when delivered to the people at risk. If people not at risk are warned, they will tend to ignore future warnings. Thus, if tornado or flash flood warnings, for example, are issued for a county or larger region, but only a small percentage of the people who receive the warning are ultimately affected, most people conclude that such warnings are not likely to affect them.

2. If warnings that are not followed by the anticipated event are inconvenient, people are likely to disable the warning device. For example, if you are awakened in the middle of the night to be warned of several events that do not ultimately affect you, you are likely to disable the warning device.

3. Appropriate response to warning is most likely to occur when people have been educated about the hazard and have developed a plan of action well before the warning (Liu et al., 1996).

4. There is a window of opportunity to capture peoples' attention and encourage appropriate action. Studies of responses to tornado warnings, for example, found that those who sought shelter did so within five minutes of first becoming aware of the tornado warnings (Balluz et al., 1997).

5. A variety of warning devices need to be used in order to reach people according to what activity they are engaged in.

6. Warnings must be issued in ways that are understood by the many different people within our diverse society.

7. The probabilistic nature of warnings, particularly for natural disasters, needs to be made clear.

The content and style of a warning message are important. An effective message should

1. Be brief (typically less than two minutes and preferably less than one minute).
2. Present discrete ideas in an organized fashion.
3. Use non-technical language.
4. Use appropriate text/graphics (if necessary) geared for the affected hazard community and general population.
5. Provide official basis for the hazardous event message (e.g., NWS Doppler Radar indicates tornado, police report of chemical accident, etc.).
6. Provide most important information first, including any standardized headlines.
7. Describe the areas affected and time (e.g., "pathcasting" for moving events such as weather systems, volcanic debris or element dispersal, etc.).
8. Provide level of uncertainty or probability of occurrence.
9. Provide a brief call-to-action statement for appropriate public response (e.g., safety instructions for protection of life and property, any evacuation instructions, shelter or other care facilities, etc.).
10. Describe where more detailed follow-up information can be found (e.g. Web site, Safety Hotline, etc.).

Effective warnings allow people to take actions that save lives, reduce damage, reduce human suffering, and speed recovery. Rapid reporting of what is happening during a disaster can be very effective in helping people reduce damage and improve response. Scientists and emergency managers are developing the capabilities to warn for more hazards and to increase warning accuracy, but ways of delivering these warnings in a timely manner and to only those people at risk need significant improvement. (The Working Group on Natural Disaster Information Systems, Subcommittee on Natural Disaster Reduction National Science and Technology Council Committee on Environment and Natural Resources, November 2000; located on the FEMA web site at www.fema.gov.)

Source: Reprinted with permission of the Association of School Business Officials International.

Guidelines for Handling Specific Varieties of Bad News

Bus Accident
— Establish a reporting procedure from the scene with all drivers and transportation officials.
— Be prepared to ask the questions to obtain the information you need. Consider having a standardized form on bus accidents next to your phone.
— Have one central location where reporters can call with specific questions.
— Don't draw hasty conclusions that students are not hurt. They can fool you before they're checked out.
— Consider sending a letter from the school to parents of children on the bus.
— Urge quick action against the bus driver if he/she is at fault. This preserves public confidence in your transportation system.

Arrest of School Employees on Criminal Charges
— Don't react until you have the facts.
— Confirm that the person is indeed a school employee. (You'll be surprised how often they aren't.)
— Get pertinent details from official sources such as police or courts or the school personnel department. Those details may include the nature of the charges, if they occurred while the employee was on duty, the type of job held with the schools, length of employment.
— Find out what, if any, disciplinary action will be taken, and why. Examples: Suspension with or without pay, placement on administrative not classroom duty, transfer, removal.
— Be aggressive getting this word to the public. It's painful but usually will die quickly if you don't stall.

"Spot News" Such as Fires, Injuries
— If it's during school hours, make sure there is a central number or contact for information.
— If it's after school hours, a spokesperson should go to the scene because reporters will not know how to reach you.
— Immediate questions to answer: injuries, damage, causes, can school continue to operate normally.
— Be aggressive with follow-up because you will need media assistance to get word to parents.
— When "the smoke clears" in the aftermath [of a crisis] like a school fire, thank the media for their help.

Source: "Media-Relations: Crisis to Non-Crisis," Myra J. Joines, Media and Public Relations Consultant, Matthews, NC.

Threat Call Checklist

Billings Public Schools
Billings, Montana

DON'T HANG UP THE PHONE
(USE ANOTHER PHONE TO CALL POLICE)

RECORD THE EXACT LANGUAGE OF THE THREAT _____

_____

_____

ASK:

WHEN IS THE BOMB SET FOR? _____

WHERE IS IT? _____

WHAT KIND OF BOMB? _____

WHY ARE YOU DOING THIS? _____

WHO ARE YOU? _____

VOICE ON THE PHONE: _____ _____

MAN _____WOMAN _____ CHILD _____AGE _____

INTOXICATED _____ SPEECH IMPEDIMENT _____

ACCENT _____ OTHER _____

BACKGROUND NOISE:

MUSIC _____ CHILDREN _____ AIRPLANE _____ ALK _____

TRAFFIC _____ OTHER _____ TYPING _____ MACHINES _____

DON'T HANG UP PHONE.

USE ANOTHER PHONE TO CALL POLICE.

POLICE PHONE NUMBER: 911.

PERSON RECEIVING CALL: IMMEDIATELY NOTIFY AUTHORITIES AND GIVE ABOVE INFORMATION, THEN NOTIFY PERSON IN CHARGE.

DATE _____ TIME OF CALL _____ RECEIVED BY _____

Source: Billings School District, Billings, MT.

Greenwood School District 50

P.O. Box 248
Greenwood, South Carolina 29648
803/223–4348

Checklist
Emergency Management Kit

The following items are listed as a basis for creating and maintaining Emergency Management Kits in every school in Greenwood School District 50. The list includes specific items that may save time in implementing a school plan to manage emergencies. Additional items may be needed by individual schools and those should be added to the emergency kit, as well.

- ❑ 20 legal pads (8.5 x 11 and 4 x 5)
- ❑ 20 ballpoint pens (not felt-tip and not pencils)
- ❑ 20 magic markers
- ❑ 500 plain white peel-off stickers (to be used to identify injured students or adults at the emergency site)
- ❑ list of telephone numbers for the district office, local law enforcement agencies, emergency medical services, fire department, and other agencies that may need to know of a school crisis
- ❑ list of telephone numbers for the portable telephones used by district staff
- ❑ list of computer, BBS, and fax lines at the district office
- ❑ list of beeper numbers for district staff
- ❑ One local telephone directory
- ❑ One current staff directory for district
- ❑ floor plan that shows the location of all exits, all telephones and telephone wall jacks, computer locations, and all other devices that may be useful in communication during an emergency
- ❑ One fully charged battery-operated bullhorn
- ❑ local street and zone maps
- ❑ for all off-campus trips, a map showing the route to be traveled to and from the off-campus destination
- ❑ for all off-campus trips, a list of students and adults on each bus or vehicle should be left at the school; students and adults must ride the same bus both ways
- ❑ list of assigned roles for school personnel and district personnel
- ❑ recent lists of students who ride buses, given by bus/route number
- ❑ summary of information that can be made public during an emergency; include Freedom of Information summary, district policy, and others
- ❑ list of professional and community contacts for organizing a "crisis care team" of counselors, ministers, and others

Source: Greenwood School District, Greenwood, SC.

Cascade Middle School Memo
(Lockdown Procedures)

DATE: January 6, 1999

TO: Staff and Site Council

FROM: Katie Legace Safety Committee Members

ADVISORS—PLEASE DISCUSS AND EXPLAIN THE RULES TO YOUR ADVISEES BEFORE THE OCTOBER 29 DRILL!!!

1. CALL POLICE AND THEN CALL THE DISTRICT OFFICES, depending on the severity of the situation.

2. INFORM SCHOOL VIA INTERCOM: Blow a whistle into intercom to alert students and staff to stop and listen to instructions.

3. COMMUNICATION WITH STAFF: Over the intercom, an administrator will say: "A lockdown is now in progress. Students stay in your classes. Students in the halls, go to the nearest classroom." Give as much relevant information about the intrusion as possible.

4. TEACHERS' RESPONSIBILITIES:
   Lock all doors and windows.
   Close blinds.
   Instruct students to stay away from windows and doors.
   No students allowed in the halls.
   No adults in the halls except to help students to safety or assigned by administration.
   Turn on Internet communication immediately.
   Wait for further instructions from administration.
   Teachers are to do an immediate roll call to insure they know where every student is located.
   Teachers e-mail names of extra students to "Cascade Staff."

5. TEACHERS ON PREP PERIOD:
   Go to nearest room with a phone and call the front office to get further instructions.

6. STUDENTS' RESPONSIBILITIES:
   Listen and follow staff instructions without argument.
   Move away from doors and windows.
   Do not leave the classroom.
   Remain quiet and as calm as possible.
   Wait for further instructions from staff.

7. HEAD ENGINEER RESPONSIBILITIES:
   Lock all doors leading into the building.

8. Notify transportation to re-route transfer buses

9. An explanatory note will be prepared for parents, as time permits.

Source: Safety Committee, Cascade Middle School, Bend, OR.

Note: This revised plan is a combination of the district guidelines for building lockdown procedures and input from the CMS Safety Committee, CMS Staff, and the CMS Site Council Members.

Lockdown (Flyer)

SIGNAL (One or more of the following):

- One continuous or pulsating bell.
- Announcement—This is a "Lockdown."
- Notification by note or in person to teacher by office.

SECURE:

IN-CLASSROOM RESPONSE:

- Students are seated, silent, and away from windows. Teachers check halls for passing students (direct students to immediately enter your room).
- Lock all doors (Do not open for anyone).
- Pull shade or place a piece of paper over door window.
- Wait for further announcement or all clear.

OUT-OF-CLASS RESPONSE:

Lunch—Passing Periods—Nutrition Break

- Go directly to the nearest lockable room.
- Follow In-Classroom Response.

PHYSICAL EDUCATION CLASSES/RECESS:

- When classes are on the field, students and teachers move to the nearest safe location. When classes are in the building, report to the locker rooms/classroom and follow In-Classroom Response.

NO STUDENT, TEACHER, OR STAFF MEMBER IS TO CONFRONT
AN INTRUDER DURING A LOCKDOWN CONDITION.

- If an intruder is observed, report by phone or intercom the location and description.

STAND-BY:

- Listen for further announcements.
- Listen for all clear.

SIGNAL FOR ALL CLEAR:

- Vocal announcement.

Physical plant design may not accommodate all of the above recommendations. Building adaptation may be necessary.

Source: Cascade Middle School, Bend, OR.

Task Check-Off List for Crisis Intervention

1. Principal is notified of crisis and verifies information. Back-up personnel: Assistant Principals Herb Genung and Denise Birdwell

2. Principal calls Head Counselor Kathy Lahlum. Back-up personnel: Social Worker Julie Edmonson

3. Principal calls both Assistant Principals

PHONE TREE IS ACTIVATED

4. Principal notifies District Office, disperses necessary information to the students, and handles any media inquiry.

CRISIS TEAM MEETS AND REVIEWS/ASSIGNS TASKS

Principal:	— Spokesperson for school, media, and family contact
Asst. Principals:	— Creation and dispersal of memo to staff to provide information, suggestions for handling, and location of crisis support teams
Head Counselor:	— Assign counselor teams to concern and caring sites (conference room, rooms 121 and 124) — Work with staff/students to identify close friend of victim — Coordinate counseling efforts — Contact middle schools; advise crisis/assess need for supportive participation
Social Worker:	— Visit classrooms of the affected student to disseminate information
Counselors:	— Provide support and counseling for students struggling with the event or personal matters magnified by the event — Take attendance; provide a follow-up list/verify absence — Identify students at "Life-Risk" to be seen individually for assessment and/or necessary parental contact by letter — Contact by letter parents of students seen in group to provide support information
Registrar:	— If necessary, remove name from computer/effects from locker, notify feeder middle school

DEBRIEF AND EVALUATE

Source: Paradise Valley High School, Phoenix, AZ.

Glenview Middle School
Emergency Calling Tree for School Closing

1999–2000
(revised 12/3/99)

Sean Wagemans informs:		Dave Stewart	555–2869
		Adrienne Curry	555–4459
Dave Stewart informs:		Spence Coleman	555–4090
		Larry Lewis	555–7448
		Janice Long	555–9921 (unlisted)
		Casey Gwynne	555–1687
		Brenda Thomas	555–4660

Adrienne Curry informs:		Spence Coleman informs:	
Caroline Case	555–4459	Phil Alexander	555–8700
John David	555–2382	Steve Douglas	555–4435
Charlotte Lauren	555–4090	Nathan Dylan	555–7878
Pete Long	555–7448	Gloria Furman	555–2845
Kristen McKenzie	555–9921	Stan Harrison	555–9649
Greg Washington	555–1687	Susan Diane Ross	555–3451

Larry Lewis informs:		Janice Long informs:	
Jim Calle	555–4560	Karen Bryan	555–6785
Gail Law	555–2238	Carolyn Clinton	555–3467
Julie Leah	555–4582	Jim Nelson	555–6834
Sharon Meyer	555–7488	Alison Piper	555–9862
Sandy Steffens	555–9121	Mark Sorsby	555–2644
Howie Stella	555–2997	Maybel Young	555–4401

Casey Gwynne informs:		Brenda Thomas informs:	
Steve James	555–4459	Roz Bolger	555–8700
Kathy Chowaniec	555–2382	Bert Emmett	555–4435
Matt Englehorn	555–4090	Patricia Hensley	555–7878
Gary Lisciarelli	555–7448	Laura McDonald	555–2845
Carlos Rodriguez	555–9921	Wilson Peyton	555–9649
Andy Ruocco	555–1687	Julie Scott	555–3451

Source: Corporate Education Consulting, Inc., Phoenix, AZ.

Crisis Procedures for
Person in Charge

Step 1   Call 911. If no response, immediately call:

Fire _____

Ambulance _____

Paramedics _____

Police/Sheriff _____

Step 2   Label all injured persons with their names. Appoint staff member liaison to accompany injured persons.

Step 3   Notify Superintendent and Community Information Director of crisis situation.

Superintendent   Office: _____

Home: _____

_____

Community Information   Office: _____

Home: _____

Step 4   If the Superintendent is not available, contact one of the Crisis Team members in the order listed below:

Office   Home

_____   _____

Step 5   Appoint staff member(s) to monitor phones.

Step 6   Implement appropriate crisis procedure.

Source: Karen Kleinz, Washington Elementary School District, Phoenix, AZ.

Guidelines for Emergency Notification

Letters sent home should include the following:

1. The crisis; a statement of tragedy. Give basic facts.

2. Information on utilization of the school crisis team, district crisis team, and community resources.

3. Description of emotional signals child may exhibit.

4. Statement that parents should be sensitive and listen to child's reaction.

5. Name and phone number of contact person who can help with referral process to agencies, etc.

6. Name of person at school or district to contact re: questions and concerns.

7. If parent meeting needs to be set up, include date and time.

Source: Monique Soria, Public Relations Director, Sunnyside Unified School District, Tucson, AZ.

Suicide Postvention Plan

Steps to be followed after a student suicide:

1. Upon being made aware of a possible student suicide or other extreme tragedy involving students or staff, you must notify the building principal.

2. The principal will convene the school "crisis team."

3. The principal, with the aid of the crisis team, will verify the information concerning the death. All suicides are referred to as "deaths." A log will be kept of all communications.

4. The principal will contact the superintendent of schools and other schools that may have affected siblings.

5. When deemed appropriate, the crisis team will prepare a formal statement based on verified facts, which is presented to the faculty with the intention that they read the prepared statement to students at a later time. The principal will contact parents in order to inform them that the school is aware of the student death, and a statement is to be read to students informing them of the death. It is the responsibility of the principal to contain the story and to protect the privacy of the family. NOTE: Some staff members may feel uncomfortable discussing a suicide with students. Respect their feelings and provide alternative opportunities for students.

6. The crisis team will notify all staff of a faculty meeting to be scheduled at the earliest possible time. If the death occurs on a weekend or evening, a phone chain will be utilized to inform the staff of a faculty meeting prior to school starting the next day.

7. The principal will inform staff of the student death and give each faculty member a copy of a prepared statement to read to all students at a designated time. All staff, including supportive staff, will be instructed to share no information with students other than the prepared statement, and efforts must be made to ensure that school functions in a normal manner.

8. All media inquiries will be directed to the building principal, and media access to student body or staff will be denied. The building principal will be the sole spokesperson regarding the tragedy.

9. The counselors will provide a designated area for severely affected students to express their feelings of confusion and grief in a safe, supportive environment. Community agency personnel may also be used in this environment.

10. In addition to reading a prepared statement to students, staff will be instructed to refer troubled students to designated crisis centers. Students who were exceptionally close to the deceased will be monitored and possible contact made through the crisis team to their parents.

11. Arrangements will be made for team members to meet with the classes of the deceased to allow for an awareness of the grief process and the discussion of student feelings.

12. The principal will designate two persons from the crisis team to inspect the student's locker and to make the contents available to the police. Teachers will return all student personal items to the principal. Do not destroy any personal materials of the student. Upon clearance from authorities, all student materials will be returned to the parents.

13. A post-staffing will be held at the end of the first day to review the day's activities and to do appropriate planning for the next two days.

14. The student name will be removed from the student roll and records finalized.

15. After an appropriate amount of time, the principal and a member of the crisis team will visit the family of the deceased student.

16. The principal will encourage the parents to have the funeral as late in the day as possible. Although school will continue to operate, all students wishing to go to the funeral will be excused (with parental permission).

17. By approximately the third day, the designated crisis center will be closed and teachers should refer to individual counselors any students who are profoundly affected by the student's death.

18. Have a closure meeting of crisis team members upon resolution of the crisis to assess appropriate procedures and decide if adjustments need to be made in the process.

19. Suicide is not a heroic act, and therefore it should not be glorified or eulogized in any manner.

Source: Magic City Campus High School, Minot, ND.

Sample Letter to Parents
(on Occasion of Death/Accident)

Date

Dear Parents:

This letter is to inform you of an unfortunate death/accident that is having a deep effect on the students and staff at our school. [Details here.]

Members of the school and district crisis teams have been working with our students and staff members today. The teams will also be available at a parent meeting tonight in the library at 7:00 PM. They will address concerns, answer questions, and assist you with support in dealing with your own and your child's grieving process.

We hope you will be able to attend. Please feel free to bring your children.

Sincerely,

Principal

Source: Monique Soria, Public Relations Director, Sunnyside Unified School District, Tucson, AZ.

Sample Letter to Students
(on Occasion of Suicide of Friend or Classmate)

Date

Dear [Name of Student]:

[Name of student]'s suicide on Thursday, May 4, touched all of us at [Name of school] High School. [His/Her] death had a personal meaning for each of us and each of us responded to [his/her] death differently. There are no right or wrong emotions, but certainly many have been affected and changed by the experience.

Our lives are always diminished by the loss of someone close to us. When suicide has been chosen as the means to end one's life, we must acknowledge that, at that moment, our friend saw no alternative to resolving deep emotional pain. This student chose a permanent solution to feelings and problems that are transitory in life's journey. [He/She] chose death rather than allowing [himself/herself] the time to heal. [He/She] reached toward death instead of the help and friendship available.

Many of you may experience moments of depression. Having "down" days is not unusual at any age. But when these feelings continue and you find yourself (1) feeling tired all the time; (2) withdrawing from people and things that used to interest you; (3) allowing grades and attendance to slip; (4) getting upset and angry over little things; or (5) feeling lonely, hopeless, and resigned, please seek help from any of the people or agencies on the attached list [provide list of resources]. You may have a friend you are worried about who is very depressed. Please encourage that person to get help. It is important also that you let an adult know [a teacher, counselor, nurse, etc.]. You are not betraying a friendship or confidence when you seek help—you may be saving a life.

I am always available if you feel you need to discuss this with someone.

Sincerely,

[Principal or Counselor or Teacher]

Source: School public relations official (now retired), Sunnyside Unified School District, Tucson, AZ.

Paradise Valley High School
Child Abuse Reporting Procedures

The following directions are quoted directly from the *Multidisciplinary Protocol for the Investigation of Child Abuse*.

School personnel are only required to obtain enough information to complete the Child Abuse/Neglect School Report Form. Unnecessary questioning or interviewing of the child victim may contaminate the investigation and create additional trauma for the child; therefore it should be avoided. The coordinator is responsible for obtaining information necessary to make the report. This information may come directly from the child or a third party. Children should not be re-questioned once the information has been disclosed regardless of which staff member received the initial disclosure. In all cases, a copy of the reporting form shall be sent to CPS within 72 hours.

a. Child as a self-reporter
   1. When it appears that a child is disclosing information about possible abuse, the person receiving such information shall listen and ask no leading questions. When possible, a quiet, private place should be provided to facilitate the conversation and document the child's statements.
   2. The person receiving the report should listen openly and speak in a positive tone at the child's level. The child should be treated with respect and support.
   3. School personnel should not make any promises to the child which cannot be guaranteed. For example, do not tell the child "this does not have to be reported to authorities," "you won't have to testify," "no one will go to jail," etc.
   4. If the child does not spontaneously provide the information about the abuse, the following questions should be asked:
      (a) What happened?
      (b) Who did it?
      (c) Where were you when it happened?
      (d) When did it happen?

THESE ARE THE ONLY QUESTIONS TO ASK!!!!

Source: Judi Willis, Public Relations Officer, Paradise Valley Unified School District, Phoenix, AZ.

12

Data Gathering

Road Map for Accomplishments

"If you don't know where you want to go, any road will get you there."

Before you and your team can decide where you need to go, you first need to know where you are. As an educator, you are quite familiar with the methodology of pre- and posttesting students to assess their mastery of skills. Yet, when it comes to the programs educators are responsible for leading, all too often, plans are based on assumptions.

It is a common aspect of human nature that most people deal more frequently with what they feel rather than what they know. However, you can't plan effective school communications and marketing programs based simply on your own gut feelings. If you are to achieve solid goals and objectives, then you need solid data as a foundation from which to work. You will not be successful in building public confidence in education and in your school until you have a clear understanding of what the public knows and expects of your school. As discussed in Chapters 1 and 2, a successful strategic planning process requires an ongoing inflow of information.

There are a number of ways to gather data as well as a number of different methods for extracting it. For example, you might begin by conducting a resource survey to help you measure the expertise available among your staff and community. This identification of available resources may determine to what extent you can implement your plan. You might wish to begin with a single-topic assessment, one that determines sentiment on one particular issue such as year-round schooling, AIDS education, changes in the length of the school day, graduation requirements, or flexible scheduling. This can be invaluable in helping you plot a course of action for issues likely to evoke strong emotions.

A more elaborate project is a climate survey, designed to provide information on how the overall environment of your school is perceived. Because climate is a determining factor in what a school is and what it can potentially become, this is the best place to begin if you're serious about a continuing process of strategic planning.

Regardless of the topic focus for data gathering, it is important that it provide accurate information on which to base subsequent plans so that you do not waste time, effort, and resources on unimportant issues. Your results will help your team determine areas of strength and weakness, as well as what skills and resources are needed to reach your goals. A side benefit is that by asking people for input, you've piqued their interest and possibly initiated their involvement and support for your school.

There are five cardinal rules for conducting school surveys:

1. Don't survey if you aren't willing to accept and report the responses.

2. Don't ask for suggestions unless you are willing to take action based on the responses.

3. Don't ask questions that imply promises that are impossible to keep.

4. Don't conduct research for research's sake.

5. Do translate survey results into targeted messages (and use the preferred medium of the target audience to deliver these messages).

Many schools use the NASSP Comprehensive Assessment of School Environments or other prepared surveys available for purchase. You can study the annual Gallup polls on education, published by Phi Delta Kappa in the *Kappan,* to get ideas. If you happen on a survey from another school or district that fits your needs, ask permission to use or adapt it for your purposes.

There are six assessments at the end of this chapter that will give you an idea of what other schools have done in this area and will help you to get started:

1. Desert Foothills Report Card

2. L'Anse Creuse Middle School North Parent Survey

3. Mountain View School Parent Survey

4. Magic City Campus Parent Needs Assessment Survey

5. The Middle School Concept (Evaluation)

6. Marion County Public Schools Parent Survey

If you live in or near a fairly large city or town and you are starting from scratch, there are several resources that could be helpful. Check nearby community colleges or universities for possible assistance from statistics or marketing classes. Mid- to large-size businesses may have research or public affairs departments that could help you or do the work for you. Political party organizations are also good sources of published handbooks on public opinion survey techniques. Businesses or political organizations can also refer you to survey companies with whom they work—a contact that might yield pro bono assistance for your project.

TYPES OF DATA GATHERING

Questionnaires. The most common assessment form used by schools is the written questionnaire. Because it is generally distributed to a targeted group (for example, to all staff or all parents), with no provisions for a guaranteed return, it will not provide a statistically valid sample, but it will give you a pretty good feel for what people are thinking. Any questionnaire designed for a mail-in response should always be accompanied by a stamped, self-addressed envelope. This will greatly increase your response level.

The Ninilchik, Alaska, Elementary/High School publishes its survey in the newspaper, in anticipation of a wider variety of people will seeing it (and in hope that they will respond). Johnston Senior High in Iowa asks parents to fill out the survey during spring parent–teacher conferences. Some schools substantially improve their return by offering incentive rewards to the class that comes closest to returning 100% of the surveys.

However, to gather information that is statistically accurate, you need to conduct your survey using random sampling. The most valid way to do this is to hire a firm that specializes in this type of activity or, using your business partnership contacts, seek pro bono assistance from a professional survey or marketing firm. If this is not feasible, consider conducting a random sampling survey by using volunteers. This will furnish a reasonably high level of validity, certainly enough to help you take the pulse of your community. Principal Susan Van Zant at Meadowbrook Middle School in Poway, California, has found the organized random survey to be very effective.

Phone Polls. Conducting a poll by telephone works well for short surveys. You will need to train your volunteers in calling techniques, and it is best to use a random sample to identify whom to call from your target audience, such as calling every seventh name in the listing.

Both questionnaires and phone polls, although relatively simple to implement, require some specific planning and involve at least a rudimentary knowledge of polling and sampling techniques. Potential sources of assistance, as well as published material, are referenced later in this chapter.

Focus Groups. A focus group consists of 10 to 12 members of your target audience who represent the various ethnic, racial, age, economic, and philosophical ranges of your school community. The purpose of the focus group is to find out what feelings are present within that representative group, not the extent to which others hold the same feelings. The group is led through a series of discussion questions by a trained leader. The leader encourages everyone to participate but does not give any personal opinions. It is the leader's job to record responses and ask probing questions that generate discussion among the group. (See Guidelines for Running a Focus Group at chapter's end.)

Focus groups can have a variety of configurations. Thomas Blair at Sauk Rapids High School in Minnesota has used "coffee meetings," site councils, and principals' nights. At Sunnyslope Elementary School in Port Orchard, Washington, John Richardson uses the school's community relations team.

Opinion Maker Interviews. Interviewing opinion makers can be very helpful for gaining insight into what influential citizens and opinion leaders think about your school. These should be one-on-one interviews, conducted in a casual atmosphere that allows for two-way communication.

Communication Audit. For a complete, accurate, unbiased assessment, a public relations professional can conduct an audit of your total communications system. This audit would evaluate the scope and effectiveness of every means you now use: staff meetings, newsletters, bulletins, parent conferences, radio spots—in short, everything. However, this takes time and money. If your district has a school public relations professional on the central office staff, enlist that person's assistance. (See Chapter 2 of this book for more about the National School Public Relations Association [NSPRA] Communications Audit).

E-Mail. Several schools are now taking advantage of gathering data using Web site and e-mail. Although the Internet may not be in every home, its use is increasing at such a rate that one cannot overlook this resource. Asking respondents to fill out a template or submit answers to questions via e-mail is a fast and simple way to gather, analyze, and compile the data. Posting results by means of a link on the school Web page can be an economical way to publish the data.

Assessment by Walking Around (ABWA). A good way to get a "snapshot" of your school on a given day is to do what Principal David A. Kergaard of Kent County High School in Worton, Maryland, did—take time to "visit" your school. Kergaard left the campus, then came back as a visitor and looked at his school through new eyes. He looked to see if the building and grounds were well maintained and whether signs were welcoming and easily visible. Was the office staff friendly and the lobby area inviting? Were the classrooms clean and students on task? Did the staff and students appear happy and enthusiastic? Kergaard points out that "it's the little things that make big impressions on the public—so don't overlook them."

Participation and Personal Observation. For an unscientific but commonsense approach to assessing how others feel about the school, ask yourself these questions: Are the students enthusiastic? Is attendance at a high level? Are disciplinary referrals from the staff at a low level? Do students show pride in their surroundings by using receptacles for litter and picking up after themselves? How easy is it to find faculty volunteers to sponsor non-required activities? Do parents chaperone student dances? Are the phone calls received from parents and patrons mostly positive or negative? Do bond issues/overrides/levies usually pass?

Student Surveys. If you want to get a fresh assessment of your school, you might follow the example of Guernsey Sunrise High School in Wyoming and Murray High School in Kentucky by sending a follow-up survey to recent graduates. If you can sort through the chaff, you'll get a good idea of how your school looks to an insider. In a simplified form, this survey could even be effective with elementary or junior high/middle school graduates.

The Rumor Mill. Although you don't want to lend credibility to rumors and speed them along the local grapevine, you should at least be aware of what is being said, because rumors often can serve as early warning signals that either something is "up" or it has been miscommunicated. It is not wise to act on the basis of rumor, but it may be worth investigating to determine the source.

IDENTIFYING YOUR TARGET AUDIENCE

Before you begin to draft questions for gathering data, you should first identify your target audience or audiences. Whom do you want to survey? This will help you focus your plan on developing appropriate methods for communicating with each group. You may want to develop several different versions of the assessment and target specific questions to each audience, such as one for staff, one for parents, and one for business and community leaders. Every three years, L'Anse Creuse Middle School North, in Macomb Township, Michigan, conducts a separate survey of parents, students, and staff; the survey is given to a different group each year.

The personal interviews conducted by the administration and guidance staff at Archbishop M. C. O'Neill High School in Regina, Saskatchewan, provide the data to develop a discipline tracking system that helps determine if there is an increase or a decrease in certain patterns of behavior. Questions developed to gather these types of data from students are going to be different from those for other target audiences.

Every survey instrument should begin with a letter/memo/notice addressed to the target audience, requesting respondents' participation and explaining the reason for the survey. A sample Needs Assessment notice from John Jacobs Site Council can be found at chapter's end. There is also a sample Assessment Participation Letter to Parents from Magic City Campus High School inviting them to participate in an on-campus survey.

DECIDING WHAT TO ASK

Once you have identified your target audience and the type of data you want to generate, you need to ask yourself five questions:

1. What exactly do I want to know?

2. Will the information I obtain be useful?

3. How will I use the information?

4. How will I report the results?

5. Who will benefit from my actions?

It is important that data-gathering questions be designed in a way that does not lead or influence the respondent. Stay objective and keep your questions simple and concise. Close-ended questions give answers to choose from and are easy to tabulate. Open-ended questions can provide interesting and useful data, but will be more time consuming to interpret and record. Be sure to include demographic questions as well; that is, ask the respondents to provide their gender, age range, educational level, how long they have lived in the community, whether they have children in school, whether they work in the community, and so forth.

It is always a good idea to pretest your survey on a small group of people to ensure that the questions are easily understood. If the meaning of a question is subject to several interpretations, the data will be skewed and not very useful.

COLLECTING DATA FROM OTHER SOURCES

To build a complete picture, you also should collect other available information about your community. This could include school board election data and other relevant election statistics for your school area and for the community at large. Also, you can evaluate census data from your school and district attendance areas to provide demographic breakdowns. Contact the U.S. Bureau of the Census in Washington, D.C., at 301-763-7662.

If your school or district has conducted any surveys in the past, get copies of those as well. They could be helpful in identifying trends or changes in your community. By comparing these data, you can form a picture of your school's community and determine how this picture varies from that of the larger area.

EVALUATING AND REPORTING THE RESULTS

Record the dates on which the surveys are returned to you.

> Knowing when a survey was filled out is important because the environment at the time of the survey affects the outcome of the answers given. . . . For example, if a climate survey goes out to parents in your schools for a three-week period, what happens in world events during that three weeks is important to take into consideration. Environmental factors can affect the outcome of the answers you receive. If you send out a survey on how safe parents feel their students are in your schools, and that week a story breaks about a school shooting in Finland, for example, that event may affect how parents answer those questions during that particular time period. Knowing the date that [people] responded to a survey and what environmental factors may have influenced those responses gives you important information. (Dianne Bowers, Director of Public Relations and Marketing, Gilbert Public Schools, Arizona)

Take the time to analyze the information carefully. You may want to enlist the help of a research specialist and break down the results into different groupings using your demographic data. Pages from the award-winning *Statistical Report* from Rex Bolinger, principal at Angola High School in Indiana, are included at the end of this chapter. The table of contents and introduction are examples of the breadth and depth of a successful data-gathering process.

It is important that you report the results of your assessment and provide information on how you plan to address the needs that were identified. Keep the data you collected close at hand as you begin to plan or expand your communications program. Information that is sitting on a shelf or in a drawer is of no help to anyone and is a waste of human and fiscal resources.

Memorize several of the more important or surprising statistics from your report and take the opportunity to plead your cause when speaking with individuals or to groups. Showing that you have a finger on the pulse of the community, as well as the school, makes you even more of an expert and adds credibility to your message.

SUGGESTED READINGS

Campbell, G. (1986). *Community research: The foundation for your marketing strategy* [Topic paper]. Tacoma, WA: Tacoma Public Schools.

Grossman, B. (1985). *Ten-step communication planner* [Workbook]. Evergreen, CO: BG Communications.

Grossman, B., & Guber, G. (1993). *Strategic communications: The key to successful site-based management.* Evergreen, CO: BG Communications.

Kergaard, D. (1991). A step back provides insight, big ideas for smaller schools. *NASSP Bulletin, 75*(533), 22–24.

Levesque, K., Bradley, D., Rossi, K., & Teitelbaum, P. (1998). *At your fingertips: Using everyday data to improve schools.* Berkeley, CA: MPR Associates.

National School Public Relations Association. (1986). *Planning your school PR investment.* Rockville, MD: Author.

Phi Delta Kappa International. (1999). *Polling attitudes of community on education.* Bloomington, IN: Author.

Sherwin, R. M. (1989). *Identify and survey school publics* [Topic paper]. Portland: Oregon Public Schools.

Siccone, F. (1997). *The power to lead: A guidebook for school administrators on facilitating change.* Boston: Allyn & Bacon.

Stickney, J. (1991). *Surveying your community using focus groups* [Topic paper]. Toronto: East York Board of Education.

A Data-Gathering and Execution Plan for Coping With Changes in District/School Boundaries and/or Student/Community Demographic Shifts

In the past two decades, District 80 has changed from 32 percent students living in low-income households to 74 percent. This has created several challenges to our staff who mostly come from middle-income households. After attending a conference in 2001 to hear one of Dr. Ruby Payne's top trainers, Kim Ellis, talk about poverty, I purchased *A Framework for Understanding Poverty* to read. The in-service and book had a profound influence on the way I felt we should work with our children from poverty. When I attended the first training, we had already increased to 63 percent students from low-income households, and I knew our staff must learn how to better meet the needs of these students.

After reading more of Dr. Payne's work, I became more convinced that in order to meet the No Child Left Behind (NCLB) requirement of students in all subgroups meeting or exceeding State Standards, our teachers and support staff had to understand the framework of poverty. The key concepts from the poverty research that I felt our staff needed to fully understand were: hidden rules among classes, registers of language, characteristics of generational poverty, support systems, relationships, and the role of language.

In the fall of 2003, I sent a team of key district employees to a week-long training in Dallas to become certified trainers about Ruby Payne's research on poverty. When they returned, we designed a plan to provide the full three-day training to all 200 of the District 80 teachers and support staff who work with students. An agreement was reached with the unions to support mandatory attendance at all three of the training sessions provided by the nationally known Ruby Payne trainers.

During the 2004–2005 and 2005–2006 school years, the District 80 trainers reviewed the important concepts with staff from each building during their monthly school improvement meetings. Now, each year during the new teacher orientation, the District 80 trainers present the key concepts so all staff will have the knowledge and skills to work with our students from poverty.

Some specific examples of implementing this research to strengthen education in District 80 follow:

a. Research: Children from poverty do not have support systems.

   Change: We increased class periods at the Middle School so students would have time to do most of their homework with their teacher and have the material to do it.

   Result: Students' grades increased during the 2005–2006 school year and have remained high because of the significant increase in completed homework assignments.

b. Research: Children from poverty talk in the casual language register.

   Change: Staff understand the need to talk to students in the adult voice, not the judgmental parent voice, which avoids putting them in a defensive mood.

   Result: The number of office referrals and suspensions for disrespect to staff decreased.

c. Research: Families from poverty value material things and live for the present.

   Change: Staff now understands why children from poverty have things (expensive tennis shoes, cell phones, etc.) but do not have money to buy school supplies or school lunches.

   Result: Staff now do not judge the parents on middle-class values, and the relationship between many parents and staff has improved.

(Continued)

(Continued)

d. Research: Students from poverty are motivated by relationships.

Change: Staff have learned to find out about students' backgrounds and find ways to "connect" with them.

Result: Students stay more engaged with the learning process because they know their teacher cares about them.

All staff members of the Mount Vernon City Schools understand the framework of poverty. By implementing these ideals, the education in District 80 has been strengthened by the results noted above. Perhaps the most significant result, at least according to the No Child Left Behind Act, is that the number of low-income students meeting or exceeding on the ISAT test has generally increased in all grades in both reading and math the past few years when compared to the previous three years for which data exists. All three attendance centers were designated as Illinois Honor Roll Schools for 2008 because of the improved academics.

Source: Contributed by Superintendent Dr. Kevin Settle, Mount Vernon City School District #80, Mount Vernon, IL.

Superstars in Education

POLYTECH High School

Woodside, Delaware
POLYTECH Advisement Support System (PASS)

INTRODUCTION

Breaking Ranks, first published in 1996, provided 80 recommendations for the vision of a dramatically improved American educational system that would highlight more student-centered personalized programs, expand support services, and heighten intellectual rigor for all students. The main thrust of *Breaking Ranks II* (2004) is "the need for current high schools to engage in the process of change that will ensure success for *every* high school student." Of the seven cornerstone strategies to improve student performance in *BR II,* five are directly or indirectly addressed by the POLYTECH Advisement Support System (PASS), first implemented at POLYTECH High School in 1995. These include establishing the essential learning a student is required to achieve prior to graduation; increasing the quantity and quality of student, teacher/staff, parent, interactions; implementing a comprehensive advisory program that ensures each student has frequent and meaningful opportunities to plan and assess her or his academic and social progress with a faculty member; instituting structural leadership changes that allow for meaningful involvement in decisions by students, teachers, family members, and the community; and continual professional development programs to help staff increase their content knowledge of the instructional strategies required to prepare students for graduation.

Additionally, the Achieve, Inc. publication, *An Analysis of Delaware's High School Standards and Course Requirements* (January, 2005) highlighted the need for Delaware to "raise academic standards, improve assessments, and strengthen accountability to prepare all young people for postsecondary education, work, and citizenship." Also, the Southern Regional Education Board (SREB) publication, *Best Practices for Implementing HSTW and MMGW* (September 2005), emphasized the need in high schools to have "effective guidance and advisement program(s) (that) ensures all students meet individually with their parents and a school advisor during each year of high school."

NEEDS IDENTIFICATION/ASSESSMENT

By the late 1980s, career/technical education in southern Delaware was struggling for survival. Although the area was blessed with a stable and growing economy, the existing half-day career/technical center was not adequately serving students, their families, or the business community. Career/technical students were usually in the general track at their sending schools, where they were enrolled in only low-level academic courses. At the same time, they were losing valuable class time moving between schools. These circumstances resulted in poor student performance. Statewide analysis of student achievement showed that career/technical students were being shortchanged, and enrollments at the half-day career/technical center had been steadily declining for ten years. Something clearly had to change.

After recognizing the need for change, one of the first steps the district took was to become an early member of the Southern Regional Education Board's *High Schools That Work* network in 1989. This decision was instrumental in helping school leaders develop a vision of the kind of school they wanted to create, based on the *HSTW* key practices. At the recommendation of *HSTW,* the Kent County School District joined forces with a team of experts from the National Center for Research in Vocational Education to review the current state of its programs and to develop a comprehensive improvement plan.

(Continued)

(Continued)

The result was a four-year transition, beginning in 1991, that led to the creation of POLYTECH High School, a fully comprehensive, technical high school. Students (and their parents) from five school districts would choose to attend the school at the end of eighth grade and to complete both their academic and career/technical studies there. Guided by the motto, "Power of Knowledge for Work and College," POLYTECH created a challenging learning environment based on high standards and a commitment to teach career-oriented students a college-preparatory academic core. The teaching staff continues to lead the development of the vision and proudly takes ownership of it. All school policies and practices reflect the vision.

POLYTECH decided that the best way to achieve its goals was to emphasize applied learning, integration of curriculum, smaller learning communities, flexible schedules with longer class time, state-of-the-art technology, a strong student advisement program, community partnerships, work-based learning experiences, and alternative assessments. To do this, POLYTECH created four "Pillars of Support" as a foundation upon which to build a strong academic and career/technical institution. The "Pillars" included the staff, facility, parents, and the students at the first level. The "second story" supported by the pillars included the climate, curricula, and a strong advisement program (PASS). The "top floor" is student achievement in preparation for life success. This model included all the important stakeholders as integral parts of the overall program.

ACTION PLAN

The PASS program focuses on career planning by developing a culture of success with *every* student. Since its implementation in the 1995–1996 school year, this program has remained one of POLYTECH's most beneficial according to parent surveys. PASS is a model career-planning program represented by six essential components: vision, commitment, comprehensiveness, collaboration, program management, and program evaluation.

VISION

The purpose of the PASS program is to help students become successful, supportive, productive citizens. A Master Plan for the PASS program was initially completed through a committee consisting of counselors, school administrators, district administrators, teachers, and parents. The PASS Committee was responsible for the development of the school and student goals.

The school goals for the PASS program are

- expand awareness of educational and career alternatives,
- decrease student dropouts,
- improve school climate,
- reduce behavioral problems,
- increase parental involvement and support,
- improve student achievement, and
- identify At-Risk students.

The student goals for the PASS program are the following:

- Organize career development into a manageable time frame
- Provide opportunity for shared responsibility for career and educational development by including parents, students, teachers, and counselors

- Enable students to gain skills and background necessary to make good educational and career decisions
- Increase students' choices and access to jobs and post-secondary education through adequate knowledge
- Encourage students to set career goals as well as to set a plan to meet these goals
- Improve relations between school, parents, business, industry, and other community members
- Improve self-esteem

The overall program emphasizes the need for students to plan for career choices early on in their education. The POLYTECH School District mission statement summarizes that commitment to career planning:

The POLYTECH School District mission is to provide the highest quality learning experience through the incorporation of applied learning and the integration of academic and technical subjects. Further, the District's purpose is to develop individuals with the skills necessary for (1) self-improvement and further learning; (2) entry or advancement into their chosen career field or educational level; (3) adaptability in later employment in fulfilling occupations, new occupations, and emerging, high-status occupations at various levels of competence; and (4) post-secondary education.

In addition, the strategic plan for POLYTECH School District addresses a vision for 2010:

POLYTECH School District will set the standard of excellence for comprehensive technical education in Delaware as evidenced by high rates of job placement and acceptance in post-secondary education.

As a result of the PASS program, students and parents are informed of the many career and education choices available. The PASS advisors work with the students to develop a Six-Year Career Plan and to determine the students' program of study based on their chosen career fields.

COMMITMENT

As the PASS program is a premier career advisement program, administrators at all levels at POLYTECH are in full support of it. The commitment is evidenced in the placement of its description and procedure in the Staff Handbook. The faculty's commitment is in the form of their role as advisors for the program. All teachers, support personnel, and administrators are advisors to approximately 10 students. During the PASS events, teachers meet with their advisees to assist them in making career and educational decisions. Teachers, as advisors, go beyond their required duties as they meet with parents on their planning periods and before and after school. Through a "whole school" involvement, each staff member becomes more aware of state and school graduation requirements and the need to meet all academic and technical criteria for the POLYTECH Technical Diploma.

Parents are also deeply involved in this program. During PASS event #3, parents and students meet with the advisors to discuss career plans, programs of study, and student progress. These individual meetings ensure that students get individual attention and that the parents' concerns for their children's education and career plan are being met. Students in meeting with their PASS advisors are able to make their own decisions concerning career planning. With the help from teachers, students can become aware of possible career choices. To get students to begin thinking about future careers, many teachers/ PASS advisors use career-planning strategies, such as the use of surveys.

(Continued)

(Continued)

COMPREHENSIVENESS

All POLYTECH students participate in the PASS program. As incoming freshmen, these students are guided through the PASS program with help from the PASS advisors. During their conferences, they discuss possible career choices and the career/technical areas that would support their career choice. They develop a Six-Year Career Plan (four high school years and two years beyond high school). They become more familiar with the Career Exploratory program in which they participate in the ninth grade that helps them to make a career/technical program of study selection.

For the upperclassmen, advisors assist these students in reviewing and revising the Six-Year Career Plan that addresses technical and educational concerns. They also become familiar with the School-to-Career program that is available to juniors and seniors. Once eligible, juniors or seniors may take advantage of the School-to-Career choices of cooperative work, internships, or job shadowing.

In the senior year, as part of the PASS program, seniors begin to fully develop their career and educational choices. All students develop and continually revise the Six-Year Career Plan through the PASS program, and their individual guidance counselors consult and further assist in planning as needed.

All students, as part of the PASS program, get a copy of the Panther Plan. This document outlines the types of diplomas available to the students, information about general career planning, career information resources available at POLYTECH, and programs of study.

COLLABORATION

In order for the PASS program to be fully meaningful, all stakeholders must be a part of the planning and revising of the career-planning program. At POLYTECH, career/technical programs of study are under the guidance of Craft Advisory Committees. These advisory committees, which consist of community members, business people, teachers, parents, and students, are helpful in keeping the technical areas abreast of current trends in business and industry. Based on advisory recommendations, changes are continually occurring in the course selections that prepare students for employment in their chosen career/technical area. Students are made aware of the most current needs through advisement in the PASS program.

The advisor's role in the PASS program is to assist the student advisees in making career plans and selecting a program of study that will support those aspirations. Advisors are able to assist students with course selections that fulfill their technical needs.

The Guidance Team, consisting of the five guidance counselors, is there to assist advisors in checking for proper credits needed for graduation and necessary course work needed for planned careers. In addition, the guidance counselors are responsible for training the PASS advisors for the yearly PASS events.

A crucial component of the PASS program is the parents. Keeping them well informed of their children's career goals and school progress is a highlight of the PASS program. At PASS event #3, conferences are held where the parents and students get one-on-one individual attention focused on the child's future.

PROGRAM MANAGEMENT

During the ninth-grade year, students meet with the PASS advisors to begin the process of planning and applying for a chosen career/technical area. As the students become full members of a technical area in Grade 10 and Grade 11, they are advised during the PASS events as to what courses are needed or required in gaining skills in the chosen career areas. In their senior year, many students are advised during the PASS events of job placement or further required education. By this time, many students have already been offered or are participating in job shadowing, cooperative jobs, or internships. Overall, their advisement is continually focused on student achievement, career plans, and aspirations.

PROGRAM EVALUATION

Surveys are used to evaluate the PASS program. Specific surveys were used to gather information from stakeholders, including students, parents, and teachers as PASS advisors. The parent surveys are one indicator of the PASS program's success. Follow-up graduate surveys at the 6-month and 18-month point further support the viability of this important program.

RESULTS

According to the Southern Regional Education Board's September 2005 "Best Practices" newsletter, of those students who participated in a mentor or advisor program for all four years of high school, 55 percent said the mentor or advisor helped them plan a high school program of study and reviewed their progress annually. These students had significantly higher achievement than students at schools that did not offer a staffwide advisement program. At POLYTECH High School, 100 percent of the students and staff are deeply involved in the PASS program and have six-year plans developed to assist in "life after high school." Dunham and Frome (2002) felt that such a plan ensures that students know what is necessary to succeed in high school and beyond. In 2006, the *HSTW* consortium named POLYTECH High School as one of its top 44 schools (of over 1,300 nationally) and a Gold Award winner, because of the accomplishments of its students and positive climate that pervades the school.

While we are not claiming that PASS in itself is solely responsible for the dramatically improved student achievement at POLYTECH over the past ten years, it has promoted a mechanism for all stakeholders to collaborate and set achievable and measurable goals for individual student success. An extensive body of research suggests that students who set academic and career goals in high school are less likely to drop out. This is particularly important in a school where many of the students are in the first generation to attend college. Many of these students have enrolled in post-secondary education at Delaware Technical and Community College where POLYTECH has the largest contingent of any school in Delaware (85 former POLYTECHers) and the largest number on the SEEDS scholarship program (70).

POLYTECH High School enjoys the lowest dropout rate of all the public high schools in Delaware over the past six years (approximately 0.3%); traditionally has the highest graduation rates for all students (and the major demographic groups), normally between 92 and 96 percent; is the only public high school that does not have (or need) a Resource Officer (patrolperson) roaming the halls; is consistently in the top three schools in student achievement on the Delaware Student Testing Program (DSTP); and has literally closed the achievement gap between white and African American students in writing and social studies (math, reading, and science are approaching closure).

POLYTECH High School and the POLYTECH School District have not had to expel a student in the past four years, and they enjoy an enviable educational environment rich in opportunities for staff and students due in large part to the relationships cultivated by the PASS program. From parent surveys, over the ten years of PASS, 91.6% of the parents rated the PASS program as being *very beneficial*. The attendance rate over the years for the parent/student/PASS advisor conferences (event #3) has been 90.5%.

As is evident by the following charts, student achievement for *all* students has improved dramatically. In late 2005, the entire staff was organized into eleven teams to aggressively address the quantifiable goals, which were organized under three major objectives. Using the 2003–2004 school year as a baseline,

(Continued)

(Continued)

POLYTECH has shown constant positive progress, thanks in large part to the PASS program. Additionally, the safe environment enjoyed by POLYTECH staff and students continues to be one of the school's strengths. By maintaining a strict discipline policy that empowers individual classroom teachers to take direct and appropriate action, the climate at POLYTECH has become enviable. The PASS program structure, which has been engrained in the fabric of POLYTECH High School, should be the model for the entire state because it works!

CONCLUSION

POLYTECH has embraced the challenge of preparing students for the competitive job market, postsecondary education, and/or military service. The career/technical areas of study offered at POLYTECH are areas of need in Kent County and the surrounding areas. Students are continuously advised throughout their careers at POLYTECH through the PASS program, which helps their planning for success. By keeping the POLYTECH students and parents informed of the programs, options, careers, and services available to them, POLYTECH does indeed live up to its motto:

"The Power of Knowledge for Work and College"

Source: POLYTECH High School, Woodside, DE.

Student Achievement

Delaware Student Testing Program (DSTP)

Percentage of Students Meeting or Exceeding State Standard			
	1997–1998	*2004–2005*	*Gain*
Math	28.7%	60.1%	+31.4%
Reading	57.5%	82.6%	+25.1%
Writing	33.9%	88.3%	+54.4%

Gap Analysis

2005 DSTP Disaggregated Data
(Percentage of Students Meeting or Exceeding State Standards)

	African American	*White*	*Gap*	*Gap Reduction (since 2004)*
Reading	71%	85%	14%	8%
Writing	88%	88%	0%	4%
Math	52%	61%	9%	3%
Social Studies	61%	62%	1%	9%
Science	52%	70%	18%	2%

Scholastic Aptitude Test (SAT)

	1995–1996	*2004–2005*	*Gain*
No. of Test Takers	52	124	+72
% of Seniors Testing	39%	53%	+14%
Mean Verbal Score	430	462	+32
Mean Math Score	411	461	+50

Discipline

	1995–1996	*2003–2004*	*Improvement*
Dropout Rate	1.7%	.9%	0.8%
Referrals	1620	1343	277
In-School Suspensions	127	27	100
Out-of-School Suspensions	84	28	56
Expulsions	8	0	8

Source: Delaware Department of Education.

Desert Foothills
Report Card

As parents of a Desert Foothills student, your input is important. We would like you to complete a report card on how we are doing as a school. The school's Site Council is committed to providing a quality education. This report card will enable us to look at our strengths and weaknesses in planning future goals.

Return the completed report card to your student's reading teacher by Friday, April 10. It is permissible to leave a question blank if you feel you cannot answer it adequately.

SAFE AND ORDERLY ENVIRONMENT	A	B	C	D	F
School is an orderly and safe place					
Student activities are adequately supervised					
School rules for student behavior expectations are fair					
Discipline consequences are fair and consistent					
Discipline on the school bus is fair and consistent					
School buildings and grounds are well maintained					
School climate is positive and conducive to learning					
School administrators are visible and accessible					
Evaporative cooled rooms provide a healthy environment for learning					
Comment: _____					
HIGH EXPECTATIONS FOR SUCCESS					
Teachers expect all students to learn					
Teachers hold expectations for achievement consistent with student ability					
Teachers and staff motivate students through caring attitude and recognition					
Teachers and staff respect the dignity and worth of each student					
Comment: _____					
OPPORTUNITY TO LEARN					
Course offerings are relevant and of sufficient variety					
Classroom learning activities are relevant					
Teachers direct and supervise student learning					
Teachers are effective instructors					
Classroom time is productively utilized					
Students learn essential skills					
Homework is given in an appropriate manner					
Homework assignments are relevant					

Extracurricular sports and club activities are available and accessible					
A set of textbooks at home helps student complete homework					
Comment: _____					
MONITORING OF STUDENT PROGRESS					
Progress reports are informative					
Reports are effective in communicating student achievement					
Parent/Teacher conferences are productive					
Teacher-initiated communications are timely					
Teacher-initiated communications are effective					
Teacher response to parent-initiated communications is timely					
Teacher response to parent-initiated communications is effective					
Comment: _____					
HOME/SCHOOL RELATIONS					
Administrators are effective decision makers					
Student Advisors provide meaningful and helpful services					
Office staff is pleasant and efficient					
Back-to-school mailers and newsletters are informative and comprehensive					
Orientation and Open House activities are informative and productive					
Written information regarding curriculum is informative and comprehensive					
Opportunity exists for parent input to school issues					
Comment: _____					
Your overall grade for Desert Foothills					
Overall grade you think your child would give Desert Foothills					

What is the most pressing problem facing Desert Foothills?

_____
_____
_____

In your opinion, what could be done about it?

_____
_____
_____

What is Desert Foothills' greatest strength?

_____

Parents of   **7th grader**   **8th grader**

_____   _____   _____

Source: Desert Foothills Junior High School, Washington School District, Phoenix, AZ.

L'Anse Creuse Middle School
North Parent Survey

Directions: Place an "X" in the numbered box of the answer you select. When a question calls for a written response, use the space provided.

1. How many children do you have attending L'Anse Creuse Middle School North?
    [1] one
    [2] two
    [3] three or more

2. What grades are they in? [MARK ALL THAT APPLY.]
    [1] 6th
    [2] 7th
    [3] 8th

3. How well informed are you about what's happening at Middle School North?
    [1] well informed
    [2] somewhat informed
    [3] not too well informed

4. Where do you get most of your information about L'Anse Creuse Middle School North?
    [MARK ALL THAT APPLY.]
    [1] my child or other students
    [2] my child's teachers
    [3] my child's counselor
    [4] Mr. Dooley/the principal
    [5] other school employees
    [6] the school's parent newsletter
    [7] the Parent Handbook (calendar)
    [8] self/firsthand knowledge
    [9] newspapers
    [10] Parent Advisory Council
    [11] other (please specify) _____

5. What types of school news are especially interesting to you? [MARK ALL THAT APPLY.]
    [1] how my child is doing in general
    [2] how our school/students compare to others
    [3] what's being taught
    [4] classroom activities
    [5] after-school activities (sports/clubs/etc.)
    [6] growth and development of adolescents
    [7] music and art
    [8] student success stories

[9] school calendar
[10] information about staff
[11] other (please specify) _____

6. About six times during the school year, the Middle School North Parent Newsletter is mailed to students' homes. Have you ever received a copy?
[1] yes
[2] no [SKIP TO QUESTION 9]

7. All things considered, would you say the newsletter is . . .
[1] very worthwhile
[2] somewhat worthwhile
[3] not at all worthwhile

8. How, if at all, would you change the newsletter?

9. Students are often given the grades A, B, C, D, or Fail to show how well they're doing in school. Suppose Middle School North were graded the same way. All things considered, what grade would you give the school?
[1] A
[2] B
[3] C
[4] D
[5] Fail

10. In your opinion, what's the single biggest problem at Middle School North?

11. And, on the positive side, what would you say is the single best thing about the school?

(Continued)

After each of the following statements, please indicate the degree to which you either agree or disagree. Mark the neutral column if you neither agree nor disagree.

	strongly agree	agree	neutral	disagree	strongly disagree
12. When I ask a question of school staff, information I receive can be trusted to be complete and accurate.	[1]	[2]	[3]	[4]	[5]
13. School discipline is not a problem at this school.	[1]	[2]	[3]	[4]	[5]
14. Activities in which parents are invited to participate are usually scheduled conveniently enough that even working parents can take part.					
15. Parents are encouraged to share ideas for school improvement with administration and staff in this school.	[1]	[2]	[3]	[4]	[5]
16. The overall purpose, direction, and priorities of this school are clear to me.	[1]	[2]	[3]	[4]	[5]
17. Student achievements in all areas are proudly publicized by this school.	[1]	[2]	[3]	[4]	[5]
18. Class sizes at this school are just about right.	[1]	[2]	[3]	[4]	[5]
19. The building and grounds around Middle School North are neat, clean, and well maintained.	[1]	[2]	[3]	[4]	[5]
20. The extracurricular programs available to students provide enough variety that there's something for every child who wants to participate.	[1]	[2]	[3]	[4]	[5]
21. The district's bus-pass policy is a good idea.	[1]	[2]	[3]	[4]	[5]
22. The amount of emphasis the school places on winning is just about right.	[1]	[2]	[3]	[4]	[5]
23. The school provides plenty of opportunities for parents to get involved in their child's education.	[1]	[2]	[3]	[4]	[5]
24. The Special Education program in L'Anse Creuse is doing a good job of meeting the needs of students with special needs.	[1]	[2]	[3]	[4]	[5]
25. School rules are applied fairly to all students.	[1]	[2]	[3]	[4]	[5]
26. Students at this school are given opportunities to voice their opinions about what happens at the school.	[1]	[2]	[3]	[4]	[5]
27. Teachers at this school expect the best from students.	[1]	[2]	[3]	[4]	[5]
28. Administrators at this school expect only the best from teachers.	[1]	[2]	[3]	[4]	[5]
29. When students leave this school, they'll be well prepared to enter high school.	[1]	[2]	[3]	[4]	[5]
30. Instructional support staff members (counselors, media specialist, social workers, at-risk coordinator, etc.) at this school are courteous and helpful.	[1]	[2]	[3]	[4]	[5]
31. Noninstructional support staff members (bus drivers, cooks, custodians, etc.) at this school are courteous and helpful.	[1]	[2]	[3]	[4]	[5]

Please answer the following questions as they pertain to the oldest child you have at Middle School North.

32. Which of the following best describes the average grades your oldest child at the school receives?

   [1] A   [5] C
   [2] A– to B+   [6] C– to D+
   [3] B   [7] D
   [4] B– to C+   [8] D– or lower

33. Does your child participate in any of Middle School North's after-school extracurricular activities?

   [1] yes [SKIP TO QUESTION 35]
   [2] no

34. Why do you think your child *does not* participate in any after-school activities?

35. How much time does your child generally spend on homework each day?

   [1] none   [4] 61–90 minutes
   [2] 30 minutes or less   [5] 91–120 minutes
   [3] 31–60 minutes   [6] more than 2 hours

36. Do you think the amount of homework your child is assigned is . . .

   [1] too little
   [2] too much
   [3] just about right

37. How often do you check to make sure your child's homework is complete?

   [1] always
   [2] most of the time
   [3] occasionally
   [4] seldom
   [5] never

38. Did your child participate in this year's Morley Candy sale?

   [1] yes
   [2] no

39. Morley Candy sale totals were significantly lower this year than they've been in the past. Why do you think sales were down?

(Continued)

For each of the following, indicate the degree to which you agree or disagree. Mark the neutral column if you neither agree nor disagree. Remember to answer questions as they pertain to your oldest child at Middle School North.

	strongly agree	agree	neutral	disagree	strongly disagree
40. I believe my child's time at school is well used.	[1]	[2]	[3]	[4]	[5]
41. I feel free to contact my child's teachers.	[1]	[2]	[3]	[4]	[5]
42. Staff at Middle School North seem to be genuinely interested in my child's future.	[1]	[2]	[3]	[4]	[5]
43. My child understands school rules.	[1]	[2]	[3]	[4]	[5]
44. My child understands classroom rules.	[1]	[2]	[3]	[4]	[5]
45. I generally know what my child is learning in school.	[1]	[2]	[3]	[4]	[5]
46. The things my child is learning in school will help him/her in life.	[1]	[2]	[3]	[4]	[5]
47. I'm generally satisfied with what my child is learning.	[1]	[2]	[3]	[4]	[5]
48. My child enjoys school most of the time.	[1]	[2]	[3]	[4]	[5]
49. My child feels safe at school.	[1]	[2]	[3]	[4]	[5]
50. The report cards and progress reports my child gets from Middle School North provide a clear picture of how well my child is doing in school.	[1]	[2]	[3]	[4]	[5]
51. My child's teachers are willing to provide additional help whenever it's needed.	[1]	[2]	[3]	[4]	[5]
52. The dittos or copies my child is asked to complete are usually of high enough quality that they're easy to read.	[1]	[2]	[3]	[4]	[5]
53. My child is generally satisfied with the variety and quality of food available in the school's lunch program.	[1]	[2]	[3]	[4]	[5]
54. I'm satisfied with the bus service provided my child.	[1]	[2]	[3]	[4]	[5]
55. My child's teachers are well qualified to teach and they do a good job of teaching.	[1]	[2]	[3]	[4]	[5]
56. Parent–teacher conferences provide valuable information about how well my child is doing in school.	[1]	[2]	[3]	[4]	[5]
57. My child's counselor has been very helpful, assisting my child with course selection.	[1]	[2]	[3]	[4]	[5]
58. My child has received sound advice and guidance from the counseling staff whenever he/she has asked for it.	[1]	[2]	[3]	[4]	[5]

These questions about you and your family will give us a profile of the families we serve.

59. Are you the child's . . .
    [1] mother
    [2] father
    [3] stepmother
    [4] stepfather
    [5] other (please specify) _____

60. Is the household headed by two parents (even if one is a stepparent or a guardian) or by just one person?
    [1] two parents
    [2] two parents (one is a stepparent)
    [3] mother only [SKIP TO QUESTION 62]
    [4] father only [SKIP TO QUESTION 62]
    [5] other (please specify) _____

61. If the household is headed by two people, are both employed at least part-time?
    [1] yes—both are employed
    [2] no—only the father/stepfather employed
    [3] no—only the mother/stepmother employed

62. What's the highest level of education you have completed?
    [1] high school not completed
    [2] high school graduate/GED
    [3] some college, technical, or trade school
    [4] technical or trade school completed
    [5] associate's degree
    [6] bachelor's degree
    [7] master's degree
    [8] specialist's degree or doctorate
    [9] other (please specify) _____

63. Have you ever attended a meeting of Middle School North's parent group—the Parent Advisory Council (PAC)?
    [1] yes [SKIP TO QUESTION 65]
    [2] no

64. If you've never attended a PAC meeting, what's the *main* reason you have never participated?

65. Please add any questions or comments you have about the school that weren't covered by this survey:

That concludes our survey. Thank you very much for taking the time to help. Now fold your completed survey and staple or tape it closed. Then please have your child return the survey to Middle School North on *November 13* to receive a candy treat.

Source: L'Anse Creuse Middle School North, Macomb Township, MI

Mountain View School
Parent Survey

READING: Reading readiness, word recognition, comprehension, and personal enjoyment of reading.

1. Do you feel your child is learning to read through the Reading Mastery Program? _____YES _____NO

2. Would you like more information on the reading program that we are using? _____YES _____NO

3. Does your child read to you at home? _____YES _____NO

4. Does your child sound out words on his/her own? _____YES _____NO

5. Do you and your child share and talk about books? _____YES _____NO

6. Is your child making progress in reading this year? _____YES _____NO

7. Has the school encouraged an interest in reading for your child? _____YES _____NO

Comments: _____

_____

LEVEL OF SATISFACTION WITH YOUR CHILD'S READING

VERY HAPPY	5	4	3	2	1	VERY UNHAPPY

WRITTEN LANGUAGE/SPELLING: Grammar, punctuation, and capitalization.

1. Are you satisfied with your child's writing at school? _____YES _____NO

2. Do you feel your child is learning to use printing or cursive writing? _____YES _____NO

3. Does your child write stories, letters, or notes? _____YES _____NO

4. Is your child using new words in his/her writing? _____YES _____NO

5. Do you feel there has been an improvement in your child's spelling? _____YES _____NO

6. Would you like more information on the writing and spelling programs? _____YES _____NO

Comments: _____

_____

LEVEL OF SATISFACTION WITH YOUR CHILD'S WRITING/SPELLING

VERY HAPPY	5	4	3	2	1	VERY UNHAPPY

MATH: Number concepts, counting, computational skills, and mathematical relationships.

1. Are you satisfied with your child's math program? _____YES _____NO

2. Would you like to receive math instruction during the school day with your child? (Family Math) _____YES _____NO

3. Would you rather receive math instruction after school?   _____ YES   _____ NO

4. Are you satisfied with your child's progress in math?   _____ YES   _____ NO

5. Does your child use math in daily activities such as games, grocery shopping, making change, video arcades?   _____ YES   _____ NO

Comments: _____

LEVEL OF SATISFACTION WITH YOUR CHILD'S MATHEMATICAL PROGRAM

VERY HAPPY   5   4   3   2   1   VERY UNHAPPY

MULTICULTURAL: Understanding, awareness, and respect for likenesses and differences among various cultures within our school community.

1. Do you feel the school has helped your child improve his/her concept?   _____ YES   _____ NO

2. Has your child been made aware of the likenesses in people?   _____ YES   _____ NO

3. Has your child become more accepting of differences in people?   _____ YES   _____ NO

4. Are you more accepting of cultural differences in people due to your child's awareness in school?   _____ YES   _____ NO

What do you feel our school could do to help *your* child develop a better understanding and acceptance of different cultures?

Comments: _____

LEVEL OF SATISFACTION WITH YOUR CHILD'S MULTICULTURAL PROGRAM

VERY HAPPY   5   4   3   2   1   VERY UNHAPPY

STUDY HABITS: School work at home.

1. Does your child bring home homework?   _____ YES   _____ NO

2. Can your child complete homework in a reasonable length of time without becoming frustrated or bored?   _____ YES   _____ NO

   (If no, please comment)

3. Are you satisfied with your child's study habits?   _____ YES   _____ NO

Comments: _____

(Continued)

(Continued)

LEVEL OF SATISFACTION WITH YOUR CHILD'S STUDY HABITS

VERY HAPPY	5	4	3	2	1	VERY UNHAPPY

ACADEMIC EXPECTATIONS:

1. Are you satisfied with your child's overall academic progress? _____YES _____ NO

2. Are you satisfied with your child's social and emotional progress? _____YES _____ NO

3. Do you feel that your child is a success in school? _____YES _____ NO

4. Does your child share his/her school experiences with the family? _____YES _____ NO

   Are they positive?

5. Do you believe an extended school year program would be beneficial to your child's learning (Year-Round School) _____YES _____ NO

6. Would you be interested in investigating the possibilities of year-round school? _____YES _____ NO

Comments: _____

LEVEL OF SATISFACTION WITH MOUNTAIN VIEW'S APPROACH TO ACADEMIC EXPECTATIONS

VERY HAPPY	5	4	3	2	1	VERY UNHAPPY

PARENT PARTICIPATION: Parent involvement and home/school relationships.

1. Do you feel the following school communications are informative and interesting to receive?
   A. Newsletter _____YES _____ NO
   B. Letters written by children themselves _____YES _____ NO
   C. Letter from classroom teacher _____YES _____ NO
   D. School programs (back to school night, recitals, plays, etc.) _____YES _____ NO
   E. Personal contacts _____YES _____ NO
   F. Student Newspaper _____YES _____ NO
   G. Visitations to school _____YES _____ NO
   H. Telephone calls from teachers _____YES _____ NO
   I. Other—please specify _____YES _____ NO

2. Are you informed of school events in a timely manner? _____YES _____ NO

3. Have you felt included in school activities such as P.T.O., barbecues, and student programs? _____YES _____ NO

4. When you volunteer your time, do you feel your time is valuable to:
   Students _____ School _____ Teacher _____

   _____ YES   _____ NO

5. Do you feel welcome when you come to Mountain View School?

   _____ YES   _____ NO

6. When you call, do you feel your concerns are handled in a courteous manner?

   _____ YES   _____ NO

7. Do you review information about upcoming events?

   _____ YES   _____ NO

8. In place of school sales would you be willing to donate a tax deductible amount of money to the P.T.O.?

   _____ YES   _____ NO

   If yes, please circle amount of money you would be willing to donate

   $10 _____ $15 _____ $20 _____ $25 _____ Other _____

Comments: _____

LEVEL OF SATISFACTION

VERY HAPPY	5	4	3	2	1	VERY UNHAPPY

PARENT EDUCATION: If the school provided the following classes, which would you be interested in?

INTERESTED IN ATTENDING

Parenting Skills	_____ YES	_____ NO
Reading Classes for Adults	_____ YES	_____ NO
Graduate Equivalent Degree (GED) Day _____ Night _____ class	_____ YES	_____ NO
English as Another Language	_____ YES	_____ NO
Child Growth and Development	_____ YES	_____ NO
Children's Literature	_____ YES	_____ NO
Family Math–Family Reading	_____ YES	_____ NO
Nutrition Health and Hygiene	_____ YES	_____ NO
HIV/AIDS Education	_____ YES	_____ NO
Alcoholics Anonymous	_____ YES	_____ NO
Money Management	_____ YES	_____ NO
Foreign Language	_____ YES	_____ NO
Narcotics Anonymous	_____ YES	_____ NO

Please list any suggestions you may have for classes: _____

_____

Comments: _____

(Continued)

(Continued)

LEVEL OF SATISFACTION WITH OUR APPROACH TO PARENT EDUCATION

VERY HAPPY   5   4   3   2   1   VERY UNHAPPY

GENERAL INFORMATION:

Grade level of your child   PRE-K   1   2   3   4   5   6

How long have you been at Mountain View?   _____ Years

Have you visited your child's   _____ YES   _____ NO
classroom during the school day?

Did your child attend pre-school?   _____ YES   _____ NO

If yes, which one? _____ Head Start _____ Praise _____

How long? _____

DISCIPLINE:

1. Have you read the school handbook?   _____ YES   _____ NO

2. Are you familiar with Make Your Day (MYD)?   _____ YES   _____ NO

3. Do you believe Make Your Day (MYD) is   _____ YES   _____ NO
   effective with your child/children?

Comments: _____

LEVEL OF SATISFACTION WITH THE SCHOOL DISCIPLINE PROGRAM
VERY HAPPY   5   4   3   2   1   VERY UNHAPPY

FOOD SERVICES:

1. Are you satisfied with the quality of food service at   _____ YES   _____ NO
   school?

If not, please make suggestions.

Thank you very much for your time and commitment in completing this survey. On our part, we pledge to make good use of your responses.

Source: Mountain View Elementary School, Washington Elementary School District, Phoenix, AZ.

Magic City Campus
Parent Needs Assessment Survey

Please fill out this form at your earliest convenience and return to Magic City Campus, 1100 11th Ave. S.W. It is extremely important that educators seek and use input from parents as they collaboratively attempt to provide quality education for all students. Thank you!

Assessment Key
(Circle appropriate response/share additional comments):

A = Excellent   D = Poor

B = Good   F = Failing

C = Average   X = Don't Know

1. The school building, supplies, and maintenance are: A-B-C-D-F-X

Comments:

2. The counseling staff is: A-B-C-D-F-X

Comments:

3. The curriculum (courses offered; educational activities provided students) is: A-B-C-D-F-X

Comments:

4. The principals (administrative staff) are: A-B-C-D-F-X

Comments:

(Continued)

(Continued)

5. Services to parents are: A-B-C-D-F-X

Comments:

_____

6. Services to students are: A-B-C-D-F-X

Comments:

_____

7. Student activities (clubs,   A-B-C-D-F-X
   organizations, etc.) are:

Comments:

_____

8. Student discipline is: A-B-C-D-F-X

Comments:

_____

9. The teaching staff is: A-B-C-D-F-X

Comments:

_____

10. My overall assessment   A-B-C-D-F-X
    (evaluation) of Magic City
    Campus is:

Comments:

_____

Source: Magic City Campus High School, Minot, ND.

The Middle School Concept

Royal Palm school is organized as a middle school with students assigned to a team. Each team consists of a reading, English, math, science, and social studies teacher. Teachers teach five classes, have an individual preparation period, and meet daily during a team planning period. The purposes of the team planning period are as follows:

1. Increase the number of parent/teacher and parent/student conferences to discuss academic and behavioral progress.

2. Increase the number of teaching units that integrate all subject areas.

3. Increase the teacher/teacher communication concerning students and their needs.

4. Increase the number of phone contacts to parents to share student progress.

What suggestions do you have for enhancing or changing the current middle school concept now being offered?

_____

_____

_____

_____

_____

_____

_____

_____

Source: Royal Palm Elementary School, Phoenix, AZ.

Guidelines for Running a Focus Group

1. Approximately 10–12 individuals make a manageable group. Try for a mixed composition.

2. The physical setup of the room is important. Use a round or square table. Refreshments are a nice touch.

3. Your group should meet for between one and one and a half hours.

4. The first few minutes are crucial. Use an icebreaker and have people introduce themselves. Establish an atmosphere where everyone feels comfortable to talk. Set ground rules for participation. You can get off topic easily in the first 10 minutes. Show leniency at first and accept something that may be off topic to build group confidence and set tone.

5. Tape the group session.

6. Assure anonymity.

7. The Board is truly interested in their opinion. Ask open-ended questions.

8. You want an honest response from everybody so don't let one person dominate.

9. Ask for comments from quiet members, such as, "What do you think about that, Mary?"

10. Don't agree or disagree. Say "thank you" without giving away your position.

11. There is no need for agreement. Two radically different ideas can be expressed. The object is not consensus. We are looking for perceptions, not the truth.

12. Probe for depth. Ask for clarification. Play down personal stories, get to the heart of the topic, such as, "We do not have enough time to hear everyone's personal stories, even though that would be interesting. Could you please summarize your idea in one sentence?"

13. There are three kinds of group personalities: the good group cooperates; the nice group says nothing; the loud group is opinionated.

14. The biggest risk is to lead the witness. You must be neutral. You are not there to defend the Board.

15. Start with a basic awareness of the topic and expand on it. Always check to see if anyone has anything to add before moving on to the next topic.

16. End the group with, "What would be the one message I could take back to the Board?"

Source: Director's Office, East York Board of Education, East York, Ontario, Canada.

John Jacobs Site Council
Needs Assessment
Education Is a Good Prospect!

The goals of the John Jacobs Staff and Site Council include providing the best education for our children, meeting your needs as a family, and promoting good communication among the school, home, and community. Join us as partners in working toward achieving each of these goals.

Please complete this needs assessment and return it to the school in the attached envelope. If you have more than one child attending John Jacobs, fill out one survey completely. Please fill out additional Academic Sections for each child. Each student returning a survey to their homeroom or the office will receive a reward and will have his/her name put in a drawing for a gift certificate. If you do not have children attending John Jacobs, return the completed survey to our school office or mail to this address.

John Jacobs Elementary

14421 N. 23rd Avenue

Phoenix, AZ 95023

Grade of the student _____

How many years has (have) your child(ren) attended John Jacobs?

I do not have any children attending John Jacobs.

JOIN US!

Source: John Jacobs Elementary School, Phoenix, AZ.

Assessment Participation Letter to Parents

Mr. and Mrs. John Doe
23 Parkway
Minot, North Dakota

Dear Mr. and Mrs. Doe:

You are one of two hundred Magic City Campus families invited to provide parent input into the Minot High School focus on fostering school improvement. It would be appreciated if *one* parent from each of the invited families meets with us on Wednesday, February 24. Other school-oriented groups providing input into this important process include students and educators.

All participants in the school improvement process will fill out two assessments. The parent assessments will take approximately an hour to complete and include the following:

— a School *Climate Survey* of 55 items to assess the perceptions of students, teachers, and parents about 10 characteristics of the school and its members
— a Parent *Satisfaction Survey* of 58 items to assemble parent perceptions on nine dimensions of school operation and services

The assessment timeline includes working with Minot High School staff on Feb. 23, parents on Feb. 24, and students on Feb. 25. In an effort to enable invited parents to be a part of this significant school improvement project, two times have been scheduled for Wednesday, Feb. 24:

— 2:30 p.m. in the Magic City Campus Theatre
— 7:00 p.m. in the Magic City Campus Theatre

Once all the assessment data has been reviewed to identify perceived strengths and weaknesses of the school, goals will be developed and action plans written to move the school in the desired direction. Please accept our school's invitation to become involved in this important educational endeavor. We'll see you on February 24!

Sincerely,   Sincerely,

Mike Gessner   Richard J. Olthoff
NCA Lead Teacher   Principal

Source: Magic City Campus High School, Minot, ND.

ANGOLA HIGH SCHOOL · ANGOLA, INDIANA

STATISTICAL REPORT

"Indiana's Only Blue Ribbon High School"
Awarded by:
The Indiana Department of Education and
The U.S. Department of Education

Indiana's Most Outstanding Successful High School
Awarded by:
The Indiana Association of Teacher Educators and
The Indiana Association of Colleges of Teacher Education

A North Central Association Member Since 1935
Visit Our Home Page
www.msdsteuben.k12.in.us/ahsialls.htm

Table of Contents

Table of Contents (Con't.)

Introduction

The 1997–1998 school year was an exceptional one for Angola High School. After three full years of restructuring around a 4 Block schedule, many significant improvements have occurred. Compared to two years of baseline data prior to our restructuring, improvements are significant in overall student grade point averages, attendance, semester exams, honor roll rates, library usage, and disciplinary referrals. Angola High School was named Indiana's Only Blue Ribbon High School by the Indiana Department of Education and the U.S. Department of Education. We are proud of our achievements and will work hard for continued improvement.

Over 630 teachers representing 91 schools have visited Angola High School during the past three years. Our teachers have hosted guests during the school day, presented inservice sessions at other schools, and directed several workshops during the summer. Focusing instruction for active learners in 90 minute blocks of time has become the area of interest for many educators. Our new restructuring has created much potential for positive things to happen with student learning. The Workplace Participation Program is one example of community partnerships enhancing student education, made possible by our 4 block schedule.

The following report is prepared for a variety of readers. Parents, community members, and students should find the profile accurate and understandable. Persons unfamiliar with our school and community should find the profile helpful in understanding our demographical make-up.

The statistical analysis, shown by graphs and explanations, is merely a small portion of the data being collected on our school. A baseline of data from 1993 to 1995 was collected to compare with current results. The outcomes are positive and readers should find them helpful in understanding our transition. The data include a collection of numbers as well as results of surveys given to parents, students, and teachers.

Angola High School will continue striving for improvements in all areas. Readers of this report are encouraged to contact us for more detailed responses or for assistance in similar restructuring efforts.

Sincerely,

Dr. Rex W. Bolinger
Principal

School/Community Profile

Steuben County is the home of three school corporations. The Metropolitan School District of Steuben County is the largest, with a student population of 2,917 students. This district is composed of five schools: Carlin Park Elementary, Hendry Park Elementary, Pleasant Lake Elementary, Angola Middle School, and Angola High School. The district is also a member of the Steuben County Educational Opportunity Center, an alternative school that serves four surrounding school districts.

COMMUNITY

Steuben County contains a unique set of characteristics which may not be found in other areas of Indiana. Four major factors influence the county: a resort atmosphere, Tri-State University, recent industrial growth, and an agricultural heritage.

Steuben County is the home of 101 lakes which provides summer and winter recreational opportunities. Pokagon State Park, which features Lake James, Potawatomi Inn and a winter toboggan run, is also located in Steuben County.

Tri-State University provides academic, sporting and cultural opportunities for the residents of the county. Tri-State facilities and faculty are a resource for Angola High School teachers and students.

Industrial growth in Steuben County in the last ten years has been termed "phenomenal." Over 45 new manufacturing companies have located in Steuben County since 1983. Manufacturing jobs in Steuben County have increased from just under 30% of the job market in 1982 to 49% in 1997. Retail jobs, which account for 20% of the job market, have increased about 70% since 1986. Factors which contribute to the increase in manufacturing jobs include a proximity to the Indiana Toll Road (I-80/90) and I-69, local and regional marketing, and a proximity to Michigan and Ohio which are higher-cost environments.

An agricultural heritage is still an important influence in Steuben County. Although only about three percent of the population still earns an income through farming, many students live in rural areas of the county and participate in a variety of agricultural classes and programs at Angola High School.

LOCATION

Angola is located in the lake area of Northeastern Indiana. Lake James, the second largest natural lake in the state, is located only five miles from the city. Interstate 69 is accessible slightly west of Angola, while the Indiana Toll Road access is directly north of the city. Ohio borders Steuben County on the east and Michigan borders the county on the north. Neighboring school systems include Prairie Heights, Hamilton and Fremont Community Schools.

SUPPORT SERVICES

Social services are available within the school district community and in surrounding counties. Local agencies include Project Help, Steuben County Welfare Department, Cameron Hospital and Treatment Center, The Northeastern Center, Operation Shelter, The American Red Cross, and Rise Incorporated. Other social services are available in neighboring counties including Branch, Dekalb, and Allen counties.

(Continued)

(Continued)

PHYSICAL PLANT

The Angola High School building is a relatively new facility. Built in 1990, it is located on 60 acres directly east of the city of Angola. The building area is 162,600 square feet located on three levels. The main level includes academic classrooms, special education classrooms, administrative offices, fine arts classrooms, the gymnasium, and the auditorium. The lower level contains the student commons, dining and food service, practical arts, and maintenance facilities. The upper level includes a wrestling and weight room as well as housing mechanical rooms. The school pupil capacity is 1,060; the gymnasium seats 3,000; the auditorium seats 500. The average space per pupil is 154 square feet per student. A wooded area on the south side of the school property accommodates outdoor lab facilities and a challenge course.

STUDENT POPULATION

Steuben County in general is an expanding county. Increased employment opportunities as well as access to the Indiana Toll Road and I-69 have drawn large numbers of new residents to the area. The U.S. Census Bureau estimated the July 1994 population of Angola at 8,171 people. This is an increase of 39.7% over the 1990 census number of 5,851. Indiana University determined that the city of Angola is one of the fastest growing communities in Indiana over a five year period. Local estimates of the 1995 Angola population show additional increases. This population increase in the Angola area is reflected in the student population that Angola High School services. The student enrollment at Angola High School has increased from 724 students during the 1991–92 school year to 838 students during the 1997–98 school year based on average daily attendance figures. This is an increase of nearly 16 percent in the last seven years.

Angola High School reflects the general ethnic demographics of Steuben County. There are relatively few minorities of school age in the county, and so there are few minority students enrolled in Angola High School. The gender demographics of Angola High School reveal an almost 50–50 split between male and female students. The socioeconomic status of the student body can be illustrated by the fact that 94 students qualify for free or reduced lunches or 11 percent of the student body.

STUDENT ACHIEVEMENT

The "Gold Card" program has been an effective reward for honor roll students at Angola High School. Students achieving honor roll status with a "B" average at the end of nine weeks are given a gold card that entitles them to discounts at local businesses. This system not only rewards outstanding students, but also involves the community with the school in a positive way.

ISTEP scores at Angola High School have increased consistently in reading, language arts, and math over the past three years in block scheduling Our total battery scores have risen from the 76th national percentile to near the 80th national percentile. Our scores have led area and state scores on a consistent basis.

Over half of Angola High School seniors have taken the SAT for the past seven years. The most recent scores place our students above the state and national average in the verbal and math portions. In addition, our students taking the ACT have made significant improvements from scores during our baseline study.

Post-graduate plans for the 1997–1998 graduating class included 62% to a four year college or university, 9% to a two-year trade or technical college, 2% to the military, and 27% to work. The trend during the past five years has shown an increase in those students planning to continue their education, while the number of students planning to go to work immediately after graduation has remained fairly stable.

DAILY SCHEDULE AND CURRICULUM

Angola High School is an intensive 4-block scheduled school. The day consists of four ninety minute periods. Traditional semester courses are taught in nine weeks and traditional year-long courses are taught in a semester. Students have greater flexibility for learning and more opportunities to take a variety of courses.

The curriculum includes over 120 different course offerings and allows students to design academic programs to meet their individual needs. Advanced Placement classes are available in English, calculus, chemistry, physics, and biology. A partnership with TriState University allows students to connect their AP courses in English, calculus, and chemistry. This unique program offers college credits from Tri-State University without the necessity of the AP exam. In addition, a workplace participation program offers students opportunities to learn within a variety of business/industrial settings in Angola. Angola High School students have a comprehensive offering of courses which has been designed to meet their needs into the 21st century.

ATHLETICS AND ACTIVITIES

Angola High School is a member of the Northeast Corner Conference (NECC), and the Indiana High School Athletic Association (IHSAA). Boys' varsity sports include cross country, football, soccer, wrestling, basketball, tennis swimming, golf track, and baseball. Girls' varsity sports include volleyball, cross country, soccer, basketball swimming, track, tennis, golf, gymnastics and softball.

Extra-curricular clubs exist for student participation according to interest. Activities include Student Council, HI-Y Teens, FFA, Pep Club, Marching Band, Art Club, Swing Choir, French Club, Drama Club, Color Guard, Speech Team, Chess Club, Mainstage Players, Jazz Band, Environmental Task Force, and Cheerleading. Academic activities include National Honor Society, Spell Bowl, National French Society, Academic Super Bowl, Math Teams, and Varsity Scholars.

SUPPORT OF BUSINESS AND INDUSTRY

Members of the business community have shown strong support for programs at Angola High School. The Varsity Scholars program, which rewards students with monetary incentives and a trip to The Bahamas, was initiated and organized by leaders in the business community. In addition, the Workplace Participation Program is a unique offering, made available because of the capabilities of our 4 Block schedule.

Representatives of the business community serve as advisors for several Angola High School Committees. Local businesses and industries also participate in career programs, job fairs, and curriculum planning. They continue to be an integral part of vocational programs such as ICE, and HOE.

(Continued)

(Continued)

FACULTY/STAFF

Angola High School has an experienced, certified staff. Of a total of 51 staff members, there are 29 individuals with over ten years of experience and only seven with under five years of experience. A majority of the certified staff has achieved a master's degree or more. Most attend workshops and conferences regularly. With the initiation of the new block schedule, many teachers have made a special effort to explore innovations in teaching strategies and methods to make the most effective use of the longer class periods. The level of professionalism is high among staff members.

CLIMATE

Attitudes of students, parents and teachers toward the new block scheduling and the learning environment at Angola High School are very positive. Surveys taken five times since 1995 show an increased satisfaction with the new schedule and the learning environment. The students, parents, and teachers, on the average, agreed or strongly agreed that "this school motivates students to learn." When the group was asked about the previous seven period day, they were generally undecided. Later, when the group was asked the same question about our new block schedule, the majority showed positive responses. This indicates a much higher level of satisfaction with the new schedule. In addition, all three groups showed a much higher level of satisfaction with the block schedule when asked if the ninety minute block schedule is "better for student learning." We can only conclude that students, teachers and parents are more satisfied with the new schedule and the learning environment.

CONCLUSION

Angola High School has many strengths and will continue to strive for academic progress and achievement. We will also continue to provide an atmosphere in which all students can learn and mature into adults who will be able to participate in society as productive citizens and lifelong learners.

School Improvement Efforts

Since Angola High School's accreditation in the fall of 1990, the following improvement goals have been set for each of the following school years:

School Years: 1990–1996

1. Our attendance policies are consistent, manageable, and effective.

2. Technology is integrated into the curriculum.

3. A systematic method is in place for staff members to interact with other staff members and administration.

School Year: 1990–1991

1. Language arts and math skills are strengthened

2. Graduation rates are improved.

School Years: 1992–1994

All school policies and rules are consistent with desired student outcomes.

School Year: 1993–1994

Renewed focus on the use of technology in the classroom.

School Years: 1994–1996

The "Four Block" schedule is investigated, evaluated, and implemented.

School Year: 1996–1997

Teaching strategies are studied and implemented, to address active learners and multiple learning styles

School Year: 1997–1998

School-to-Work Programs and School-to-College Programs are developed; new technology is integrated *into* the curriculum.

Our most successful effort in school improvement has been the new "Four Block" (alternative) schedule. We feel this is due to the careful planning, visitations, discussions, in-services, and quantities of professional literature and videotapes which were provided to aid in our preparation for this change. Also, the staff members have been provided with an opportunity to take part in several in-service sessions to focus upon varied teaching models and strategies. It seems to be working well.

(Continued)

(Continued)

Mission Statement

The Angola High School mission statement has been developed from the Metropolitan School District mission to reflect the unique environment of Angola High School. Our mission is revisited and reaffirmed many times throughout the school year by individual staff members as they plan for groups and by committees as they progress toward their various goals.

Angola High School is a partnership of staff, students, parents, and community. Our mission is to provide a comprehensive quality educational program enabling students to become successful lifelong learners and contributors to society.

We, the staff and administration of Angola High School, recognize that it is our responsibility, along with parents and community, to support and nurture our students to their fullest individual potentials. Our goal is to have all students become successful life long learners and positive contributors to society.

Our Statement of Beliefs

We Believe That . . .

1   *All individuals can learn.*

2   *Individuals learn differently.*

3   *Each individual has value.*

4   *The family is the primary influence on the individual's development.*

5   *Attitude of the individual always affects performance.*

6   *Each student has a responsibility to contribute to society.*

7   *A nurturing and caring environment enhances a student's confidence in oneself and contributes to his/her **success.***

8   *Learning is a lifelong process.*

Desired Learner Characteristics
A GRADUATE OF ANGOLA HIGH SCHOOL IS A . . .

1. **Person Who Learns and Applies Critical Knowledge**
   - exhibits a knowledge of the basics
   - exhibits ability to locate needed information
   - demonstrates ability to move from factual recall to practical applications
   - applies information, knowledge, and skills
   - demonstrates ability to problem solve and plan effectively
   - utilizes appropriate technology

2. **Person Who Communicates Effectively in All Content Areas**
   - applies the skills of listening, speaking, reading, writing, and illustrating in correct forms

3. **Person Who Is a Self-Directed Learner**
   - demonstrates initiative, personal responsibility, and pride in completing tasks
   - learns for the purpose of personal growth
   - responds positively to constructive suggestions

4. **Person Who Shows Respect for Others**
   - demonstrates an ability to work cooperatively
   - understands the rights and responsibilities of citizenship
   - exhibits a knowledge and willingness to participate in activities at the local, state, and national levels

5. **Person Who Prepares for a Career**
   - demonstrates employability skills
   - contributes to society
   - transfers academic success to life
   - understands the value of continuous learning

Tech Prep addresses the need for students to prepare for careers in an ever-technical society. Our curriculum guides students to be responsible, cooperative, and able to apply critical knowledge—basic skills needed in preparation for any career.

(Continued)

(Continued)

Angola High School Average "GPA"

Over 16,000 grades were collected and averaged from 1993 to 1995. Over the four semesters during this time, our schoolwide GPA ranged from just under 6.8 to slightly over 6.8 (on a 12 point grading scale).

During the twelve grading periods from 1995 to 1998 on a 4 Block schedule, our schoolwide GPA ranged from slightly over 7.4 to nearly 8.0 on the same 12 point scale. This is a significant improvement to nearly a "B" average schoolwide.

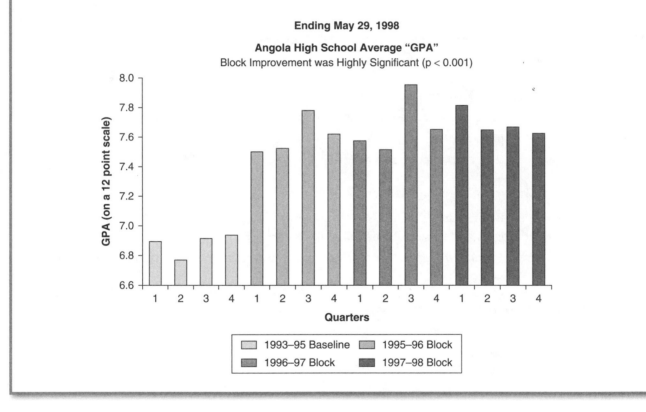

Ending May 29, 1998

Angola High School Average "GPA"
Block Improvement was Highly Significant (p < 0.001)

Departmental Average GPA

Nine of our ten departments have shown highly significant improvements in grades over a three year period. While changes in physical education/health grades are not significant, perhaps some course restructuring has accounted for this data. Generally, departments with lower grades see all students where some departments are elected by students. The graph below shows the statistical comparison. The improvements are readily noticeable.

Ending May 29, 1998

Angola High School "GPA"

All Departments in 1995–98 Except Health/P.E.

Had Significant ($p < 0.05$) Improvement

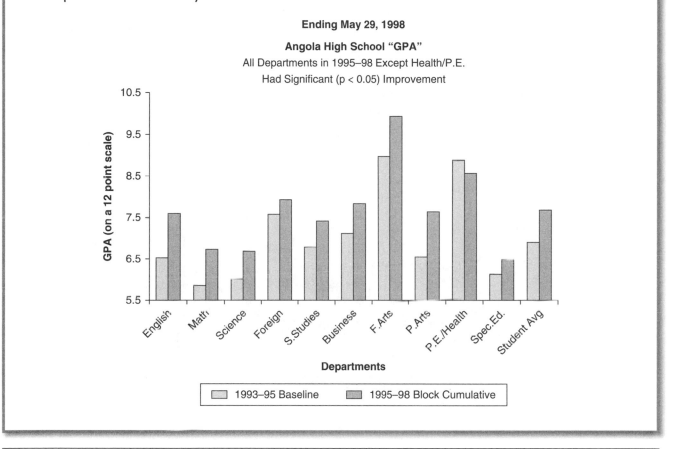

(Continued)

(Continued)

Angola High School Semester Exams

Some persons may suggest that our grades were inflated over the past three years or that the "newness" of the schedule caused the improvement. However, we asked that the same semester exams given in the past be used during our first year on the 4 Block schedule. Some adjustments had to be made for new classes, courses not taught during the baseline, or for curriculum adjustments. But, essentially the same exams were given. Since these are the evaluation of exit skills, our students have improved.

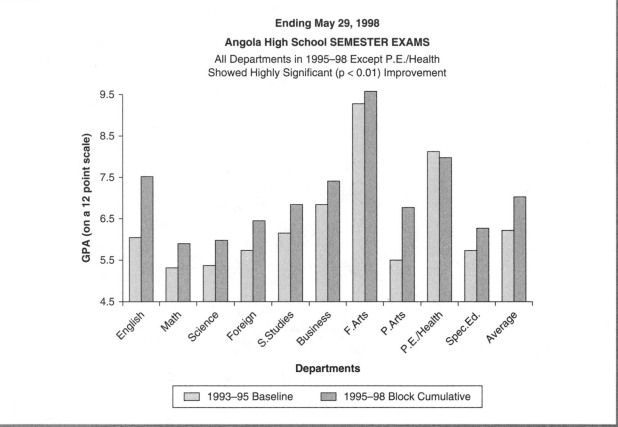

Ending May 29, 1998

Angola High School SEMESTER EXAMS

All Departments in 1995–98 Except P.E./Health
Showed Highly Significant (p < 0.01) Improvement

Angola High School Honor Roll

Our students must maintain a "B" average to be eligible for the Honor Roll. The following graph compares ninth graders to ninth graders and so forth. Note the improvement from the baseline percentages. We believe students do better when focusing on fewer courses for longer periods of time.

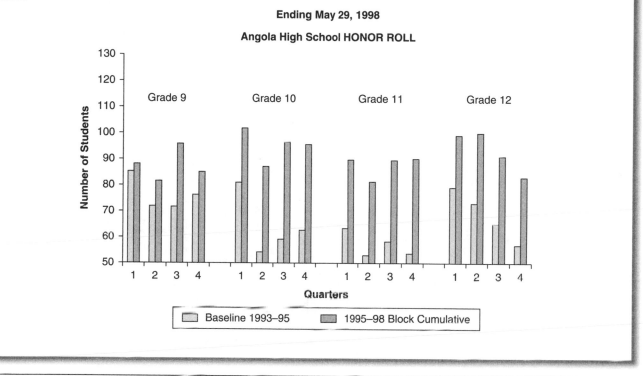

Ending May 29, 1998

Angola High School HONOR ROLL

(Continued)

(Continued)

Angola High School Attendance

A monthly review of our attendance during three years of 4 Block scheduling shows overall improvement. We were lower in January during the past three years. However, every other month was higher, giving us an improved attendance rate over 95%. We will continue to study this area for trends such as sickness, weather related absence, and other issues. Generally, we believe more success improves students' attitudes toward attendance.

Ending May 29, 1998

Angola High School ATTENDANCE

Highly Significant (p < 0.01) Improvement Was Seen

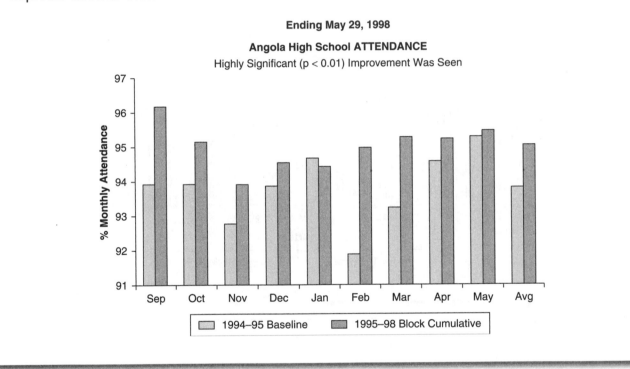

Angola High School

"ISTEP+, SAT, 8 ACT" SCORES

(Indiana Statewide Test of Educational Progress)

The I STEP+ has been given to sophomores throughout Indiana from the fall of 1995 to the fall of 1997. Our results were some of our very highest. Last year's scores from Angola High School sophomores were some of the highest in our area and ranked within the top percentage of Indiana's high schools. However, we expect fluctuations from year to year. These scores vary from group to group, often based upon numerous factors beyond the type of schedule a school follows. We are pleased with our results.

We have shown improvement over the past two years with SAT and ACT scores. Our scores were above both state and national averages in the verbal and math sections. However, a similar response will be given as with ISTEP+ scores. We believe several years of review will be necessary to draw any general conclusions regarding these scores and our daily schedule.

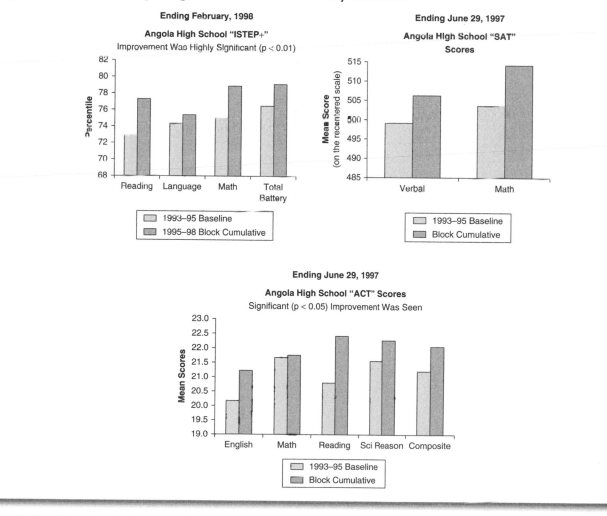

MARION COUNTY PUBLIC SCHOOLS

PARENT SURVEY

Marion County Public Schools -- School Improvement Surveys

Marion County Public Schools
School Improvement Survey
2007 - 2008

MCPS Home > School Improvement > Survey Pages

**2007-2008 School Improvement Questionnaire
Parent Version**

Thank you for taking the time to fill out our survey. Please carefully answer the questions below; we need the information for school improvement planning. This is an anonymous survey. Please only participate in this survey once per child. If you have more than one child in Marion County Public Schools, please fill out the survey for each child's school and grade level.

**Please give us some demographic data that will allow us
to interpret the results of this survey:**

Indicate your child's school name: Choose the school

Indicate your child's grade level: Choose the grade level

Parent Survey

1. I believe that the principal is the Instructional Leader in my child's school.

Strongly Disagree O   Disagree O   Agree O   Strongly Agree O

2. The principal clearly communicates the school's goals and priorities to me.

Strongly Disagree O   Disagree O   Agree O   Strongly Agree O

3. I believe the school's administration is visible in my child's classrooms.

Always O   Usually O   Seldom O   Never O

4. I believe the school's administration supports and attends extra-curricular activities (parent nights, sports, plays, SAC/PTA meetings, etc.).

Always O   Usually O   Seldom O   Never O

5. The principal actively involves parents in planning and reviewing school programs.

Always O   Usually O   Seldom O   Never O

6. The teachers communicate and demonstrate that they believe all students can learn.

Always O   Usually O   Seldom O   Never O

Marion County Public Schools -- School Improvement Surveys

7. My child's school offers a variety of programs to assist students with different kinds of needs to meet high academic standards.

Always ○   Usually ○   Seldom ○   Never ○

8. The school staff encourages me to set high expectations for my child's overall achievement.

Strongly Disagree ○   Disagree ○   Agree ○   Strongly Agree ○

9. My child's teachers expect and promote academic excellence.

Always ○   Usually ○   Seldom ○   Never ○

10. Teachers in my child's school are focused on FCAT excellence.

Strongly Disagree ○   Disagree ○   Agree ○   Strongly Agree ○

11. I believe that my child is actively engaged in teacher-planned learning activities during the school day.

Always ○   Usually ○   Seldom ○   Never ○

12. I believe that in my child's school, teaching is focused on Sunshine State Standards for which all students are held accountable.

Strongly Disagree ○   Disagree ○   Agree ○   Strongly Agree ○

13. I understand the District's Continuous Improvement Model.

Strongly Disagree ○   Disagree ○   Agree ○   Strongly Agree ○

14. I believe that the ongoing Focus Calendar Assessments are an important part of my child's academic success.

Very Important ○   Important ○   Of Little Importance ○   Unimportant ○

15. My child feels safe at school.

Always ○   Usually ○   About Half the Time ○   Seldom ○   Never ○

16. My child's teachers are focused on teaching and learning.

Always ○   Usually ○   About Half the Time ○   Seldom ○   Never ○

(Continued)

(Continued)

Marion County Public Schools -- School Improvement Surveys

---

17. I have read the District's Code of Student Conduct.

Yes ○   No ○

---

18. I believe that the District's Code of Student Conduct is strictly enforced across the district.

Yes ○   No ○

---

19. I believe that the District's Code of Student Conduct is equally applied to all students in the district.

Yes ○   No ○

---

20. The staff at my child's school encourages positive social interaction among and between students.

Strongly Disagree ○   Disagree ○   Agree ○   Strongly Agree ○

---

21. I am regularly informed of my child's progress in addition to receiving an interim and a report card.

Strongly Disagree ○   Disagree ○   Agree ○   Strongly Agree ○

---

22. Students in my child's school have the opportunity to receive additional help with skills they have trouble mastering.

Always ○   Usually ○   About Half the Time ○   Seldom ○   Never ○

---

23. My child's report card accurately reflects academic achievement in a way I can understand.

Strongly Disagree ○   Disagree ○   Agree ○   Strongly Agree ○

---

24. My child's teachers provide opportunities for me to discuss my child's overall progress.

Always ○   Usually ○   About Half the Time ○   Seldom ○   Never ○

---

25. I receive timely information about all aspects of my child's schooling.

Strongly Disagree ○   Disagree ○   Agree ○   Strongly Agree ○

---

26. I have adequate opportunities for involvement in different activities at my child's school.

Strongly Disagree ○   Disagree ○   Agree ○   Strongly Agree ○

---

27. (Title I Parents) I know about the services offered in my child's Title I school.

Strongly Disagree ○   Disagree ○   Agree ○   Strongly Agree ○

28. Parent meetings are offered at a variety of times to meet my schooling needs.

Strongly Disagree ○   Disagree ○   Agree ○   Strongly Agree ○

29. I receive information about programs, curriculum, assessments, and proficiency levels that all students are expected to meet.

Strongly Disagree ○   Disagree ○   Agree ○   Strongly Agree ○

30. Annually, I receive copies of the school handbook and the School-Parent Compact (Title I Schools only) that describe ways the parent, student, teacher, and principal will support learning.

Yes ○   No ○

31. My child's school has an active Parent/Teacher group and/or a School Advisory Council that includes parents.

Yes ○   No ○

32. My child's school provides resources and/or training to help me work with my child(ren).

Always ○   Usually ○   Seldom ○   Never ○

33. I feel welcome in my child's school.

Always ○   Usually ○   About Half the Time ○   Seldom ○   Never ○

34. Overall, I am satisfied with Marion County Public Schools' education program.

Strongly Disagree ○   Disagree ○   Agree ○   Strongly Agree ○

Comments:
Please add any additional comments you have that weren't covered in the questions above:

When finished click here >> | Submit the Survey | << Click here when finished

Source: Used with permission from Marion County Public Schools, Ocala, FL.

13

Communicating With Technology

Going Beyond Web Sites

Change is good. You go first.

—*Dilbert* comic strip

Web sites, Web pages and e-mail, blogging, podcasting, RSS . . . the list is endless. Just within the last decade, computers have offered many new avenues for communication. Most schools and school districts around the country have Web sites or Web pages, and even in the most remote rural areas, communication now regularly utilizes the newest technology such as Web sites, e-newsletters, podcasts, Web blogs, and more for information and even socialization. Teachers help students keep track of homework on their individual Web sites, parents can monitor their students' grades and progress online, and departments have Web pages on school district Web sites for anything from course offerings, school calendars, and enrollment forms to student handbooks and employment information. Many school Web sites and Web pages within those sites are even created and maintained by technology-savvy students. Most information can be entered (or posted) and changed with ease.

For example, at L'Ouverture Computer Technology Magnet School in Kansas, Principal Howard Pitler says that each teacher updates his or her Web page weekly with information for parents on what students are studying. L'Ouverture students test software and hardware for a number of companies, and the school puts out a weekly electronic newsletter (or e-newsletter) edited by fifth graders.

Electronic mail (e-mail) is one of the easiest and quickest ways to make contact with individuals, such as key communicators, all at once, with "broadcast e-mails." Instant messenger services on the Internet offer the opportunity for two or more people to have a dialogue. A "chat room" can be made private with the use of a password or "user ID." (See Chapter 4 for more about electronic communication).

HOW HAS TECHNOLOGY CHANGED (OR IMPROVED) THE WAY WE COMMUNICATE WITH OUR STAKEHOLDERS?

Communicating via technology is instantaneous—that can be a benefit or a detriment depending on how it is used, especially in emergency situations. It can lead to inaccurate information, rumors, and speculation that can be counterproductive to the real message. That said, being able to notify families early that a school will be closed because of a local issue is just one example of how this rapid communication is a plus. Many educational staff currently use text messages, instant messaging, cell phones, and e-mail to get the word out, and older students use such technology as well; the challenge is to encourage more parents to use it.

Many people have made technology an integral part of their lives, and they tend to avoid traditional communication methods such as mailings. Who hasn't had the challenge of safely pinning notes to young students' clothes or trying to get middle school and high school students to carry home important flyers? As advantageous as instant communication has proven to be, it is critically important that messages be thoroughly reviewed before a "send" button is ever pushed. Many people have faced the embarrassment of sending e-mails to the wrong people or not giving enough thought to the message being conveyed.

Technology saves money on paper and postage, but it is important to assess if it should be used as a supplement to a mailing or public meeting or any other communication techniques commonly used. Keep in mind that today's rapid-fire communication via the Internet means that e-mail "mailboxes" can quickly become overloaded with messages. Knowing how parents and community members access information will provide the answer to the question of the best way to communicate with your audiences.

Another consideration is keeping up with the knowledge level students have of technology. Most students have a mastery of technology that adults may not have achieved. They can text message in class without even looking at their phone, take pictures and video secretly, and access inappropriate content on the Web. So, today, using technology to communicate is a given, but putting protections in place such as filters, school technology use policies, and careful observation is a must.

TECHNOLOGY TERMINOLOGY

Wiki? Podcast? Social networking? Here are a few definitions that can help you decipher the jargon.

One hallmark of the Digital Age is the creation of new words. Many terms you hear in discussions of 21st Century Learning and Classroom 2.0 (education curriculum discussions) may be strange to the ear. Here are brief definitions of several expressions used in "techno lingo" that you might need to know.

What does "asynchronous" mean?

Asynchronous literally means "not at the same time." Blogs, threaded discussion boards, and e-mails are examples of asynchronous tools. An asynchronous event on the Web allows participants to access, process, and respond to information and discussion at times they choose, by downloading or viewing multimedia and text files or reading and posting to message boards and electronic mailing lists.

What is a "blog" and how is it used?

A **"weblog"** or **"blog"** is an "Internet journal" that enables the user to publish comments, images, and ideas instantly for other people to read. Bloggers frequently include Web links to other materials to enrich the content of their postings. Teachers and students may use blogs to extend class discussions, pursue collaborative projects; publish the products of their work; or communicate with parents, experts, students in other schools, and so forth. Free, easy-to-use weblog services like "Edublogs" (edublogs.org) make it simple and safe for the nonexpert to create a blog. One popular use of classroom blogs is the *Scribe Post*.

In the past few years, blogs have established themselves as a key part of online culture. Two surveys by the *Pew Internet and American Life Project* showed the popularity of what has become known as the "blogosphere." By the beginning of 2005,

- 7 percent of the 120 million U.S. adults who reported using the Internet said they had created a blog or Web-based diary. That represented more than 8 million people. (With the rapid growth of social networking sites, that number has increased exponentially.)
- 27 percent of Internet users said they read blogs—a 58 percent jump from the 17 percent who had reported they were blog readers just months before. By the end of 2004, an estimated 32 million Americans were blog readers.
- 5 percent of Internet users said they used "RSS aggregators" or "XML readers" to get the news and other information delivered from blogs and content-rich Web sites as posted online.
- the interactive features of many blogs are attractive to "bloggers." Twelve percent of Internet users reported they had posted comments or other material on blogs.

What is "filtering"?

Filtering is the process of controlling access to a network by analyzing the incoming and outgoing packets of information from the Internet. School systems often use filters to guard against objectionable content reaching students.

What is "podcasting"?

Podcasting is a method of distributing multimedia files, such as audio or video programs, over the Internet for playback on mobile devices and personal computers. Podcasts are often distributed using RSS (defined below) feeds. Teachers and students use tools like digital recorders and editing software to produce audio/video podcasts about things they are teaching or learning.

Web 2.0 or the Read/Write Web are labels used to describe the evolution of the World Wide Web from a medium used primarily to find or post information to a medium where those with shared interests can communicate, collaborate, and form temporary or long-term social networks. One key tool in the growth of the read/write Web is RSS—Web-based software that lets users keep track of new postings on the Web.

RSS is a "Rich Site Summary," also called "Really Simple Syndication." According to the technology experts, "RSS" *is* really simple. RSS is a text-based format, a type of XML, a common computer syntax used for writing Web content. (In fact, RSS files are often labeled as "XML, or sometimes as "RDF.") RSS files (also called RSS feeds or channels) simply contain a list of items. Usually, each item contains a title, summary, and a link to an URL (e.g., a Web page). The most common use for RSS files is for news and other Web sites such as "blogs." An item's description may contain all of a news article, blog post, and so forth, or just an extract or summary. The item's link will usually point to the full content (although it may also point to what the content itself links to). When a Web sites has an RSS feed, it is said to be "syndicated." The most popular applications for RSS feeds are for displaying headlines on other Web sites, creating search engines, or aggregating data from multiple Web sites (RSS information above came from www.faganfinder.com/search/rss.shtml). Here are some other helpful Web sites that explain the basics of RSS and give tips about how to set up RSS feeds, and also give some perspective on blogs:

www.digitaldivide.net/articles/view.php?ArticleID=68

www.dartmouth.edu/~libacq/News_Center/ncrss.shtml

www.iupload.com/news/rss_overview.asp

www.xml.com/pub/a/2002/12/18/dive-into-xml.html

What does "social networking" mean?

Social Networking—Social network theory emerged in the 1950s to describe the ways people are connected through family, work, community, and so forth. In the context of the World Wide Web, social networking refers to the communications and relationships that develop through the use of social software—Internet applications that help connect friends, business partners, teachers, students, and others using a variety of tools (see below).

What is "social software"?

Social Software is any digital tools that promote social networking, allowing people to "rendezvous, connect, and collaborate" and to form online communities. "Old-fashioned" examples include electronic mailing lists, message boards, and the like. More recent examples range from publishing tools like blogs and wikis, to information-sharing sites like Flickr or Delicious, to social network services like Ning or (for students) Think.com and more commercial kid networks like Webkinz and Club Penguin. A more advanced approach to social networking can be found at Second Life and Teen Second Life, networks that present a videogame-like virtual world where participants (over 7 million at last count) create "avatars" to represent themselves and move about to participate in events and activities. Educators are beginning to use Second Life to create *innovative learning environments* for students and faculty.

What does "wiki" mean?

Wiki is the Hawaiian word for "quick." A wiki is a Web sites that anyone can edit at any time. Users can easily and quickly add, remove, or otherwise edit all content on a wiki page. Most wikis include discussion pages where visitors can leave comments. This ease of interaction and operation makes a wiki an effective tool for collaborative writing, brainstorming, and project development. Typically, a wiki Web sites provides an easy way to monitor changes and restore earlier versions of pages. Some free wiki services (such as the Wikispaces service) offer the option of password protection to prevent non-participants from editing pages. Several Alabama schools use Wetpaint, a wiki-like free service with more flexibility to add graphics and special features.

INTERNET BEHAVIOR TRACKING

According to the *Pew Internet and American Life Project* (www.pewinternet.org), a non-profit initiative of the Pew Research Center to examine the social impact of the Internet, in 2004, an estimated 6 million Americans reported getting their news and information fed to them through "RSS aggregators" (when they were defined for them), but 62 percent of those online did not know what a blog was. Today, with the more prevalent use of political blogs, and as more Americans are becoming technology-savvy communicators, education leaders need to stay informed of the way technology has become integral to how we communicate with each other and about our schools.

Resource A

CONTRIBUTORS

American Association of School Administrators (AASA), Arlington, Virginia

American Federation of Teachers (AFT), Washington, D.C.

Association for Career and Technical Education (ACTE), Alexandria, Virginia

Association for Supervision and Curriculum Development (ASCD), Alexandria, Virginia

Vern Ahrndt, Principal, Plymouth Middle School, Plymouth, Minnesota

Fred Anderson,* Custer County High School, Miles City, Montana

Jeff Athey,* Dodgeville High School, Dodgeville, Wisconsin

Richard Bagin, Executive Director, NSPRA, Rockville, Maryland

John Baldwin,* Caddo PM Senior High School, Shreveport, Louisiana

Karen Bangert,* Wagonwheel Elementary School, Gillette, Wyoming

Pat A. Bell, Evansville-Vanderburgh School Corporation, Evansville, Indiana

Deborah Binder-Lavender,* Thornton High School, Broomfield, Colorado

Thomas D. Blair,* Sauk Rapids High School, Sauk Rapids, Minnesota

David Bolger, Corporate Education Consulting, Inc., Phoenix, Arizona

Rex Bolinger,* Angola High School, Angola, Indiana

Tyler Brown, Mount Vernon City Schools, Mount Vernon, Illinois

Herb Bunch,* Seventh Grade Building, New Castle, Indiana

Judy Cameron, Principal, Bonanza High School, Las Vegas, Nevada

Peter Carparelli, Superintendent, Billings Public Schools, Billings, Montana

Rachel Carter, Corporate Education Consulting, Inc., Phoenix, Arizona

Kem Cazier, Assistant Principal, Star Valley Junior High School, Afton, Wyoming

Alan Chmiel,* Fall Mountain Regional High School, Alstead, New Hampshire

Kevin Christian, Marion County Public Schools, Ocala, Florida

Larry Clark,* Halifax County High School, South Boston, Virginia

Panfilo H. Contreras, Arizona School Boards Association, Phoenix, Arizona

Corona-Norco Unified School District, Norco, California

Gary Crowell,* Georgetown High School, Georgetown, Texas

Barry Curry, Polytech High School, Woodside, Delaware

Marilyn Curry, Corporate Education Consulting, Inc., Phoenix, Arizona

John Jay Daly, Daly Communications, Chevy Chase, Maryland

Gary Damore,* Paradise Valley High School, Phoenix, Arizona

Delta Kappa Gamma, Austin, Texas

Bill Denkinger,* Mt. Edgecumbe High School, Sitka, Alaska

James Dooley,* L'Anse Creuse Middle School, Mt. Thomas, Michigan

Tom Dougherty,* Mainland Regional High School, Linwood, New Jersey

Thomas Downs,* Johnston Senior High School, Johnston, Iowa

Arne Duncan, Chicago Public Schools, Chicago, Illinois

Daniel Durbin, Director, Signature Learning Center, Evansville, Indiana

Robert Ericson,* North High School, Sheboygan, Wisconsin

Orin K. Fulton,* Agua Fria High School, Avondale, Arizona

O.B. Garcia,* South Park Middle School, Corpus Christi, Texas

Celeste Garrett, Chicago Public Schools, Chicago, Illinois

Ben Grebinski, Archbishop M.C. O'Neill High School, Regina, Saskatchewan, Canada

Ken Griffith,* Guernsey Sunrise High School, Guernsey, Wyoming

Bernie Gurule, Mt. Edgecumbe High School, Mt. Edgecumbe, Alaska

Vaughn Heinrich,* Vallivue High School, Caldwell, Idaho

David H. Ibarra, Washington Junior High School, Toledo, Ohio

Richard Janezich,* Brooklyn Center High School, Brooklyn Center, Minnesota

Sharon Jayne,* Greenacres Junior High School, Greenacres, Washington

Kevin J. Kapp, Prescott Unified School District, Prescott, Arizona

Bob Kenison,* Wauconda Grade School, Wauconda, Illinois

David Kergaard,* Kent County High School, Worton, Maryland

Karen Kleinz, Associate Director, NSPRA, Rockville, Maryland

John Lammel,* Millard South High School, Omaha, Nebraska

Gwendolyn Lee,* Thornridge High School, Dolton, Illinois

Sharon Lewis, Teacher, Simpson Elementary School, Phoenix, Arizona

Alan Linford,* Star Valley Junior High School, Afton, Wyoming

Los Angeles Unified School District, Los Angeles, California

Bret Lovejoy, Executive Director, ACTE, Alexandria, Virginia

John "Mac" MacCurlee,* Pearl High School, Pearl, Mississippi

Andrea Martin,* Winnfield Kindergarten School, Winnfield, Louisiana

Nick Miller,* Buffalo High School, Buffalo, Minnesota

Alvin Montgomery,* Grace King High School, Metairie, Louisiana

Marion Morehouse,* Cascade Middle School, Bend, Oregon

National Association of Elementary School Principals (NAESP), Alexandria, Virginia

National Association of Secondary School Principals (NASSP), Reston, Virginia

National Association of State Boards of Education (NASBE), Alexandria, Virginia

National Congress of Parents and Teachers (PTA), Chicago, Illinois

National Education Association (NEA), Washington, D.C.

National School Boards Association (NSBA), Alexandria, Virginia

National School Public Relations Association (NSPRA), Rockville, Maryland

Richard Olthoff,* Magic City Campus High School, Minot, North Dakota

Orange County Public Schools, Orlando, Florida

Robert Patton,* East Burke Middle School, Icard, North Carolina

Leonard Paul,* Clark County School District, Las Vegas, Nevada

Elizabeth Pawlitschek,* Plymouth Middle School, Plymouth, Minnesota

Kimberly Peoples,* Golightly Vocational/Technical Center, Detroit, Michigan

Gary Phillips,* Fayette County High School, Fayetteville, Georgia

Douglas Pfeninger,* Dartmouth Middle School, Dartmouth, Massachusetts

Phi Delta Kappa, Bloomington, Indiana

Howard Pitler,* L'Ouverture Computer Technology Magnet School, Wichita, Kansas

Bill Ratliff, Texas Business and Community Leaders, Austin, Texas

John R. Richardson,* Sunnyslope Elementary School, Port Orchard, Washington

Nancy Richmond,* Amsterdam Elementary School, Belle Mead, New Jersey

Linda Robertson,* Aurora High School, Aurora, Ohio

Robbinsdale Area Schools Education Service Center, New Hope, MN

Thomas Ronning, Fall Mountain Regional High School, Charlestown, New Hampshire

Laura Roth, Corporate Education Consulting, Inc., Phoenix, Arizona

Peter B. Sack,* Swampscott High School, Swampscott, Massachusetts

Nancy Saltzman,* Broadmoor Elementary School, Colorado Springs, Colorado

Kenneth Satre,* Ninilchik Elementary/High School, Ninilchik, Alaska

Patrick E. Savini,** Sussex County Vocational-Technical School District, Georgetown, Delaware

Emmett Sawyer,* Logan-Rogersville High School, Rogersville, Missouri

Frank R. Scalise, Owen J. Roberts School District, Pottstown, Pennsylvania

Teri Schroeder, www.isafe.org

Charles Schuetz,* Don Bosco Technical High School, Boston, Massachusetts

Mary Ellen Scully, Copernicus Interactive, Inc., Phoenix, Arizona

Kevin Settle, Mount Vernon City Schools, Mount Vernon, Illinois

Nedda Shafir, Cave Creek Unified School District, Cave Creek, Arizona

Phil Silsby,* Belleville West High School, Belleville, Illinois

William D. Smith, Director of Educational Administration, Saint Xavier College, Chicago, Illinois

Gerald Tirozzi, Executive Director, NASSP, Reston, Virginia

Susan Van Zant, Principal, Meadowbrook Middle School,** Poway, California

Cathy Watson,* Ravenel Elementary School, Seneca, South Carolina

Brenda Welburn, Executive Director, NASBE, Alexandria, Virginia

Bill Wells,* Murray High School, Murray, Kentucky

John Wherry, President, The Parent Institute, Fairfax, Virginia

Judi Willis, Paradise Valley Unified School District, Phoenix, Arizona.

Jennifer Winter, Corporate Education Consulting, Inc., Phoenix, Arizona

*State Principal of the Year
**U. S. Department of Education Blue Ribbon School